Praise for Lu Ann Darling's
DISCOVER YOUR MENTORING MOSAIC

"Most people think of mentoring as a formal organizational process leading to a better job. However, few are ever involved in this formal process, yet we are mentored and mentor all our lives—most often not 'naming' the process. We have been mentored by a teacher, our child, our favorite grocery store clerk, a friend, and, of course, ourselves. Likewise, we have provided mentoring to numerous people, often never realizing the impact our words and actions had.

"In this exceptional book, Dr. Darling outlines the ever-changing, transformational and often subtle and hidden elements that form each person's unique Mentoring Mosaic, a process that is ongoing and evolving from childhood to old age. There are insights for every age group—with new perspectives on traditional mentoring, mentoring in later life, self-managed mentoring, and non-people mentors. Readers will benefit from well-researched information, tools, and strategies that can be used to improve both personal and professional effectiveness. It's a must-read."

Suzanne P. Smith, Ed.D., RN, FAAN
Editor-in-Chief, The Journal of Nursing Administration and Nurse Educator

"*Discovering Your Mentoring Mosaic* offers a fresh perspective on mentoring. Based on sound research, Lu Ann Darling's book shows us the complete process of mentoring, illustrating it with extremely relevant examples. The women in management with whom I work in Japan and Korea both want and need to understand this process so they can apply it to their own careers and organizations. Dr. Darling describes the process of mentoring in easily understandable language that people can immediately apply. The book's unique approach and cross-cultural applicability make it a stand-out among mentoring books. It is a valuable addition to the literature."

Jean R. Renshaw, PhD
Management Consultant and Author of
Kimono in the Boardroom: The Invisible Evolution of Japanese Women Managers

BST

More Praise for *Discover Your Mentoring Mosaic*

"*Discover Your Mentoring Mosaic* puts the process of advice, guidance, coaching, and planning all together. I had a strong idea for a career path but was not sure which road to take at each junction. The many pieces in the puzzle are sorted out by Lu Ann Darling, who guides the reader in putting the pattern together in an expeditious manner.

"What are the varieties of mentors? Do they all have to be people? Can you self-mentor? All of the steps necessary to reach your goal are outlined with wonderfully touching examples. I recommend this book for those starting, choosing, thinking of switching, or even closing a career. In a way, this book should be required reading for everyone embarking on the journey of finding their place in the world."

Allan Ebbin, MD, MPH
VP of Healthcare Quality & Education at Sierra Health Services; and Emeritus Professor of
Pediatrics & Family Medicine at the University of Southern California

"I have been mentored, and I've been a mentor. I have been lucky in both ways: to find people willing to guide me, and to find people who can value what I've learned and can share. Dr. Darling's book removes some of the elements of luck and happenstance and makes transparent the 'mystery' behind mentoring.

"The sciences have always relied on an apprentice process. The more unlike one is from the traditional participants in these fields, the greater is the need for mentoring through the professional life cycle. What is seldom realized is the role of mentoring in getting one to the point of daring to be a pioneer. Dr. Darling's book helps us understand the messengers and the messages that can lead to success and fulfillment of one's life work."

Shirley M. Malcom, PhD
Director, Education and Human Resources,
American Association for the Advancement of Science (AAAS)

"In my role as president of a regional non-profit organization, New York Women Composers, which is in the process of reorganizing and re-energizing itself, I have found great value in *Discover Your Mentoring Mosaic*. I have been able to use the ideas presented in the book, both in seeking help from a leader of another group and in leading membership meetings. The thoughts on co-mentoring are especially valuable for women who rarely receive traditional mentoring if they venture beyond traditional careers. As a composer, I had only male teachers and nearly all male colleagues. Teachers preferred bonding with their male students, and I had no female role models and advice-givers to turn to. Also, as a geographical outsider, it was difficult for me to 'learn the ropes.' Dr. Darling's book has helped me think of ways to use our organization to correct such problems."

Marilyn Bliss
President, New York Women Composers

"*Discover Your Mentoring Mosaic* is a much-needed book and guidance tool. Most of the mentoring resources that we identified as part of our research on mentoring in the sciences are aimed at mentors, not the mentee. Also, many of the existing resources focus on mentoring during a particular educational stage or as part of a workplace program. *Discover Your Mentoring Mosaic* recognizes that mentoring is a continuous process that begins during the school years and continues throughout the career years."

Yolanda Scott George
Deputy Director, Education and Human Resources and Program Director, Human Resources Programs, American Association for the Advancement of Science (AAAS)

DISCOVER YOUR MENTORING MOSAIC

A Guide to Enhanced Mentoring

Lu Ann W. Darling

Booklocker.com Inc., 2006
Visit www.mentoringmosaic.com for more information.

DEDICATION

To my mother,

who gave me the enduring legacy

that learning is a privilege and reading is a joy

ABOUT THE AUTHOR

Lu Ann W. Darling, Ed.D., is a consultant in leadership, mentoring, and organization development. She has researched, taught, and consulted on mentoring for more than two decades. She can be reached through www.mentoringmosaic.com.

ACKNOWLEDGEMENTS

The book first took shape under the tender guidance of Kathy and Marty Rubin, who helped me form and organize the book. Others read the manuscript from cover to cover and gave me thoughtful advice that helped in the shaping process. Allan Ebbin tested its practical application both as a mentor and mentee in clinical practice and medical education. Suzanne Smith gave me suggestions and advice both as a professional editor and as a one-person rooting section. William Gray and Sheila Wellington reviewed the manuscript from the viewpoint of mentoring professionals. Jean Renshaw made herself available to test ideas, concepts and writing flow—and was there to consider any writing conundrums I might have. Eva Rubin pulled herself away from graduate studies long enough to set up my Web site, www.mentoringmosaic.com, and coach me in its management. My daughter, Martha Darling, stepped up to do content editing and make sure the book would be accessible for people on different career paths. My son, Steve, provided constant support and encouragement, as did all my family.

I am indebted to my professional editing team as well: Samantha Wall, who designed the book cover and graphics; Andi Lucas who managed the copy editing/formatting process; Marilyn Bliss, master indexer; Angela Hoy of Booklocker.com publishers; Julie Duffy, who advised on book promotion; and photographer, Craig Ferré.

Most especially, I want to thank the 200-plus people who allowed me to come into their lives, shared with me their mentoring experiences, and in so doing taught me much of what I know about mentoring.

CONTENTS

PART II: ENHANCING YOUR MENTORING 305

INDEX

DISCOVER YOUR MENTORING MOSAIC

A Guide to Enhanced Mentoring

PART I
THE MENTORING MOSAIC

Chapter 1

EMBARKING ON THE MENTORING JOURNEY

Discover Your Mentoring Mosaic is an easy-to-follow guide for understanding and managing your mentoring throughout your life. It provides a framework that allows you to identify your unique mentoring pattern as well as to design a mentoring plan that best fits your life pattern, current mentoring needs, and available resources. The result is a self-empowering mentoring process that is creative, systematic, and timely for the 21st century.

Many books on mentoring focus on finding a mentor, being a mentor, or developing mentoring programs. In contrast, this book takes a comprehensive approach, covering experiences and environments that are mentoring as well as people who are mentors. Grounded in research, the book provides a structure for understanding mentoring as a lifelong process. As you read this book, you will discover:

- how your mentor-bonding experience impacts your mentoring process;
- how your mentor-bonding pattern shapes the form and characteristics of mentors in your life;
- how the kinds of mentors to whom you gravitate will change during your lifetime;
- why mentoring relationships are just a part of the mentoring process;
- how your own mentoring experiences can be as significant in your life as relationships with mentors;
- how people who have had no mentors are able to be very successful in their lives;
- how self-mentoring begins and how it can be developed;
- how mentoring needs continue throughout life;

- the mentoring strategies most available and helpful in middle and later life;
- how self-mentoring strategies can help you manage your mentoring;
- the reasons for taking an active role in managing your mentoring; and
- the tools and strategies that are available to help you in the process.

In summary, this book provides you, the reader, with a basic structure—the **Mentoring Mosaic**—to use in tracking your mentoring history and in determining how best to manage your mentoring process to meet present and future needs as well as to enrich your life.

WHY MENTORING? WHY NOW?

In previous eras, many large organizations had well-defined pathways to success—definite rungs on the ladder to climb, preferred routes to take, tickets to be "punched," and mentors available to advise and counsel the neophyte on the long career journey. This progression is no longer true. Changing cultures and organizations across the globe have disrupted previous patterns of mentoring, leaving us with far too few systems and supports to ensure charting a successful mentoring journey.

Few organizations have the vision or the resources to plan and direct effective mentoring. In the process of streamlining operations, entire layers of middle managers, those who traditionally assumed mentor roles, have been eliminated. This is not unlike what happened to the native peoples of the North American continent upon contact with the white man. In succumbing to European diseases, native cultures lost up to 90% of their "memorizers"—those elders responsible for transmitting the culture to younger generations. The upheaval from organizational restructuring has been similar.

New technology companies have proliferated, many with inexperienced managers and minimal organizational infrastructures. Mentoring under these conditions has been catch-as-catch-can. The mentoring gap widened still further when hundreds of these companies folded with the collapse of the economic bubble at the end of the 1990s.

Twenty years ago, "mentoring" itself was an uncomfortable word. Now, the pendulum has swung in the opposite direction. One indication is the designation of the month of January as "National Mentoring Month."[1] Although attitudes toward mentoring are changing and a groundswell of public-spirited ads and other promising moves are fostering mentoring programs, the numbers remain woefully small compared to the need. Present programs are usually geared to a narrow niche of the population, such as "gifted" or "at-risk" youth or people in specific professional fields. Few organizations have the interest or ability to manage an employee's career or plan well-ordered career paths. As a result, individuals must plan much of their own career development.

The concept of self-managed mentoring actually may fit better with today's culture of independence and self-reliance, not waiting or expecting a paternalistic "big brother" — whether a government agency, corporate organization, or philanthropic institution — to "do it for you."[2] We are more educated, more resourceful, and more knowledgeable in

---

[1] So designated by the Office of the President on January 9, 2004, and now ongoing; see The White House: Proclamation Archives. Available at: www.whitehouse.gov/news/releases/2004/01/20040109-12.html. Accessed July 16, 2006.

[2] See, for example, Ronald Inglehart, *Modernization and Postmodernization: Cultural, Economic, and Political Change in 43 Societies*, Princeton, NJ: Princeton University Press, 1997.

this new century than ever before. We are better equipped than even the best of mentors to chart a course that is right for us. What anthropologist Margaret Mead said is even more pertinent today than when she made the observation several decades ago:

> "Children today face a future that is so deeply unknown that it cannot be handled as a generation change within a stable, elder-controlled, and parentally modeled culture. …We would do better to apply the pioneer model, the model of first-generation pioneer immigrants into an unexplored and uninhabited land. But for the figure of geographic migration, we must substitute migration in time. Within two decades, 1940 to 1960, events occurred that have irrevocably altered men's relationships to other men and to the natural world. Until recently, elders could say, 'I have been young, and you never have been old,' but today, young people can reply, 'You never have been young in the world I am young in, and you never can be.'"[3]

Younger people are indeed "pioneers" today. The wise, seasoned mentors of yesteryear cannot know what it is like to grow up, and grow old, in today's world. Wisdom from the past must be preserved, treasured, and transmitted to current generations, but transmitted as rich information to be thoughtfully considered and acted upon according to its relevance today. As we manage our own mentoring through our lifetime, we want to cherish the values that are important to us and apply them in ways that are fitting for today and for tomorrow's world.

Mentoring needs in early life—in school, work, and career—are more obvious, more discussed, and given more attention than any other part of the life span. The words "mentor" and "mentoring" rarely are used in later-life discussions, even though the mentoring process continues throughout our lives. Mentoring in later life is of particular interest as

---

[3] Margaret Mead, *Culture and Commitment: A Study of the Generation Gap*, Garden City, NY: Natural History Press/Doubleday & Co, 1970, pp. 62–63.

huge numbers of Baby Boomers[4] are approaching their 60s, as their Generation X children move into their mature years, and as vast numbers of seniors in second careers or active retirement live well into their 70s, 80s, and even 90s.

My research data underscore the reality of life-long mentoring. Although mentoring does not cease in later life, it transforms as needs change and different forms of mentoring are available to meet those needs. As we look forward to decades of life beyond retirement, mentoring takes on new importance. What is the process of mentoring in later life, what are our mentoring needs during these years, and how can they be met? What we learn now can help us manage our later life paths with sureness, agility, and confidence.

THE UBIQUITOUS NATURE OF MENTORING

As a first step, let's examine the terms "mentor" and "mentoring" as they are used in this book. Mentoring is a process we engage in, are involved with, and spend time on whenever we feel the need for learning, guidance, and/or support.

- We are mentored, we mentor others, and we mentor ourselves.
- We do this consciously and unconsciously.
- We vary in the success of our efforts.

We can't not engage in mentoring. It is as natural as breathing. We learn, develop, and grow; we share and pass along things we have learned. We support, encourage, and foster ourselves—and usually others. When things go well, we have positive experiences with mentoring. Sometimes

---

[4] Baby Boomers born 1946–1954 are considered "leading-edge" Boomers; the 1955–1964 group is considered the "trailing" Boomers.

we have bad experiences. We differ in what life brings us, what we bring to our efforts, and in our degree of success.

Understanding the mentoring process makes it possible for us to consciously manage our own mentoring. We do not have to be passive. After we reach adulthood, who better? We are the only persons there, always, for ourselves. Not to say we don't reach out to others for assistance—we do. But we also can actively direct the course of our mentoring process. Although it is true that a mentor is traditionally viewed as a person older and wiser—a teacher, a leader, a guide—this view is limiting and does not explain the research data. Many of us have found other sources of mentoring equally rewarding.

Instead of focusing on the mentor, this book examines mentoring as an active process, a way of connecting with a source—whether with a person, an experience, a model, a book, or, most often, a combination of these—in order to find guidance, to learn, and to grow. The possibilities are almost endless. What is important to understand is that it is the mentoring process that provides meaning and guidance, not a specific person. Throughout this book, we will look at mentoring as an action-oriented, ongoing, dynamic process.

DISCOVERING YOUR MENTORING PROCESS

Becoming aware of and understanding your mentoring process is essential in managing your own mentoring. Bringing into your consciousness various aspects of your mentoring, of which you might be only dimly aware, will enable you to construct a historical time line of your mentoring life and of the people, events, situations, and relationships that have inhabited it. Patterns and connections will emerge. Yet that image has too static a quality. More apt is viewing mentoring as an ever-changing, never completed, transformational art form as each of us designs and reworks the main elements of our unique Mentoring Mosaic. It is a work in progress.

The design of your Mentoring Mosaic is shaped by your genetic material, your family, societal factors, and other external influences, and it is created, consciously and unconsciously, by you. This one-of-a-kind creation will be dense with design in some areas and thin, even skimpy, in others. It is constantly shifting and changing, though the underlying structure remains solid and firm. In this book, you will find ways to discover your Mentoring Mosaic.

MANAGING YOUR OWN MENTORING

To manage your own mentoring effectively, you need to understand the pattern of your Mentoring Mosaic as well as your current situation. You use awareness of that pattern and your present mentoring strategies to take charge of your mentoring. You become the director and coordinator of your mentoring, deploying the resources available to you, both internally and externally, in the way that you see fit. You also scan resources potentially available and determine how best to tap into the ones of most value to you and to expand your mentoring repertoire.

It is like managing your own health. You have general overall knowledge of your health and personal history. Like a good personal physician, you are concerned with your total health and well-being. You will seek out your doctor or other health professional to advise you and, when indicated, to refer you to a specialist for diagnosis and treatment. You monitor your progress and keep informed so you can decide when or if another course of action is needed.

Managing your own mentoring is like that. It is empowering in that you take charge. You are not dependent on someone else to make decisions and provide for you. As you manage your total mentoring process, you will tap into available mentoring resources. Occasionally, you will decide to sit at the foot of a "master." Other times, you will decide to learn on your own. Some of the things you will do:

- You will understand your mentoring pattern.
- You will use what comes naturally and determine what must be more consciously developed.
- You will decide when to focus on mentoring relationships and when not.
- You will survey mentor resources that are available or potentially so.
- You will find or develop mentoring relationships.
- You will identify the mentoring aspects of experiences and environments.
- You will be aware of and draw on your self-mentoring strategies.

THE FOUNDATION OF THIS BOOK IN MENTORING RESEARCH

I have been involved in mentoring research since the early 1980s. When I started, the term "mentor" was viewed as an archaic word, and "mentoring" was unfamiliar in many occupational fields. In the years that followed, a spate of literature developed, and "mentoring" became the new buzzword.

The term "mentor" goes back a long time. Originally, it was coined to describe the comprehensive role of Mentor,[5] the wise and trusted counselor of Odysseus and the tutor of his son, Telemachus. His name is identified with a close, trusted, and experienced counselor or guide. The role of Mentor was apt in the ancient world's traditional society and traditional roles.

---

[5] Mentor, we are told, was really Athena in one of her many guises.

When I began my research, the pace of societal change was accelerating. New groups—women and minorities—were entering the labor force in significant numbers. I observed that many of these individuals were not content with being pigeonholed into narrow occupational roles; yet, they were not finding mentors or mentoring programs that could guide them. At the same time, there was a tremendous upheaval in organizations as whole layers of management were being eliminated. New organizational forms, roles, and structures also emerged from the technology revolution. Notions of traditional mentoring being available, whether fantasy or not, were no longer realistic.

However, the need to grow and develop, the yearning for positive guiding influences in our lives, did not disappear. The needs became even more apparent while the solutions became more elusive. The literature focused on the value of having a mentor, what to look for in a mentor, and what a mentor can do for you. Many articles expressed a sense of urgency. But nobody was trying to understand the process of mentoring or how it works. Just get a mentor, and all of your problems will be solved.

This gap between the idea of mentoring and the reality of mentoring was the motivating force and focus of my research. This book is a distillation of my findings about mentoring: what it is, how it works, and how you can use the information to manage your own mentoring.

These conclusions are drawn from my research of the past 20 years.[6] During that time, I have conducted more than 200 interviews with

---

[6] Most informants in the original sample were in professional or managerial roles in their mid-20s to mid-50s; two-thirds were women. The sample included physicians, nurses, and dietitians. All interviews were taped; they were open-ended, 1^{1}/$_{2}$–2 hours in length, designed to elicit each person's

people in the professions, academe, and business. The majority of the interviewees in the original study were in the helping professions; many were women. Subsequent interviews enlarged the database to include other occupational groups and more men. A related project has been a longitudinal study examining consistency and variability of mentoring patterns over time. I also have studied the mentoring patterns of men and women in their 70s and 80s to better understand mentoring with the aging of our society. Also, wherever I have cited interviews in the book, the names have been disguised.

WHO IS THIS BOOK FOR?

I intend this book as a practical source of information and enlightenment for anyone interested in mentoring, especially in managing their own mentoring—both as mentors and mentees—through career stages and into later life. Whether you are still in school, early in a career, contemplating a career change, or migrating to more meaningful work or a different combination of work and other interests, this book is for you. The book may be particularly apt for Baby Boomers now approaching late career stages and retirement. But it is also a useful guide for parents and for those responsible for developing and managing formal mentoring programs. Given the nature of the research sample and the examples given, the book may be especially pertinent for women and for people in health and human services. At a fundamental level, the book is for all of us.

---

mentoring history and to weave together the threads of that history into a pattern. My research is based on the grounded theory and methodology developed by Barney Glaser and Anselm Strauss, *The Discovery of Grounded Theory: Strategies for Qualitative Research*, Chicago: Addison-Wesley, 1967. Conclusions are also supported by data from later studies as well as by seminars and mentoring workshops.

THE ORGANIZATION OF THE BOOK

Since the image of the Mentoring Mosaic is used to organize this book, a brief summary is indicated.

Each of us has a unique mentoring process that I call the Mentoring Mosaic—a one-of-a-kind design as unique as a fingerprint. Although many similarities exist from one person to another, the overall pattern is never repeated precisely. It is a mélange or tapestry that has some principal motifs and other designs less prominent.

The Mentoring Mosaic develops out of our mentor-bonding process; it is here that our pattern first becomes visible. The process of mentor bonding creates an immense divide between those of us who developed strong positive bonds with adult figures in early years and those who did not. Furthermore, how mentor bonding developed influences the way our Mentoring Mosaic evolves.

In the first part of the book, emphasis is on the seven basic elements or motifs of the Mentoring Mosaic. We start with Mentor Bonding (Chapters 2–4), establishing this process as an overall framework. The succeeding sections examine various elements of mentoring through the lens of the mentor-bonding experience. These elements are Mentoring Messages (Chapters 5–7), Mentoring Models (Chapters 8–10), Mentoring Relationships (Chapters 11–14), Mentoring Experiences and Environments (Chapters 15–16), and Self-Mentoring (Chapters 17–18).

Below is a graphic map that shows the component parts of the Mentoring Mosaic and the sequence in which they are discussed in the book. Mentor bonding is in the center to emphasize the primacy of the mentor-bonding experience in our mentoring lives. Surrounding it, from left to right in a clockwise direction, are the six elements that complete the Mentoring Mosaic.

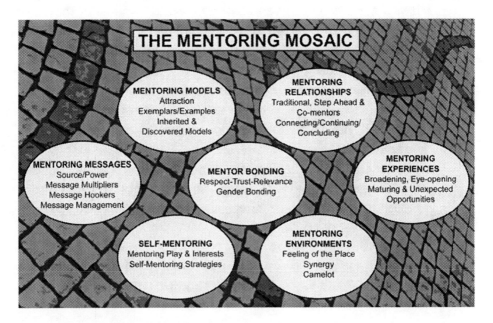

Figure 1. The Mentoring Mosaic

The emphasis in the book's second part is on Enhancing Your Mentoring. The first section, Taking Stock, looks at ways of "Identifying Your Mentoring Mosaic" (Chapter 19), "Mentoring Needs and Life Stages" (Chapter 20), "The Mentoring Mosaic in Later Life" (Chapter 21), and "Life-Long Mentoring Vignettes" (Chapter 22). The Trends section surveys "Trends Impacting Mentoring" (Chapter 23) and "Networking and Mentoring" (Chapter 24). We then turn to strategies for Taking Action: "Managing Your Mentoring—as a Mentee" (Chapter 25), "Managing Your Mentoring—as a Mentor" (Chapter 26), and "Enhanced Mentoring" (Chapter 27).

Whatever your reading purpose, I suggest that you start with the Mentor Bonding section and then turn to the chapters that interest you.

- If you are a browser, you can hop around sections of the book without too much difficulty. The chapters do build on each other, but I believe you can jump around without a serious break in the thought process.
- If you are interested in the mentoring discovery process for yourself or others, I suggest you go through the book systematically in order to build continuity and foster insight development.
- If you find you are one of the non-bonders among us, you might want to skim through the chapters on mentoring relationships and focus more heavily on the chapters dealing with non-people mentors.

In order to link the book chapters together, you will find at the end of each chapter a bridging paragraph briefly summarizing the content of the current chapter and looking ahead to the next.

BRIDGE

This chapter summarizes the purpose and organization of the book and ways it can be helpful to you. The concept of the Mentoring Mosaic is introduced as a creative structure containing the elements of each person's evolving mentoring pattern. The next section examines mentor bonding, that important base element of the overall mentoring design: what mentor bonding is and how it comes about.

Chapter 2

IT ALL STARTS WITH MENTOR BONDING

"I never had a mentor ... "

In this chapter, we explore mentor bonding, what it is, how it evolves, and why it is key to understanding the mentoring process. The discussion includes the essential requirements for mentor bonding to occur, degrees of bonding, and characteristic behaviors of bonders compared with non-bonders.

I learned about mentor bonding early in my research. One of my early interviews was with a successful entrepreneur who had been a pioneer in the cable television industry. I really was looking forward to what I would learn from him, but we were only 10 minutes into the interview when he told me he wasn't sure how much help he could be to me because he never had a mentor!

I was dumbfounded, thinking, There goes my research. But instead of packing up and going home, I listened intently to what he was saying. Out of that interview and many others has come my understanding and appreciation of the mentor-bonding process. So much so that sometime later, when the director of women's studies in a major university declared firmly and positively during a seminar I was conducting that she never had a mentor, I could readily respond. I told her that about 15% of the people I've interviewed report having no mentoring relationships with people. Yet, they, like her, are functioning very well. How does this happen?

Mentoring starts with the early relationships with adults in our lives in a process I call mentor bonding. This is the great divide that affects how each of us goes about mentoring and where people fit into the process. So, if we are to make sense of mentoring, we need to look at mentor bonding—where it all starts.

Most of us have bonded or connected with adults early in our lives and continue to do so throughout our lives. A small number do not bond at all with adult figures. Our early experiences with adults influence the nature and extent of our connections with people mentors. General understanding of the values, knowledge, and acceptable ways to get along in the culture are handed down from our elders. When this happens in an accepting, valuing atmosphere, trust develops, and the young person can easily turn to adult figures for advice whenever it is important to do so.

However, when the young person experiences a lack of relevance, trust, or respect with adults, bonding is not likely to occur. Such persons commonly report having no mentors. Although there are many reasons for non-bonding or limited bonding, this occurs most frequently with children of immigrant parents, regardless of country of origin. Because of the dislocation of the family from the original culture, the wisdom of the elders does not seem relevant to the young person, who develops a number of self-mentoring strategies instead.

Understanding mentor bonding is key to understanding mentoring relationships, the kinds and types of mentors we are drawn to, and whether we have any at all. This is where mentoring starts.

I've had the opportunity to watch the mentor-bonding process in action with my young grandson, Ricky. Here is how I described that process:

> Ricky is 3, and he has a thousand questions about the world in which he lives. He is blessed with parents who respect him and answer his questions at an appropriate level. "Where does the (electric) light come from?" "Why is … ?" I am always at a

loss to answer such questions, but his mother patiently explains as much as she feels is appropriate at his level, and my son does the same.

Ricky likes to be around where his dad is working, wanting, even insisting on "helping." "I want to do that," "Let me," and "I want to help" are common expressions. When I see him with his dad, who might be fixing something or working around the house or yard, I think of the classic imprinting studies of ducklings, who will follow an imitation mother even of another species, so strong is the instinctual imprinting process. So Ricky follows along, wants to do whatever Dad (or Mom) is doing. Ricky is lucky; the adults around him don't dismiss his efforts, but they instead help him participate and try out skills. Feeling respected and valued—or the reverse— starts very early.

Parenting relationships are usually the beginnings of mentor bonding. Alternately, the bonding could be with a parent surrogate—someone with whom the child connects with emotionally, such as a grandparent, an older sibling, or a non-family member close to the household. Lucky for Ricky, all of the necessary ingredients for mentor bonding are there: respect, trust, and relevance. We can answer "yes" to all of these questions:

- Is the adult respectful of the young person?
- Is the adult reliable and trustworthy?
- Is the information or advice relevant to the life of the young person?

When the answers are affirmative, positive mentor bonding is almost assured.

THE ESSENTIALS FOR MENTOR BONDING

Whether or not we bond at all with adult figures in our lives depends on what we experience, consciously or unconsciously, regarding these three factors of respect, trust, and relevance. If we experience the advice of our elders as relevant to our world, if we trust the elders and feel trusted and respected, we are likely to bond naturally and turn to elders for advice, guidance, and help. In this way, we gain access to the "wisdom of the tribe." If we find one or more of these missing, we are likely to turn away from adult figures to someone who is safer, more respectful, or more relevant. We might turn more to peers or people slightly older than ourselves, or we could turn away from people completely and elect to go it on our own.

Our relationships with adults start very early in life and influence the extent to which we connect emotionally, gravitate toward, and feel comfortable with adult figures. The pattern of age, gender, and personal characteristics of adults we seek out as mentors is generally formed during those growing-up years. Those early relationships provide the continuity and set the stage. They provide the first glimpse of our mentors-to-be and also our first glimpse of people who would not be acceptable as mentors.

Respect

Respect cuts two ways: respect for the adult figure, and respect from the adult for the young person. Respect must be present for bonding to occur. Admiration, love, valuing, and appreciation are all terms we use in describing important adult figures when respect for the person is present and mentor bonding takes place. We need to receive respect from figures in our world if we are to bond effectively with people. When a child feels like "nobody listens to me," bonding is hard to develop. The absence of respect provides poor soil for mentor bonding to occur, either lack of respect for the adult figures, or lack of respect from them.

Lack of respect for adult figures:

- Wil's immigrant parents did not measure up to his expectations; they weren't as capable as he wanted to be. His lifelong motivation was to surpass his father.
- Ray said his relationship with his father was "non-existent" because his father traveled most of the time. "Even when he was in the room, we would ask my mother, 'Where's Daddy going next?' We wouldn't direct the question to him; he wasn't an approachable person."
- Russ never wanted to go any place alone with his father. "In some way," he said, "I was clearly rejecting my father. Without being explicit, I was saying that he didn't measure up. I was searching for someone I respected to give me unconditional positive regard and also to study as a model."

Lack of respect from the adult for the young person:

- Respect is what Fran did not get from her parents, but she found it from her brother and cousin.
- Nor Diane, from the relatives with whom she was forced to live and who treated her as a poor relation.
- Nor Molly, from her mother who treated her as "a klutz."

Trust

Is the adult figure trustworthy? Two aspects of trust figure here: being available and approachable, and not turning against you. Can the young person count on the adult being there on a consistent, dependable, and reliable basis? Not causing injury or harm, not betraying you, not violating your trust?

Lack of trust examples:

- Barry couldn't count on his mother. Her violent mood swings, linked to a diabetic condition, made her very erratic and unpredictable.
- John learned he couldn't count on people to be there for him. His father died when he was a teen, and later, several mentors died just as he had formed a relationship.
- Lewis found it wasn't "safe" to learn from other people.
- Farveez's father frequently exploded with emotional outbursts, and Farveez could not reason with him.

Barry, John, and Lewis became largely self-mentoring; Farveez turned away from his father and instead bonded with his trustworthy grandfather.

Relevance

Is the advice, counsel, instruction, or direction from the adult figure relevant? Does it fit with reality as the young person sees it—with the culture the young person lives in or imagines living in? Does it fit with the personality and style of the young person?

Limitations to relevance can result from a variety of causes:

- Advice given is not seen by the young person as useful in the current situation and is either discounted or dismissed.
- The young person has a good mentor-bonding base through positive connection with adult figures, but the adults do not have the resources, skills, or motivation to be helpful in the specific instance of need.
- The young person has never had experiences where adults were a resource, so they are not sought out.

Advice Not Seen as Useful

Well-meaning parents can provide gratuitous advice that they believe is relevant to the young person without questioning its relevance for the young person today. "When I was your age ... " or similar comments that point to the adult as all-knowing can quickly be a turn-off, as many parents have discovered. When that advice is delivered in a heavy-handed way, respect between parent and child can be seriously undermined, and resistance or rebellion is likely.

The factor of relevance is increasingly important in our rapidly changing world. Margaret Mead pointed this out some years ago with reference to the nuclear age into which children were being born.[7] A more recent book on the digital economy asserts, "For the first time in history, children are more comfortable, knowledgeable, and literate than their parents about an innovation central to society."[8]

Relevance is especially difficult for immigrant parents and children who must move quickly into the new culture. Immigrant children have to sift through the advice of their parents. Much of the advice relevant in the home country does not fit the new environment. Also, home country customs can alienate immigrant children from other kids. Wil was "an immigrant kid and dressed funny," so instead of playing with other kids, he would "hang out" in the town library.

The relevance factor looms so large for children of immigrant parents that I've included Chu's story for illustration. Chu's mother, born in China of a wealthy family, went to college in Beijing but never expected to support herself. In 1947, her physician husband came to the United States on a fellowship, and the rest of the family stayed with the mother's parents.

---

[7] Mead, op. cit., p. 5.

[8] Don Tapscott, *The Digital Economy: Promise and Peril in the Age of Networked Intelligence*, McGraw-Hill, 1996, cited in *Future Survey* 18:1/037.

Two years later, with the establishment of the People's Republic of China, Chu's father was caught on one side of the Cold War alignment and her mother on the other. Her mother was left to fend for herself and her children for eight years before the family could reunite.

Later, when the whole family relocated to the United States, Chu's mother was an important mentor in encouraging her daughters to have careers so they could fend for themselves. Chu did follow her mother's career advice but learned to disregard other messages that did not fit her situation:

> "My mother was a good influence if you had problems or became discouraged. She was a good person to talk with, but I needed to think for myself and make decisions for myself. I had to keep in mind that my mother was not brought up in this country, and certain things in this country were quite different than where she came from. Her idea was that the right time to get married was when your education was behind you—then, magically, there was always going to be somebody just right for you. That's what it was like in China, but in the United States, that's not the way it is. So I got married while I was still in medical school, and it took her quite a few years before she totally approved."

Advice Not Available

A young person can be actively searching for a mentor but not able to find one who fills the need in the situation at hand. This is especially true for those who want to enter new or unusual fields. If there is a mentor-bonding base of respect and trust for adults, the person is likely to be receptive to mentor connections later when someone does appear who can provide the needed information, instruction, resources, or guidance. This was true for Don and Kay:

- Don lived on an isolated farm in the Midwest. He had good relations with his mother and stepfather, but he had interests far beyond his school's and family's resources. He filled the gap by taking correspondence courses, then going away to college. When an appropriate mentor appeared in a graduate school of architecture, he connected immediately.

- Kay wanted to work in the realm of public policy, a field that, at that time, was traditionally not open to women. Unable to find anyone available or motivated to guide her, she plotted her own course. Some years later, in a large organization where there was a well-developed mentoring tradition, she was able to connect easily to male mentors.

<u>Adults Not Seen as Mentoring Resources</u>
Young people who have had to assume adult roles or responsibilities early in their lives become used to making decisions on their own, so seeking the advice of elders might not even occur to them. In some cases, the reversal of normal parent/child roles might be so pronounced that the young person ends up in a parenting role.

- Brenda learned Spanish before she learned English. From the age of 6, she served as translator for her Anglo parents when the family was living in Mexico. In the process, she often made decisions on her own without telling them.
- Alice was the oldest of six children, responsible for managing all the younger children and the house when her mother was at work.
- Joan was thrust in the role of marital counselor to her mother from the age of 10.
- From the age of 15, Fernando provided for his two aunts as well as himself; there was no one else.
- As a teenager, Al was the one in his family who went to school to talk to the teacher about his younger brother and later told his parents they should get a divorce.

Unless they had other mentor-bonding relationships, such young people are not likely to seek the advice, opinions, and counsel of adult figures. The idea would not occur to them. They are more likely to go on their own, possibly finding other adult figures as useful resources.

DIFFERENCES BETWEEN BONDERS AND NON-BONDERS

Compared with bonders, non-bonders are unlikely to see people as mentoring sources. Instead, they learn from observation, books, experiences, or by experimenting and developing self-mentoring strategies.

Mentor Bonders	Non-Bonders
Accustomed to seeking help from others	Accustomed to doing it on their own
Tap into people as rich sources of guidance and support	Tap into people for information only
Find other people good sources of information	Rely on books and other impersonal sources of information
Comfort and familiarity in seeking out others	Comfort and familiarity in seeking own answers
Receptive	Selective
Willing to be guided and influenced	Avoid influence of others
Actively seek and develop relationships	Generally avoid building relationships
Relationships broad, can be far-reaching	Relationships with others carefully limited

DEGREES OF MENTOR BONDING

Mentor bonding is rarely an all or nothing proposition. We range from none at all to extensive bonding. Most of us are somewhere in the middle. Looking at mentor bonding as a continuum makes visible the degrees of mentor bonding.

The gradations of mentor bonding follow a bell-shaped curve with few people on either end. About 10% to 15% of the people interviewed said they had no mentors. There is almost an equal number at the other end—people who have many learning and growth-inspiring relationships with people of both genders and a variety of ages and experience. Most of us are somewhere in between, finding a few or a cluster of people to be good mentoring sources. We enlarge our mentor group to the extent we have positive experiences with people and we find their advice trustworthy, respectful, and relevant. Our mentor collection does not stay static: There is a steady inching toward the right side of the continuum as our comfort with people increases.

Mentor-Bonding Continuum

NONE----------------->SELECTIVE------------->EXTENSIVE

No bonding   **Bonding with**   **Bonding with**
with people   **some people**   **many people**

EXPLORING YOUR MENTOR-BONDING HISTORY

How can you identify your mentor-bonding pattern? Often, the pattern is very apparent, and we easily recall early relationships with parents and other adults who were important to us. Many times, though, the pattern is more elusive. Gayle's bonding pattern was obvious; Cory's was not.

Gayle's Mother

I knew Gayle had had a very special relationship with her mother, and I wanted to learn more about it. "If 'mentor' means someone who encouraged you and was a role model and nurtured you, then I would say that my mother was my first and most important mentor," Gayle told me. I asked her to explain. Here is Gayle's story of her early mentor bonding, a tribute to a remarkable mother:

"She was an extremely loving woman, very emotionally connected. I got a lot of very good feelings about myself, which is key and core for me. I always felt I was everything that she wanted in a daughter. I always felt complete approval and acceptance. She gave me an extraordinary amount of freedom to be who I was. I remember, as a child, she let me have all the freedom to dress as I wanted to dress. I was very strong-willed, and I would only wear certain dresses or dress in my brother's cast-off clothes and play with the boys. I have pictures of myself in cut-offs with a boy's haircut because it was cool and comfortable in the summer, and I wanted to be included with my brother. I never had any expectations or thoughts that little girls can't do 'this,' or little girls had to be 'that,' which was common for girls.

"She was not overprotective. I rode horseback all over our little town from the time I was 3. I was out in the caves with my brother and his friends and swimming in the little canal. She said that it was one of the hardest things for her not to be overprotective. But she didn't want me to be fearful, so I grew up feeling competent."

Gayle's mentor bonding with women started with her mother and was reinforced by her Mexican "second mother," who was a key member of the family when they lived in Brownsville, Texas. Sometimes, however, our mentor-bonding pattern is less obvious, even obscure. We might need to start with a look at our mentoring in our adult life and work backwards; this was true for Cory.

Cory's Cluster

I had nearly finished my interview with Cory, but I was puzzled. He reported a veritable stream of mentors who had been important in his life: five men, one woman, and later, two mentors who were his peers. Yet Cory said he grew up without much guidance or parental interaction. His father was "always working and never got involved." His mother was very loving and warm, but, he said, "I don't think either of them were terribly interested." *So, how did this rich mentor-bonding pattern develop?* I wondered aloud. It had to come from somewhere in his past. Here, in his words, is what we teased out:

- "My grandfather was a Russian immigrant, a very neat guy, very warm."
- "My uncle was an army officer in the artillery. He was glamorous. I had a relationship with him whenever he was visiting."
- "I was in love with a teacher in elementary school, Mrs. Dunn; I suppose because she was loving."
- "My neighbor used to take me fishing out on the Berkeley pier. Maybe I was 10. He must have liked me, because he took me with him, and I knew his son."
- "My chemistry professor in high school liked me. He gave me free rein in the laboratory."
- "I admired my girlfriend's father. He was a good friend of mine, like a contemporary. He was involved with the teen group, played piano, and was very approachable. I was part of that family all the way through high school."

So it turns out that Cory had a stream of early relationships that were warm and nurturing and set the stage for later connections. Relevance, trust, and respect were all present in these early adult relationships, even though they did not stem from close mentoring relationships with parents.

The multitude of adult figures in Cory's life seemed to fill his parent void. The transition from early nurturing relationships to mentoring relations was a natural progression. Mentor bonding took place and was continuous, in contrast to Wil, the entrepreneur we met at the beginning of this chapter, where mentor bonding was absent. But as we have seen, most of us experience something in between.

Teasing out your own mentoring history can be as easy or difficult as the examples suggested. In Chapter 19, you will find guides to help you think through your mentor-bonding history.

BRIDGE

Mentor bonding is the base element in our Mentoring Mosaic. It is the ground on which all other mentoring elements come into play, interact, and rest. We start our ever-changing art form, our mosaic, from this base. Not to say that it is fixed permanently and cannot change; we will find otherwise. But it does shape the way we approach mentoring—the way we use, develop, and apply all the other elements in our Mentoring Mosaic. In this chapter, we looked at the three key requirements for mentor bonding to take place: respect, trust, and relevance. The next chapter focuses on another striking finding from the data: the gender and age patterns among our mentors. We will explore what they are and how they come about.

Chapter 3

THE ROLE OF GENDER AND AGE IN MENTOR BONDING

One of the striking differences in the interviews is the gender and age of our mentors. Some of us have only male mentors, some only female mentors, and others have a scattering of both. A few of us have no people mentors at all. Because our early experiences in relationships are with parents and extended family, the focus of this chapter is on examining those early patterns of gender and age bonding. We also look at the personal characteristics of the key people with whom we bonded early in life.

The gender and age pattern of our mentors is usually set in childhood by the nature of the relationships we form with adults, starting with our parents—whether they were with men or women or both, and whether they were with our parents or others of that generation, or with older siblings or peers.

For most of us, our natural mentor connections stem from those early experiences. Did we bond primarily with the parent of the same gender, the opposite gender, with both, or with neither? If bonding did not occur with parents, did it occur with other family members who filled that role, who were substitutes? Were there grandparents, aunts and uncles, older siblings, or cousins? Our experience, whatever it is, sets up a pattern likely to continue through our middle adult years. In our mentor-bonding mix, most of us have a little of this and a little of that. Some of us have none of "that." What we make of our mentor-bonding mix is the tilt, the emphasis, and how it all fits together.

Having a pattern of mentor bonding with both genders would seem to be ideal. The young person who has respectful, trusting, and relevant relationships with both men and women has a larger potential mentor pool from which to draw.

Four pattern possibilities of gender bonding are obvious:
- same-gender bonding;
- cross-gender bonding;
- both-gender bonding; or
- non-bonding.

Also, age differences are notable in bonding patterns. When we put together these two factors of gender and age, we see a number of possible variations. Although gender bonding offers multiple possibilities, in our early years, one or two patterns tend to dominate. In the research data, three patterns for each gender predominate.

Common Patterns of Mentor Bonding

Men	Women
Boys with Fathers/Father Surrogates	Girls with Mothers/Mother Surrogates
Boys with Mothers/Mother Surrogates	Girls with Fathers/Father Surrogates
Boys with Older Brothers or Cousins	Girls with Older Brothers or Male Cousins

We look first at the variety of gender-bonding patterns of men, then at those of women. Examples are drawn from mentoring interviews.

GENDER-BONDING PATTERNS OF MEN

Boys with Fathers/Father Surrogates

The relationships that boys have with their fathers can be close, distant, conflicting, or missing altogether. Boys like Tony were fortunate in the positive bonding they had with their fathers.

<u>Positive Father Bonding</u>

Tony picked up a lot of his work habits from his quiet, hard-working father—"the old work ethic," he calls it. Both of his parents were born in Italy, and Tony was the first of the children born in the United States. He spent a lot of time with his father.

> "We had vegetable gardens, we built our own house, we worked on projects with the house, and we had a big basement where we used to make wine and sausage. It was a good time for me growing up; I enjoyed it, and I learned a lot. We didn't have a lot of money, but we made the best of what we had and learned to enjoy the blessings we did have. I learned that all from him."

Tony was indeed lucky, others not so. What happens then depends on the availability of father surrogates or substitutes. When Bob lost his father very early in life, his uncle filled the void:

> "Uncle Ted would come by and visit. He had a sense of obligation that his brother's widow needed assistance. He would come by in real lean times with a can of pears or something like that—it was quite a treat. He had a great concern for his nephews and nieces. He was my surrogate father. I could see a lot of my father in him in the pictures I had seen. Ted was very close and tender about that; he understood how I felt about him."

Absent or Distant Fathers

By contrast, when the father is absent, distant, or negative and there are no positive substitutes, no bonding of this type can occur. A number of men reported distant relationships with their fathers. Fathers worked long hours or spent many hours away from home. They were too busy, too tired, too ill, too passive, or just not interested.

- David had a limited amount of interaction with his father. He couldn't recall doing things with him, nor could he think of any other men who were mentors to him.
- Bruce's father was passive and made no effort to counter the domineering role taken by his mother. As Bruce sadly concluded, "I don't think I ever had a mentor in terms of a close personal relationship."
- Jim's father had a chronic health problem. Jim said, "I think I've always wanted a mentor, and I think that comes from not having a mentor in my father." There was an emptiness, a wistfulness that came through.

Unless there were other compensating male figures in their lives, such as a neighbor, a scoutmaster, or a teacher, few such men developed close mentor relationships with other men.

Negative Father Relationships

Other fathers were very active with their sons but in a way that was experienced as critical and controlling. Such relationships often are stormy and difficult and can create problems for the young person later in dealing with authority figures, particularly those who are male. Those early experiences tend to turn the young boy away from mentor relationships with men.

— *"He had a tendency to impose his will."*

Gary's father was more or less absent during his adolescence, and when he was there, Gary didn't want to get his father's attention because his father would impose his will. Gary was quite candid in admitting his authority problems: "In college, I don't think I had good relations with faculty, a function of my relations with my father. I have difficulty relating to authority figures; I avoid them." He did, however, bond with his mother and other female figures, and his later mentors were all women. In his chosen field of health care administration with a social service focus, this bonding pattern has worked reasonably well for him.

— *Distrustful; "If they look gruff … "*

Todd could not remember any men a generation older that he ever really respected, starting with his father. "I tend to approach them, especially if they look gruff, with a distrustful and a superior feeling—that I don't really care what you have to say unless you prove that it's worthwhile." Although he had a good relationship with his mother and feels comfortable with women, that was of no help in his oil corporation post where there were no women mentors. Instead, he has followed a self-mentoring path.

Boys with Grandfathers

Grandfathers can play an important role in the mentoring of young boys, either as a male surrogate or substitute. Or, if there is already good father bonding, the presence of the grandfather can provide a multiplier effect. A young person who is comfortable with and seeks out the advice and counsel of "elders" stands to gain from their wisdom.

I've heard a number of very moving stories from men about their grandfathers. I include Sam's story because of the effects of that relationship on his unusual ability to relate to older mentors later in his life.

— *"He was a very rich influence in my life."*

Sam's grandfather lived with the family during his pre-teen and teen years; he was always there when Sam came home from school. "We would talk a lot, we'd go horseback riding together, and we were just really good buddies. He was a very rich influence in my life."

So much so that when Sam was a pediatric resident, it was natural for him to seek out the eminent physician, then in his 70s, who was known as the father of neonatology. "The other residents avoided him, thought he was an old fuddy-duddy, but I used to go to his clinic when he would examine babies. He reminded me of my grandfather, and he liked me. I got to know him as a mentor because he would go across town and examine newborn babies at the pediatric hospital. The other house staff didn't like to go over there. I enjoyed him because he had a lot of real wisdom. I would watch him work with newborn babies; that's how I became interested in newborns."

This relationship worked to Sam's benefit in an unexpected way. During the Vietnam War, he learned the Army wasn't going to take him, and he was uncertain what to do. His mentor said, "You like these newborns. Why don't you go to Paris to be with a mentor there and study newborns? They know a lot of things about examining the central nervous systems and EEGs. Maybe we could get you a grant." Sam asked his mentor how that could work, and his mentor said, "Here's a NATO fellowship brochure. Why don't you send this thing in and see if you can get it?"

Without the ability to relate comfortably to older people, a comfort he developed quite naturally with his grandfather, Sam would have missed out on this valuable mentoring. The more comfortable we are in relating to many kinds of people, the wider is our mentoring net.

Boys with Older Brothers and Other Relatives

In the absence of good bonding with fathers or other older men, a number of men developed close relationships with older brothers or male relations who provided support and guidance.

—*"He was gentle, soft-spoken—a scholar."*

Ned's cousin Harry lived in Ned's house during the years that Harry went to New York University. Ned was 5, Harry about

20. Because of family bickering, Ned was very unhappy. He would wait for Harry to come home because "he was very gentle, very soft-spoken." Harry would be studying, so it was quiet, and he would allow Ned to sit there, too. The idea that he was a scholar impressed Ned—that he would sit and study for hours and hours made Ned see that this was a way to learn and to get what you wanted.

Ned tells this story: "I liked the sound of ripping papers out of spiral notebooks, and once I removed all his notes by ripping every single page. When he came home, he didn't yell. He told me that what I had done was wrong, and I shouldn't do that again. That was the extent of my punishment. I knew I had done something far worse than that. He was a very mild-mannered person."

Ned's relationship with Harry set up a mentor-bonding pattern that was replicated several times throughout his career. Ned became a member of the medical faculty in a large university. He has had a long string of mentors along the way, all bearing some relation to the wise and gentle bearing of his cousin.

— *"He was very approachable; we could josh around."*
Ben regretted and resented the lack of guidance from his father, who ran the family-owned beverage business. He turned to Ken, who was eight years older. Actually, Ken was Ben's uncle, but they were close enough in age that they could do things together. Ken had to do research for his college studies, so the two would play mathematical games together. Ken was very interested in sports, and they'd play sports together. Ben admired Ken and could relate to him both as a friend and as an adult. He continued to admire Ken, and said he's "a brilliant man, a mathematical genius."

The relationship with Ken set a mentor-bonding pattern that has repeated in Ben's life: finding a mentor who is somewhat further advanced in career, yet is close enough to be available and approachable—something Ben's father never was.

After Ken came Abe, who was five years older. Ben said he was "brilliant, spoke English and Hebrew fluently, was fantastic in sports, had a mind like a whipsaw—could play intellectual games. He was into culture, an incredible person."

Then, after Ben finished his medical training, he met a young physician from Yugoslavia who also studied microbiology and was in the United States doing research. He became Ben's mentor and took Ben under his wing. "He taught me virology, and I loved it. I thrived. He was very approachable, at my level, and we could josh around."

Boys with Male Peers

Boys who did not bond with older men for any of the reasons cited above are more likely to bond loosely with boys their own age. The comfort and companionship they might find in a group of peers can lead to peer mentoring in later years. But many non-bonders also come from this group.

- Brian grew up without much guidance and was on his own after school in his small Oregon town. Both parents worked, and he spent his free time "mixing it up" with his gang, a group of boys that did things together. Today, Brian has a number of peer co-mentoring relationships.
- Lyle had a chaotic family life. His father was a drinker and womanizer. He found hanging out with peers far safer than being with his family. Today, Lyle has found that colleague support groups meet his needs better than other forms of mentoring.

In lieu of mentor bonding, each developed self-mentoring strategies, a topic that is discussed in Chapter 18.

Boys with Mothers/Mother Surrogates

Mentor bonding with women—mothers, grandmothers, and mother surrogates—has a different quality for boys than do their relationships with men. Women tend to be more influential in the areas of values and human relationships than in vocation. In some cases, the mother is described as "warm and supportive," and then she becomes a background figure unless something unusual happened. A few men had domineering mothers whom they resented.

But a number of men had mothers who were significant in their lives in opening up the world of relationships to them: how to get along with people, how to be sensitive to them, how to be responsive to their needs, how to get approval.

- Throughout his career, Paul has used the strategies of observing and listening to people that he learned from his mother. Paul could see where his own disregard of others' feelings when he was a teen-ager created problems for him. Plus, he could observe the results of his father's dogmatic and feisty behavior.
- Dennis had a living example in the way his mother would calm his fiery-tempered father.

Both Paul and Dennis are comfortable working with and learning from women, stemming from mentor bonding with their mothers. Other men also developed relationships with their mothers in a way that helped them understand and work comfortably with women colleagues and bosses:

- Sam attributes his ability to work with women to his close relationship with his mother, who had a long bout with breast cancer. About the time he was applying to college, his mother learned she was in the terminal stage with just months to live. She insisted that he attend Dartmouth anyway, and Sam resolved to write her every night. In writing those letters, he said, "She and I had a richer last two years of her life than we had ever had before." Sam works particularly well with women and cited the chief executive officer of the hospital where he was medical director as well as a physician department head that others found difficult.

- Carl's mother set the pace for hard and rewarding work. She was the most important person to him when he was growing up. "Dad was always one to say what we had to do, but just saying it doesn't influence people very much. My mother was the one who showed us how to work hard, how to accomplish things, and how to do what we needed to do to succeed."
- Ned's mother was gone many hours of the day, working with his father in the small family business. His grandmother and aunts filled the void, particularly his grandmother, who had the greatest influence on him. She was his advocate. Whenever he wanted or needed something, she would appeal to his parents for it. She was firm, caring, nurturing, and concerned about the growth and development of the children in the absence of parents who were gone 12 or more hours a day.

Boys with Older Sisters

Although older brothers are often highly valued by women, older sisters are clearly not important to men in their mentoring history. Only one man reported a connection. This suggests either that sisters have not been in a position to help younger brothers, or that there is a lack of awareness of their contribution. The latter was true for Kevin, whose sister was 10 years his senior. He didn't realize her value to him, he said, until after he was married. Now, he is very clear that she was very supportive all along.

> "She gave me her car for a spring vacation; she loaned me money for my first car. She's the one who gave me the idea of hospital administration just by talking to me about it, because she was dating a friend who was involved in it. So she was maybe a mother substitute in a sense, almost pushing me to do things. She helped me get away from the family, even though

she couldn't. She was very praising of whatever I did, and defended me."

Boys with Female Peers

I have no examples of this possible pattern from the growing-up experiences of men. Peer mentoring with women, when it occurs, is reported in adulthood.

GENDER-BONDING PATTERNS OF WOMEN

The major mentor-bonding agents for women are both mothers and fathers—almost equally so. Mothers are rarely background figures for young women, and for most informants, the relationship was a positive one.

Girls with Mothers/Mother Surrogates

In the experiences of Marisa and Bell, we can see excellent examples of mentor bonding with mothers although their backgrounds were quite different. Marisa grew up in an upper-class Hispanic society in Colombia, and Bell in an African-American community in Louisiana.

- Marisa's mother was a journalist, a "gutsy, nontraditional female," who set the tone for Marisa's mentor bonding. She said, "My mom has been a tremendous influence in my life, and she is a non-conformist female. When I look back to the women who have truly fascinated me in my life, my sense of identity had to do with being valued by non-traditional females."
- For Bell, "The most important person in my life is my mother—I could not even talk about the person I am without talking about her. She was a young lady with a 6th grade education, but a Ph.D. in life. She was 32 when my father was killed in a hunting accident, leaving her with eight children. She chose not to remarry; instead, she went to work to provide us with all the

necessities and extra things growing children need. She taught us some very specific things: 'You remain a lady under all circumstances, no curlers, don't go out without stockings,' 'I don't want you to do what I'm doing [scrubbing floors and cleaning houses], but I don't want you to be ashamed. If you have to, you can do it.' There was continuous reinforcement for my sister and me—how important it was to be self-supporting and independent. At the same time, she never negated marriage. 'I want you to get married,' she said, 'but there are other things you need to achieve before you do that.' She always believed in working for yourself and not taking a handout. She would work all day, come home, cook, and still have time to see that we finished our homework and talk to us about what went on that day."

A few women I talked to came from matriarchal families where women mentors were built right into their families. Nora grew up in a family with a strong grandmother and seven maternal aunts, all of whom provided very close and influential relationships. Among them were three Ph.D.s and one M.D. Nora joined the professional ranks of her family by becoming a pediatrician. Her aunts, particularly the physician aunt, became her mentors.

In contrast to the importance of father surrogates for men, there are few examples of mother surrogates among the women I interviewed. Clarisse was an exception. Her own mother was distant and unapproachable, but she did find a surrogate mother in her college dean of women. The nurturing mentor relationship that developed between them lasted for many years.

Girls with Grandmothers
In my interviews, there were few examples of grandmother relationships that were strong and influential for women.

Girls with Older Sisters/Cousins

Similarly, I did not find many instances of girls bonding with older sisters or female cousins. This is in contrast to the pattern of mentor bonding in men. One of the few examples: Older sister Grace was the most important person in Letitia's professional development. She trained Letitia to be a journalist, and in time, Letitia did become a freelance writer.

Now that more women are achieving career recognition and status, I expect far more bonding with older sisters and surrogates.

Girls with Female Peers

Peers do not loom as important in the lives of young girls as they do for boys. They appear usually as one or two "best friends" rather than groups or gangs. But female peers do become important in adulthood and often are the basis of enduring and significant friendships and co-mentoring relationships.

Girls with Fathers/Father Surrogates

Girls either have strong bonding relationships with their fathers and/or other male figures, or a complete void. There seems to be little in between. Women who were tomboys and spent time with their fathers in sports and intellectual matters are likely to gravitate to male mentors.

We see in women, as in men, the multiplier effect of having mentor bonding with both father and father surrogates. Look at Lucy's experience:

> "My father always seemed to say, 'You can do it!' He didn't necessarily know how I was going to do it, but he just had a lot of pride in me." Since Lucy was the only child for a long time, she was very much a part of his life. She was interested in sports, and he would spend time playing baseball and other sports with her.

41

Lucy also had a very positive relationship with her grandfather, whom she would see weekends. She describes him as a very thoughtful man, an electrician by trade but widely read with a large library. He was very interested in the anything she took to him. The grandfather-bonding pattern repeated in college with her Shakespeare professor, who was tall, austere, the scholar of the English department. "He spent a lot of time just talking about reading and writing. He gave me room to express some of my ideas. He and my grandfather were around the same age, and I related to them in the same way."

Lucy has always felt respect from men and concludes that it's probably because she feels comfortable around them. Part of it comes from her relationship with her father and grandfather, and part comes from the sports she played as a kid: "Playing side by side with guys, they accepted you if you did a good job."

Peg's relationship with her father was important but stormy during her teen-age years. Here is how she describes those years and the years that followed:

"He was a military man; he had that military mentality of structure, organization, and drive. He also was a very high achiever. He had come from a rotten childhood and was going to make sure that his girls went to college. When I was about age 12, I said, 'I'm going to be a nurse,' and he said, 'Okay, then you're going to do it right, you're going to go to college.' He drove me in terms of schoolwork. If I came home with anything less than all 'A' marks, there was a lot of explaining to do. He was strict. He taught me how to write. There was this constant pressure that one had to please Daddy.

"I was probably 25 years old before I realized he was a mentor. It dawned on me one day that he was right. He probably provided the drive behind me. 'You aren't just going to be a staff nurse; you'll do other things. You're going to get that bachelor's degree so you can be a head nurse or something else.' He's the one who made sure I applied for scholarships. We had a big fight when I was 18 about my refusal to break up with a boyfriend. I stormed out of the house with a suitcase and didn't reconnect with him until four years later."

Peg did not abandon her college plans. She took out loans and her mother slipped her a little money now and then. She supported herself and ultimately did break up with the boyfriend. A very valuable four years, she said, becoming independent, building her competence, and doing it by herself. Now Peg said she and her father are "like two peas in a pod and talk a mile a minute" when they're together. Over time, Peg moved up in her nursing career, becoming the chief operating officer of a community hospital. No staff nurse for her!

Tempering Difficult Father Bonding

Lucy and Peg are examples of positive mentor-bonding patterns of girls with fathers. Others' experiences are more mixed. Some aspects of the father bonding can be difficult, and girls who have a father surrogate to temper stresses in the father relationship are fortunate. This was true for Laurie.

Laurie was very close to her father until she turned 15. He played softball with her, wrestled with her and her sister, was comfortable with her tomboy behavior, encouraged her, affirmed her desire to write, suggested books, and read aloud to Laurie and her sister as long as she could remember. But at 15, Laurie became an instant young woman: "I got a figure in about two months." Development was so fast, her father pulled away, and Laurie was bereft. His behavior seemed phony to her.

This experience left Laurie puzzled and untrusting. However, during her growing-up years, there was also a close family friend, Keith, who was "like an uncle" to her. He taught Laurie and her sister how to fish, was a "fantastic preacher," and did not disparage her notion of becoming a minister. Instead, he shared his ministerial experience with her and said, "Go for it."

Laurie's bonding with men has been mixed. She has been drawn to mentors who were men like her father, but her experience with her father left her with trust issues to work through. The constancy of Keith's relationship with her offset to an important degree the negative aspects of her experience with her father and made it possible for Laurie to develop effective relationships with male mentors. This has been crucial in her career development because of the few women ministers available to her at the time she entered the ministry.

Girls with Older Brothers/Cousins

A number of women felt ignored by their fathers, some even rejected. All was not lost provided there were substitutes. Older brothers can play an important compensating role as they did for Vera and Lois.

- Vera's relationship with her father was minimal. From very early on, she saw her brother getting all the attention—he was good at sports and a good student. It wasn't until later that she realized how important her brother was to her and how much he supported her. "He was always kind to me. When I wanted to go to a dance, he'd always pick me up in the car. Even when I was little, he would say, 'I'm not going to play unless my sister can play.' He taught me things: We'd sit and read and do word games. I learned to be very good in sports, too. Everything he learned he would teach me so that it was quicker for me to learn. We only had each other, because our family was so chaotic."
- No matter what Lois did, she could never measure up to her father's expectations, nor to her mother's. What made it possible for her to connect with male mentors later was her bonding with her older brothers. "They were always looking out for me. It had to do with being the baby and a girl. They taught me to be an athlete, to do boy things. They took great pride in my abilities and always set up situations for me to achieve in. They taught me to throw a baseball so I didn't throw it like a girl. I ended up playing softball into high school very competently. They used to

pole vault, and they saw to it that I learned how to pole vault. I adopted swimming as my sport and swam competitively for a number of years." They also emerged as spiritual or emotional mentors, especially brother Josh. "When I was a teen-ager, I went to him with most of my teen problems rather than my parents. It was very important that he approve of my behavior and that he set the standards for me. I told him things I would never have brought to my parents. Josh would say, 'Just be yourself; you're terrific.' While he wanted me to do all these wonderful things and was teaching me how, he was also saying, 'You're just fine the way you are.'"

Girls with Younger Brothers

Siblings in a family can band together as a protective measure against upsetting relationships with parents or to deal with changing environments. In the process, deep friendships and lifelong mentoring patterns can develop. This is true for Catherine.

Catherine had virtually no relationship with her military father or any other adult males, and her mother was emotionally unstable. When her mother "would go on the rampage and start screaming and carrying on," Catherine and her two brothers would join together. "There she goes again," they'd say and try to help each other through it.

As a result, the three children became very close. Catherine's father made a career of the military, and they moved a lot. Every time they were uprooted, the three of them checked out the new turf together. They were inseparable, a practice that continues today.

From her childhood on, peers have been important to Catherine. She is a team player. She learned early that there is strength in pulling together—that you can explore things together and make good things happen. This learning is reflected in her present-day supervisory style.

BOTH-GENDER BONDING: THE BEST OF ALL WORLDS

Most of us connect more naturally with men or women mentors, usually not both. But some people seem to have the best of all possible worlds. They list an array of both men and women mentors. It is as if every relationship they have becomes, or can turn into, a mentoring relationship. In a mentoring sense, they do have the best of all worlds. When we look more closely, we can see that their experiences with mentors later in life seem to build on their early mentor-bonding patterns.

Such folks are at ease in their relationships with people. They have a history of finding people to be good sources of information and learning. They experience people as reliable and trustworthy, they are used to being treated with respect, and they have found value in the advice and counsel that they are given. And they have had this experience with both men and women.

The following are some examples of both-gender bonding.

- With three siblings 10 or more years older, Terry was practically the baby of her family. Her older sister had a tragic ending to her life: Her boyfriend shot her and then himself. Terry was 7 years old at the time. "When that happened," she said, "I was almost cocooned. I was overly protected by my mother and father and probably had a better relationship with each of them because of this." When it came to career decisions, her parents allowed her to direct her own future. From the moment she went to nursing school, she connected to instructors and supervisors, right down the line. Terry saw each of her supervisors as a mentor and cited specific learning from each. Very quickly, she listed seven mentors—mostly women, because of her profession, but also men she met when she was working on her M.B.A.

- Ned's "best of all worlds" pattern comes not from close relationships with parents, but instead, from his bonding with his cousin and his grandmother. Ned's long-standing relationship with cousin Harry started when he was 5 years old and has continued through the years. The combination of his cousin and his warm, supportive grandmother has made it possible for Ned to connect in a mentoring way with a variety of people, both men and women. They include teachers (6th grade, high school, college, private yeshiva school), a pathologist, a physiology professor, several physicians throughout his medical career, and even a retired science professor.
- Shelley's parents were very proud of her, and she always felt loved. Her parents allowed her to find her own direction. Shelley's parents were killed in an automobile accident when she was 18, and Shelley and her sisters moved in with their Aunt Kate. Even given this tragedy, Shelley continued to build strong relationships. She quickly listed an enormous array of mentors—seven from her nursing background, plus several physicians and several educators. Her husband, too. When I commented about her unusual panoply of mentors, Shelley acknowledged that she knows "how to tap into people." Doing so is one of her joys in life. She thrives in creating interactions with people that generate learning and mentoring.
- Ben's both-gender bonding was with his uncle Ken, who was eight years older, and with his "intellectually alive" mother. He relates comfortably to both men and women: His women mentors include his high school English teacher, his wife, the woman who ran the pathology lab, and the staff director of the Peace Corps. Ben's male mentors include several men who are similar to Ken. Both men and women stand out in terms of intellect, stimulus, and the values of "don't limit yourself."

PHYSICAL AND PERSONAL CHARACTERISTICS
IN BONDING PATTERNS

Two additional aspects of mentor bonding are of note: physical appearance and personal characteristics. Often, our mentors in early career—beyond the family—replicate the physical and personal characteristics of our early mentors. We seem to be drawn to people who are similar in some way. We might not be aware of the similarities. As I point out possible connections to people, they say something to this effect: "I never thought about it that way, but you're right!" Then comes the phrase, "They were all … " with an ending something like this:

As to physical appearance, "They were all … "
- "older men, like my grandfather."
- "guys a little older than I was, like my cousin."
- "gray-haired men, like my father."

As to personal traits or characteristics, "They were all … "
- "gentle and soft-spoken."
- "gutsy, non-traditional women."
- "very powerful and assertive women."
- "warm and nurturing, like my mother."
- "intellectual, zestful, alive people."
- "strict, rigorous, and demanding of hard work."
- "tall, austere, and scholarly, like my grandfather."

The descriptors are as varied as the people; these are just a few. The personal characteristics, however, are not gender specific. If you have a mentor-bonding pattern of relating both to men and women, the mentor who is "intellectual, zestful, and alive" might be a man as well as a woman. The one thing in common is the consistent characteristics. We are drawn to mentors who are similar to our earliest mentors in some or many of their personal characteristics.

BRIDGE

In this chapter, we have looked at mentor-bonding patterns in relation to gender, age, and personal characteristics, and we begin to see how these factors in mentor bonding can influence our mentoring relationships. But we need to go deeper. The next chapter in our examination of mentor bonding deals with the dynamics involved in the process: the circumstances under which mentor-bonding patterns change, the costs of excessive bonding or non-bonding, and how mentor-bonding patterns shape mentoring.

Chapter 4

QUESTIONS PEOPLE ASK ABOUT MENTOR BONDING

- How do mentor-bonding patterns shape our mentoring?
- Mentor bonding sounds very important, but how does it work?
- If mentor bonding is such a powerful force in shaping our mentoring, does the pattern ever change, or are you "stuck" with that early imprinting? Can and do you ever change?
- Is there such a thing as too little or too much bonding?
- If your mentor bonding is low or zero, is there any way to overcome that?
- Can your mentor-bonding pattern get in your way?

These are some of the many questions people ask about mentor bonding that we will pursue in this chapter.

HOW DO MENTOR-BONDING PATTERNS SHAPE OUR MENTORING?

Our mentor-bonding profile provides the foundation for our experiences with or without mentors. How we "do" our mentoring process is influenced by this basic mentor-bonding pattern. The big divide is, of course, between bonders and non-bonders and how each group approaches mentoring. From there, it's a blend of resources and opportunities—those we are surrounded by and those we make ourselves—that help shape our course.

We develop ways of behaving toward adult figures based on our early mentor-bonding experiences. These unconscious or partially conscious ways of behaving continue to play out in our life. We develop attitudes and stances that attract or turn away certain types of mentors or, in the case of non-bonders, prevent us from making mentor connections at all.

If we've had early relationships that were respectful, trustful, and relevant, we are likely to feel comfortable seeking help whenever we need it. We are open and receptive to an array of people resources.

If our relationships have been respectful and trustful, but the advice given was not seen as pertinent to our life, we will go our own way until a relevant resource appears.

But if we've had the misfortune to find the people in our world hostile, indifferent, or excessively demanding, we are more likely to turn away from people as mentors and rely on our own resources.

Where trust has been an issue, we are likely to approach relationships with caution. If we have had positive experiences only with certain kinds of people and under certain circumstances, we're likely to limit our outlook to those kinds of people and circumstances again. We are not stuck there, however, as the "It wasn't until … " phenomenon illustrates.

DO MENTOR-BONDING PATTERNS EVER CHANGE?

Thus far, we have focused on early experiences with mentor bonding, but that is not the total picture. Mentor-bonding patterns are not cast in stone. Although they tend to form a fairly fixed pattern, they do change with life experience and changed perceptions. Early mentor-bonding patterns are the rule, but as we change, grow, enlarge our experiences, and alter our perceptions of the people around us now and in the past, some interesting things happen. Later bonding can indeed take place. This could be a conscious process, or it might come upon you unaware—like the "It wasn't until …" phenomenon.

"It wasn't until …" is a tip-off phrase that suggests later bonding. There are many examples:
- It wasn't until Russ had unconditional acceptance from his male psychotherapist that he could connect with a male mentor.
- It wasn't until Bruce's wife opened up the world of relationships that he could develop a mentoring relationship with a woman.
- It wasn't until Jim observed men who were effective leaders in the company and who had mentors that he "finally realized" what he was missing out on by not being receptive to being mentored.
- It wasn't until Pat was in her 30s that she could appreciate the feminine strength and talents of her mother.
- It wasn't until Mel understood that his father was not the "bad guy" in the family dynamics—as he had thought—that he could bond effectively with men.

New experiences can generate shifts in perceptions and awareness. In mentor bonding, these shifts take place in one of the three areas of respect, trust, or relevance. These shifts open up new mentor-bonding possibilities. A similar shift might be possible for you. If your pattern leans to non-bonding, you could have new experiences that cause you to see some people in your world more positively, in a new light. As you gain new insights that modify your attitudes in one or more of the three areas of respect, trust, and relevance, you are likely to broaden your mentor-bonding base.

Yvonne is a good example of a later mentor-bonding experience. Although she is a charismatic educator and consultant, Yvonne has struggled throughout her life in keeping to a disciplined path.

Yvonne's relationship with both parents was limited, because her brother was the favored one in the family. As a result, Yvonne acted out, and neither parent gave her the steady, firm guidance she needed. Luckily, Carol—a woman friend of Yvonne's father's—came into Yvonne's life when she was 19 and in college. Carol became Yvonne's surrogate mother, a relationship that continued until Carol died many years later.

"I learned a lot of values and principles from her: how I was perceived by others, that I had a tremendous persuasive power, and that the thing that would be the most difficult for me in my life would be self-discipline. I could talk to her. She had all the things I admired in people: high standards, persistence, and follow through."

Yvonne's relationship with Carol had the three requirements for mentor bonding. Respect: Carol gave Yvonne respect and love and pointed out her potential. Trust: Carol was always there for Yvonne, always accepting no matter what. Relevance: Carol also sensed what Yvonne needed in order to make it in the world and provided discipline to meet high standards. Carol was a beacon for Yvonne. In fact, Yvonne's later mentors have been women with many of the same characteristics as Carol; some were rigorous and held high standards while others were valuing and supportive.

ARE THERE DOWNSIDES TO MENTOR BONDING?

Mentor-bonding patterns are not "good" or "bad" per se; they are just different. Advantages and potential risks exist in all forms of mentor bonding. In the same way that, when carried to excess, our strengths become weaknesses, the mentor-bonding pattern we buy into can create problems for us. Non-bonding can lead to excessive independence; strong bonding can foster mentor dependence and excessive leaning; and negative bonding can create unhealthy situations. All can have costs.

The Payoff and the Price of Non-Bonding

As children, a few of us could not find adults whom we could trust, who respected us, and whose advice was relevant. As a result, we did not connect with or learn from adults and went our own way. We taught ourselves, learned to keep our own counsel, and provided our own guidance.

The sort of independence non-bonders develop has its place. Non-bonders are not likely to follow traditional ways, and they invent themselves and their work as they go along. It's a natural for pioneers, inventors, and other innovators, as non-bonders find it easy to break away from the pack and follow their own star. But there's a price to pay for going it alone, for being independent.

- Lewis, who had reasons not to trust any adults, resisted mentoring figures and taught himself almost everything. He could learn out of books because "that was safe." But, he observes, "I'm a homemade man and, like many things homemade, sometimes they don't work very well."
- Vicki was labeled "the strong one" in her family and found she couldn't say when she was hurting or feeling vulnerable, and she ended up in a career path that was not of her choosing. "You miss out a lot when you can't put yourself at the feet of the master," she said wistfully. "A lot of that learning is trial and error, but it would be nice to sit there and say, 'Show me the way.'"
- Becky did things on her own to avoid the kind of control she was getting from her parents. She sought out resources and found the library to be her best friend; books were her mentors. It was only later that she found she had to learn how to deal with people.

- Alexa didn't realize she sent signals that she didn't need or want a mentor. She said, "I feel that way inside most of the time, but there's something missing; I want a mentor."
- Wil describes both the rewards and price he paid going it alone as a cable TV pioneer: "In almost everything I did, I was first in the field, and nobody would have known where to guide me. FM broadcasting at the beginning, TV when there was hardly any TV. It was like being an inventor—you solve the problem yourself. It was more gratifying than creating an organization that worked on the problem. But the consequence was that I was less than patient with everyone else for not being as competent as I wanted them to be. My greatest skill was doing the whole thing myself. Still, I resented working so damned hard."

The Price of Excessive Bonding

Similarly, those of us who tend to seek out people for help can overdo it. We can become mentor-dependent, leaning on others, tending to "go ask" before sufficiently studying the situation or problem or doing some preparatory work.

> Louisa looks back now and can see the extent to which she was mentor-dependent as the "baby" in the family. Whenever she ran into a problem, she learned to "go ask." Having a sister five years older encouraged this behavior. She would ask for help, not for information. The problem would be solved, but no growth took place—it simply reinforced her dependency. Her learning and growth came more in school when she was not given this special treatment.

Mentors I've talked to avoid mentees who "hang on" and are unwilling to move toward independence. They see such mentees as a drag. Excessive leaning also can result in failure to develop self-mentoring strategies.

The Price of Negative Bonding

Most of the time, our mentor-bonding pattern works on our behalf—this is our way to connect with people to form productive and satisfying mentoring relationships. Occasionally, however, a few of us find ourselves in dysfunctional mentor-bonding patterns that do not aid our growth and development as human beings. Most of the people I talked to who had negative early relationships simply rebelled, turned away, and chose to go the non-bonding, self-mentoring route. Sometimes, though, we get stuck. Several women I interviewed were caught in a destructive mentor-bonding pattern in their earlier years. Only as mature women did they break from these dysfunctional patterns. They had bought into relationships that contained the three elements of relevance, trust, and respect, but with a perverted twist. Look at Beth's story:

> Beth received a great deal of teaching from her father as well as her brother, who was 13 years older. It took the form, she said, of "training to take this hopelessly trivial person and put her on the path so she wouldn't be an imbecile. Those were the people who modeled for me and whose traits I took on. I admired them and felt that was the only way to live. Because they put down my mother a lot and made her seem stupid and trivial, it was hard for me to have women as models. So I picked harsh men. I learned from them, 'Don't trust anyone, don't look up to anyone, don't trust the bastards!'"

> Following that pattern, Beth chose therapists who were strong men and very directive—with her being "subservient." Her first time trusting women came when she was in her early 30s in a women's group. The women helped her through a divorce and in deciding what to do with her life. For the first time, she admired women and their strength. By the time I met Beth, she was long over that hurdle and had a successful career. She knows well the power of mentor bonding to influence your life in a negative way.

Mentor bonding of this sort is really mentor bondage. Luckily, it is rare.

BRIDGE

In this section, we have explored what mentor bonding is, how it develops, how it influences our relationships, and how it provides a base for the Mentoring Mosaic. Aids for exploring your mentor-bonding history as well as suggestions for altering or enlarging your mentor-bonding base can be found in Chapters 19 and 25. In the next section, we begin our exploration of mentoring messages, those edicts and statements that provide much of the underpinning of our values. In Chapter 5, we start by examining what mentoring messages are and how they function.

Chapter 5

WHAT ARE MENTORING MESSAGES?

Brigitte, an operating room supervisor, was small, blonde, feminine, and looked "sweet," but the truth was, she could be tough as nails, and the surgeons knew it! Brigitte came from a German family whose motto was: "The Helping Hand Is at the End of Your Elbow." Fiercely independent and assertive, she thoroughly exemplified her family motto.

In contrast to Brigitte, what Jane heard growing up was, "If you're good, good things will happen to you." What this message encouraged was a polite, conforming behavior, responsive to others' needs.

Family mottoes and messages are general themes drawn from experience of the elders in our world. They are intended to interpret that world to young people and to serve as rules of conduct. Messages are early forms of socialization. In this chapter, we examine the nature of mentoring messages, what they are, how they affect us, and how they influence our mentoring process. In the two chapters that follow, we will look at a sampler of messages and review the dynamics of message sending and receiving—how they affect mentoring, and where they fit into the Mentoring Mosaic.

Messages and mottoes are mentoring to the extent that they are conscious or unconscious guides or influencers of our behavior. In the examples of Brigitte and Jane, we see the impact of two different family messages on the behavior of family members. Mentoring messages are a major source of our core values and provide the underpinnings that set up the direction and substance of our life. Because they are very potent forces for most of us, we need to understand them, how they work for us, and how they get in our way. We are liberated by our messages or held hostage to them, sometimes both. Some of our mentoring messages are uplifting and freeing; others are stifling and imprisoning.

Messages serve a purpose for parents in rearing children and preparing them for the reality of the world as parents see it. As adults, however, we do not have to continue to be governed by them. To change these messages or lessen their impact, we need to be aware of our cultural imprinting—to inventory our mentoring messages and to look at them freshly as if for the first time. We are unlikely to rid ourselves entirely of some messages, even if we choose; however, once the messages and their origins are understood, we can enhance their positive effects and blunt the negative ones.

The focus of this section is on the messages we received during our formative, growing-up years. We receive many messages about ourselves throughout our lifetime. How we receive and respond to those messages often is a result of the mentoring-message pattern we formed early in our life experience. We can examine those patterns to see what they tell us about message influences in our mentoring process.

What we received and what we made of those early messages tell us a great deal about our attitudes, our values, and our sense of self, including:
- how do we view authority, and how receptive are we to being mentored;
- what balance do we give independence and community;
- what sense do we have of our competence and worth;
- how open or closed are we to new ideas;
- how wide or narrow are the parameters of our world and of our behavior;
- how broadly do we view our horizons, and how limited are our choices;
- what do we aspire to and what do we disdain;

- what values do we cherish; and
- how do we treat people.

MESSAGE INTERPRETATION

Mentoring messages—the messages we have picked up from words, actions, and behaviors of significant figures in our early lives—may come across as positive, negative, or neutral. What we make of messages is subject to our interpretation. These messages are not just verbal; they are part and parcel of the entire communication process. We make meaning by what's said and not said as well as by what's indicated by eye expression, voice tone, and body posture. We also pick up cues from the context or setting. Messages can be ambiguous and difficult to interpret; yet, all along, we try to make meaning of them.

How accurately we catch the meaning of the sender varies. Because interpretation is a subjective process, distortion can easily occur. We might take a limited message and elaborate on it in our minds or take a positive message and discount it to fit our negative self-image. Sometimes, we miss the mark completely. We also can ignore the message and let it roll off our back, or we can accept it at face value. Regardless, it's what we pick up—the meaning the message has for us—that carries the impact.

MESSAGE MULTIPLIERS

Often, mentoring messages have a multiplier effect. Messages, either positive or negative, that are reinforced by other similar messages by one sender or by messages from two or more senders, gain power. These message multipliers greatly affect our feelings of self-worth. They can be a tremendous source of joy—or of bad feeling. Rarely do we receive an excess of positive messages; usually, it's the reverse. That's when we experience problems. We can handle a single negative message fairly well, but when a pattern of negative messages develops, the result is a strong hit on our confidence and self-esteem. The negative energy has multiplied, and the message sticks with us sometimes far into the future. This might not show on the surface, but under stress, the demons pop up unexpectedly and powerfully.

> Wendy's mother usually scolded her two daughters with two guilt-inducing messages: "You ought to be ashamed of yourself!" and "You ought to know better." Although her sister let them roll off her back, Wendy took them very seriously and felt bad.

> Wendy's sister, five years older, could do all sorts of "wonderful things," and it hurt when she didn't want Wendy around. When Wendy was inept or when something went wrong, her sister would turn on her: "It's all your fault!"

> These mother/sister messages became Wendy's lifelong negative companions. When something goes wrong all these years later, those voices of the past merge inside Wendy, and she hears, "Well, it's all your fault. You ought to know better." Luckily, Wendy knows now to question and reevaluate the situation, but the awesome power of messages is illustrated by this automatic inner voice, still present years later.

Consider the toxic messages many of us have received. "You'll never amount to anything." "Why can't you be like your sister [or brother]?" "You never do anything right." "Stupid!" "You'll never make it to college." In workshop groups, I am always amazed at powerful negative messages, such as these, related by attractive, competent, and successful people.

MESSAGE CONTENT

To see the message motifs in our Mentoring Mosaic, we must bring our messages into view, much like putting them under a microscope for closer examination. Real-life examples of different kinds of messages can be helpful for comparison as we examine our own. Once identified, we can study the messages for current-day relevance.

Messages are of two types: first, general statements about the nature of the world, the way people are and should be, and the values of family or community; and second, individually directed messages aimed at each of us about who we are and how we should think, be, act, and do. The messages having the most impact on us as young children communicate something about our worth as a person, our abilities and possibilities, and the expectations adults have for us.

General Messages

General messages are meant to apply to all those involved, from the children in the family to the community to the larger world. They communicate values and expectations. Here are illustrative messages from workshops and interviews:

Excellence, Striving, and Hard Work
- Be the best you can; don't accept less.
- There's nothing you can't do if you're willing to work hard.
- No goal is insurmountable—if you want it, you work for it, and you figure out ways to get it.
- When you make a decision, stick with it—don't be easily swayed.
- If you say you're going to do it, you'd better do it!
- Be thorough at what you do; do it well enough that you're proud of what you've done no matter what it is.
- Don't give up—see it through; don't let it defeat you.

Self
- Take care of yourself.
- If you're not happy doing something, then don't do it. You have the rest of your life to work and be miserable.

Authority, Obedience
- Be obedient, listen to your parents, get good grades, and don't cause trouble.
- This is the way it's going to be!
- You have to do what I say, and don't ever cross me!

Education and Learning
- School is more important than chores.
- Study and learn.
- Respect teachers and what they stand for.
- Do well in your studies.
- There's no excuse in our family for not getting good marks.
- Education doesn't matter; the almighty dollar speaks.

Independence
- Stand on your own two feet.
- Stand up for what you believe.

Limits, Options
- Don't limit your horizons; don't be afraid to explore.
- Don't close yourself in; other people are out there.
- You'd better make do with what you have and not aspire to much.

Attitude
- Whatever happens will turn out positive even though you don't understand at the moment.
- Always try to be optimistic.

Social Relations
- A person is known by the company he (or she) keeps.
- Take the first step: Smile first, and people will smile back.

Concern for Others
- Be considerate of others.
- Take care of your brothers and sisters.
- Always do more than your share.
- Set an example for everybody else.

Individually Directed Messages

Individual messages are customized and directed to a specific person. They relate to competencies, realities, and expectations as seen by people in our lives. Children receive many personally directed messages about who they are, who they can be, who they should be, and who they must be. Messages can be positive or negative in terms of their impact. Few of us have any surplus of positives. If anything, it's the other way around: We carry baggage from the past of messages that no longer fit but that still create hurt and pain. Here are examples of messages collected in seminar groups:

Negative Messages	Positive Messages
From Parents	
"You aren't lovable."	"I'm very proud of you."
"You'll never amount to anything."	"You've been a blessing."
"Why can't you be good like … ?"	"You always care about others."
"You're a girl! You can't do that!"	"Beautiful women don't need make-up."
From Teachers and Counselors	
"You'll never be an electronics engineer."	"You should go to college."
"You're not college material."	"You're a bright kid."
"Your sister did better than that!"	"You're a leader."
"You're average."	"You'll go far."
From Siblings	
"Get out of the way."	"You've got great legs, Sis!"
"Don't bother us; we're playing."	"I'm glad you're my brother."
"Who cares what you think!"	"Not bad, kid!"
From Peers	
"Bookworm!"	"You're my friend."
"Ski-nose!"	"You always figure out math problems."
"Four-eyed metal mouth!"	"You're always there when I need help."
"String-bean!"	"I can trust you; you don't gossip."

MESSAGE CONSISTENCY

When we are small, we are so dependent on adults that we fasten on every cue that can help us get what we need and want. Beyond our survival and safety, we desperately need the attention and approval of the adults around us. For some of us, confirmation of our worth happens fairly naturally; for others, it is a constant struggle. It helps if we're surrounded by an extended family and/or community that is supportive of young children. That was the experience of Elsa, who grew up in a small Finnish community in rural Canada that provided a warm and comfortable environment for all children. Amy's experience was similar. She lived in an extended family of aunts, uncles, and cousins, all of whom supported the kids even when they got into trouble.

But most of us grew up in a nuclear rather than extended family, limited to mother, father, and children—if that. Other family members just weren't close and available. This situation is hard for new parents who are inexperienced and have few people to call on for help. The effectiveness of nurturance and guidance depends on the ability of the few available caregivers to encourage, support, and guide the young child. Just look at some of the variables:

- Parents might not have any notion of what parenting is all about.
- Parents might disagree on parenting principles and practices.
- Parents might differ in their ability and interest in raising young children.
- Parents might not realize they are each sending different messages.
- Parents might not realize they are sending inconsistent messages from one day to the next.

Families where parents have different values and expectations invariably project those conflicts onto the child, sending mixed or confusing messages to which the young person is expected to respond. When parents are divorced and have different living patterns and lifestyles, messages can be doubly confusing—the child has to sift through different contexts as well as different messages. And a single parent must do it all.

Parenting is not easy. No wonder most of us grow up with a mixed bag of messages, an indigestible message soup. Although many of the messages work for us, some of them get in our way.

BRIDGE

In this chapter, we examined the nature of mentoring messages, what they are, how they affect us, and how they influence our mentoring process. Next, we will look more deeply into the content of mentoring messages. What are the kinds of messages that impact so greatly on us in our growing-up years?

Chapter 6

A SAMPLER OF MENTORING MESSAGES

This chapter provides a sampling of mentoring messages drawn from interviews. Messages are organized by themes about worth as a person; about abilities and possibilities; about rules, discipline, and authority; about achievement and competence; about getting an education; about work and career; about responsibility; about the place of money; and about service to the community. This collection can be useful in identifying the message types with the most power and influence in our lives.

MESSAGES ABOUT WORTH AS A PERSON

We get our sense of our worth as a person from a multitude of signals from the people around us, about our "being" and our "doing." Are we valued simply for being who we are, or are there conditions laid on us that we must perform or meet in order to get the love and approval we so badly need? Our message worth comes from the love and attention that we receive, the respect and trust we are given, the expectations placed on us, and the evaluation we get about how we're doing.

As we grow and become active within our family, school, and community, we learn quickly that some of our behavior pleases adults and fits with their expectations—and some definitely does not. The messages don't even have to be verbally expressed. We very quickly learn to put up our antennae to get a reading.

Many of us cherish the love and attention received: "My parents doted on me." "I always felt loved." "From the people around me, I felt loved, needed, and wanted." "My grandmother always gave us that sense of how important we were and how neat we were."

Some of us had negative messages about our worth and importance: "My father was drinking, never around, and never took an interest." "My mother was emotionally disturbed and sometimes didn't even recognize me." "I felt I wasn't wanted in the family."

Most of us had an experience somewhat in between. Dave learned very early that he could not get love and cuddling from his faculty parents, but he could get their approval if he performed—and he did. Indeed, he performed so well that he became the darling of the university faculty. Children learn very quickly how to please caregivers.

Love, Affection, and Attention

Some mentoring messages tell us only indirectly that we are worthwhile. We need to look at actions as well as words, at the amount of time we spend with each parent or parent surrogate, and the kind of the attention paid to us.

Consider parents who patiently coach us and develop our skills, who are cheerleaders or happy responders to our achievements. Parents who sat through endless baseball games, swim meets, and other sports matches to support and urge us on. Parents who cheerfully transported us to practice, scout meetings, and school events. Parents who attended school performances where we awkwardly or skillfully performed—and gamely or enthusiastically applauded our efforts. Parents who made special efforts to see that we had opportunities not easily available because of living in a rural area or because of limited finances. Parents who worked to see that we had opportunities of which they had been deprived.

Sometimes, these supportive parent actions are so subtle that we fail to pick them up and appreciate them for what they represent. I've been interested in the positive messages that some people, especially women, received from their fathers. "How did you know you were important and valued?" I asked. By "being taken around with Dad and shown off." By "his spending a lot of time with me playing baseball and by going hiking to different places." By "sitting with him while he read to me." By "helping him work": gardening, painting, laying tile, helping build a garage, pushing wheelbarrows full of cement. Sometimes even by going to his work with him. The key is feeling important and special.

Respect

We sense our worth as a person from the love and attention displayed, the respect and trust shown to us, and the encouragement of our independence.

The family dinner table is a fertile forum for the transmission of messages in all shapes and forms. It can be used to focus on all of a child's transgressions—or his or her accomplishments. It can be used to transmit values as well as encourage communication and the thoughtful development of ideas. Topics might range from opinions on world events to lessons from Sunday school.

Respect for one's opinions—or the reverse—can stand out in these discussions. In the chart that follows, we see a range of examples. At their respective family dinner tables, some young people received respect as persons as well as for their opinions; the experience of others was withering.

THE DINNER TABLE AS A MESSAGE FORUM

—*"One-upmanship was the dinner table game ... "*

"In my family, my parents cheered when one of us scored against another. That kind of sparring was an accepted norm in the family—but it was bruising to outsiders. My wife felt put down and out of place in family gatherings. It was bruising to me, too. I had automatically incorporated confrontation into my management style in the HMO where I worked. I went 'toe to toe' with physicians. It wasn't long before I was transferred out of my management job."

—*"It was lively around the dinner table."*

"We replayed the Friday athletic events, blow by blow. We had a rehash of the Sunday school lesson and what the Bible said, and Dad—an inveterate newspaper reader—would comment on what was in the paper. You can see I come from a family of conversationalists. It was a lively place."

—*"It was a whole thought process."*

"My parents played a big part in teaching me leadership roles. At dinner every night, my father expected that we would be able to defend any viewpoint we might hold, and he would often take the opposite point of view—whether or not he believed it—just to help us think through the logic of our opinion and see the implications of what we were saying.

"It sounded like argument, but it was more whether or not the Vietnam War should be going on, or if black people had the right to live in our neighborhood or not. It was a whole thought process, really having to research my opinions and express them well.

"My father was very well read and had lunch with a variety of people, so he was apt to have an overview that we, of course, would not—whatever our teachers said was what we thought was right. He really challenged a lot of that and helped us see that we could think for ourselves."

—*"We were always taken seriously around the dinner table."*

"The whole business was the conversation. There was a rule that you couldn't read anything at the table, which always struck me as a very sound principle. You talked about what you had done during the day in an interesting way. Each person was taken seriously as an individual, as opposed to dismissing anything that kids did as being unimportant. We had quality discussions about issues and events and our thoughts about them. Our opinions were valued, especially if they were well backed up with information."

—*"I learned I didn't have the right to speak."*

"We had a formal dinner table with linen and silver. My father carved, served, and held forth. My mother never said a word. Early on, I learned I didn't have the right to speak. My voice wasn't valued. When I tried, my brother said, 'Who cares what you think!'"

Trust and Independence

Coupled with respect is the need for the growing young person to feel trusted and increasingly independent. For most of us, the messages move in this direction. But for others, adult needs for control send quite the opposite message.

On the Positive Side

—*Responsibility plus privilege*

As the oldest child, Rose carried a heavy responsibility to be an example for the rest of the kids, but there was a plus side as well. As a teen-ager, she didn't have a curfew; she was expected to come home when she was tired or when something was going on that she didn't like. It made her feel trusted as a functioning human being and not a baby.

— *Freedom to explore*

Vera's independence came from summers in Manitoba at her mother's family cabin on a lake. She recalls the things she was allowed to do when she was 5 or 6 years old. "We'd be gone with a friend who was three or four years older, going through sand hills, scouring the beach, the forest, sand cliffs, swampy areas, the train station. Just incredible things we were allowed to do on our own. At home, too, in the winter, riding toboggans for hours and hours, riding down a shallow river frozen over but also off the edge of cliffs."

— *Demonstrated ability to cope with adverse conditions*

Raphael's trust and independence came out of a traumatic childhood. His mother committed suicide when he was 16 — the family had faced a real struggle in the years leading up to the incident. His father saw how Raphael and his brother performed under adverse situations and knew that his sons had the fiber to make it on their own, so he allowed them considerable freedom.

— *Strictness but freedom to make decisions*

Liz's independence messages came from parents who were very strict but believed she should be allowed to think for herself and do for herself. She knew what the rules were and what her goals were. The messages and environment created by her parents helped her be a very independent thinker. She has no trouble saying "no" in a group, because part of her upbringing was to stand up for what she believed and defend the issue against all odds.

<u>On the Negative Side</u>
> — *Seeking to conform*
>> Lacey wanted so much to be accepted and have people close to her love her that she conformed to whatever was asked, whether or not it was good for her. She made herself "malleable," as she puts it, and allowed herself to be governed by everyone else.

> — *A life not her own*
>> Cynthia has "felt like an observer" for much of her life. The biggest message she received from the adults around her was that her life wasn't hers to run.

> — *Others charting the course*
>> Teresa is regretful: "I guess I don't know how to make decisions." Her life was always planned out by her father. Instead of charting her own course, she "let the river carry" her. Later, when she had to make her own decisions, she didn't know how, and she said that now, "I guess I still don't."

In most cases where trust and independence messages are positive and strong, the young person has been given scaled experiences that demonstrated to adults a readiness to assume increasingly independent roles. In such a step-by-step process, trust builds. Where the messages have been negative, the developmental process is ignored or offset by the adult's need to control.

Messages about Abilities and Possibilities

In interviews, I ask, "What were the messages you received from your parents and other adults about you, about your ability, what you could be, should be, or must be—the possibilities in your life?" There are many positive messages:

- "My father gave me the impression that I was capable of doing anything."

- "I got the sense from my mother that I was a good person; my father added the competition part—'You have it in you to be the best.'"
- "My mother said, 'Atta-girl, you can do it'—she always made me feel I could move that couch, paint that ceiling. I never was a limp-wristed woman."
- "My family was telling me I was smart and would do well at whatever I did, but it was entirely up to me what I did."

Yet many of us received negative messages about our abilities. All the people I talked to were functioning well in society, but the messages some had received about their abilities ran directly counter to their success. Misjudgments by parents, teachers, or counselors stand out.

- John's mother felt he "definitely wasn't bright," but he was "good with his hands." John had a difficult early life with an ailing father who died of a heart attack as well as a delinquent brother he had to manage. Although John had a hard time getting on track, he finished medical school with flying colors and is a practicing physician. Granted, he is good with his hands, but that's only one of his many abilities.
- The self-fulfilling prophecy operated with Sherry. Her older sister was a very good student, but Sherry often was told that she was an average child. She interpreted that message as "just" average, that she could do no more than barely hang on and get a two-year degree. But an important teacher challenged her, "You are going to get your B.S. degree!" Sherry told her teacher that she didn't think she had the ability to do it even though she was pulling good grades and knew it. Her teacher was shocked. It took a while for Sherry to turn her head around and view herself differently. The story had a happy ending when Sherry became the first member of her family to graduate from college.
- Lara was told she wasn't college material through a testing program. She believed them and flunked out of university.

Later, she challenged that expectation and went on to get advanced degrees and teach at the university level.

Misjudgments verbalized in such negative messages do great harm to young people—the self-fulfilling prophecy at work. Robert Merton spelled out this theory some time ago: Once an expectation is set, even if it's not accurate, we tend to act in ways that are consistent with that expectation. Often, the result is that the expectation, as if by magic, comes true.[9] Luckily, the people above were able to rise above such inaccurate and negative messages, though with much trauma and time delay.

Gender-Different Messages

Our sense of worth is heightened or diminished by the gender messages we receive. Some of us find that our value is measured by our gender.

Men

Several of the men talked about special treatment they received because of their gender. Peter was aware that his older sister was jealous of him because of the freedom he was given. Gary's father took him on business trips occasionally and gave him other special privileges since he was the only boy and the oldest. "I felt I was favored," Gary said. "I was made to feel important."

Women

When it comes to negative content, women are more likely than men to receive messages that communicate lesser worth as a child and limited options for the future. These are communicated in several ways. One is by negative comparisons, praising the boy's abilities and discounting those of the girl. That happened to Joan, whose mother

---

[9] Robert Merton, *Social Theory and Social Structure*, Free Press, NY, 1957.

said, "Well, young lady, you're not so smart. You get good grades, but your brother is much better."

Another way of communicating lesser worth is in the prioritizing of resources and energies on behalf of the male child. In Eloise's European-oriented home, the sun rose and set on the male child. The role of the female child was to look after the male, to protect him and make sure all energies went to helping him acquire skills. This was true also in Vera's family. The financial resources went first to her brother to see that he received an education. As for her, "You can learn to type and get a good job as a secretary."

By contrast, Adrienne's father was determined to give her the educational opportunities she wanted, even if it meant a financial hardship for the family. "I was ready for college the year the bottom dropped out of cotton and the Depression came on," Adrienne remembers. "My father didn't have two pennies to rub together, but he said I must go to college if I wanted to."

It was important to Marisa's parents to invest in her education as well: "You cannot spend too much money on her brain" was the message from her father. Her mother's message was, "My two daughters aren't beautiful, but they're bright." She concluded Marisa would have to make her way by her intellectual talents.

We cannot leave this discussion of "worth" messages without looking at the indirect messages communicated by the division of labor in the home. Are there strict gender roles or a more equal sharing?

- Lacey's father had more power "because he made money and ran the whole house. Everything there was to meet Daddy's needs—when you ate dinner, where you'd go on vacation."
- In contrast, Amy's mother worked, did volunteer work, and helped with school things, and Amy saw her father helping at

home. "Dad always did the dishes in the evening with our help. Mom made dinner, though sometimes they'd reverse roles. Saturday morning, we could all be out mowing the lawn and weeding together, or we could all be in the house cleaning. It was not segregated. If things were at all out of order, Dad would often start the vacuum and get things going."

MESSAGES ABOUT RULES, DISCIPLINE, AND AUTHORITY

Children store up messages about how they're treated when they get into trouble. Are they immediately scolded, severely punished, reasoned with, or corrected gently? Is discipline harsh or soft; is it perceived as fair and appropriate or unreasonable? Through the correction and discipline we receive, we build up messages about rules and authority. What follows are contrasting examples:

Contrasting Examples of Discipline

—*"I believe you should apologize to the ranger."*

"On our trip to the Grand Canyon, I was 16 and feeling my oats. My 12-year-old cousin was along, and we decided to walk to the bottom of the Canyon. When we got there, we ran into some boys who were going to a ranch three or four miles up the river. We didn't get to the ranch until 2 o'clock. We went for a swim and started walking back.

"Just as we got to the part of the walk where you start climbing, my cousin got a big blister on his heel and started complaining. He just ran out of gas. We were on the bottom of the Canyon in the early evening with no real way of communicating. I kept him going until we arrived at a midway station, and I was able to get a telephone message to the top.

"About 11:30 or so, we were roused from our non-sleep by a man who had one mule for my cousin. He was put on the mule and taken back to the top, and I was left at the station. I arrived at the top at about 7 in the morning. The only thing my grandfather said was, 'I believe you should apologize to the ranger; you caused a great inconvenience.' That was the sum total of the discussion."

—*"You break this up right now!"*

"I had just got a little red squirt gun and was told I should never shoot it in the house. One day, I squirted water all over the head of my younger brother, and he began screeching and crying. My father came out. The sheets were soaked, and I had this squirt gun in my hands. My father asked what happened, and my mother told him.

"Father told me, 'You know what I'm going to have you do—give me the squirt gun.' He gave me a hammer and said, 'You break this up right now!' I began to wail like a wounded cow and brought the hammer down and missed; I wouldn't hit the darned thing. 'You hit it! You break it up right now!' He never touched me. So I wailed terribly, closed my eyes, brought the hammer down. It broke into a thousand pieces, and I never used a squirt gun in the house again.

"That night, he brought me home another one and said, 'You won't squirt again in the house, will you?' 'No, Daddy, I won't.' So obedience to the rules, respect for authority and for people at school were all things I was taught from the very beginning— what I had to do if I was going to get along in this world."

Most of us experienced rules that were reasonably fair and firm:

- Craig knew there were rules to be abided by in the house; his mother was the disciplinarian, but the rules were not excessive.
- In Liz's strict environment, there were strong constraints about rules and where you were to go in life. But Liz was allowed to think and act for herself within that framework.

But others of us experienced parent figures as unreasonable, arbitrary, and unfair:

- Polly said that her mother would say, "'This is the way it's going to be!' She never gave you the chance to ask why. It wasn't obedience; it was fear. If my mother said we couldn't go to an event because we didn't complete something, when that night came and she had gone to work, even though my father said, 'Go ahead if you want to,' we still wouldn't go."
- Helene's father would "lay down the law," whether he was right or not. She was not allowed to question.
- Farveez's father became very emotional in arguments. "It used to infuriate me, because I could not negotiate with him. He would just bring an emotional end to the argument."
- Ned saw his father as weak. He would come home and get instructions from Ned's mother that the boy had been "bad" and should be punished. Ned would get paddled without his father being aware of what he had or had not done. All the while, his grandmother would sit crying, because she felt he was being mistreated.

EXPECTATIONS ABOUT ACHIEVEMENT AND COMPETENCE

"Do your best" is a frequent message from parents as well as "Be the best you can be." These are positive expectations looked back on with warmth and appreciation. "Be the best you can be. You can do better if you try" is a strong achievement motivator.

Carried too far, this expectation can exceed the bounds of comfort and put undue pressures on the young child.

- Trish was in her 30s and working as the administrator of a hospital radiology department when I talked to her. She had achieved a great deal in her life and credits her parental encouragement. But now and then, when she pushes herself too far, she realizes she's responding to her mother's voice inside her head that says, "Try harder!" She sees now that those early messages have compelled her to pursue goals far beyond what makes sense for balance in her life.
- Trudy was uncomfortable when we talked about parent messages and expectations. She recognized that her mother's words, "Do your best," and her father's words, "Be the best!" sent quite different messages—one achievable by effort, the other virtually impossible to attain. She could manage the pressure from her father, because she lived with her divorced mother when she was growing up and saw her father less frequently.

EXPECTATIONS ABOUT EDUCATION

Grades

Grades are often a source of conflict and disturbance. Such messages as "do your best" or "be the best" are often translated into specific report card expectations. The discrepancy between parental expectations and the student's report card or grade point average can be a continuing source of conflict between parent and child and can strongly affect feelings of competence and worth.

For a number of people, report card time was a totally unpleasant experience. If you brought home a B, why wasn't it an A? If an A, why not an A+? And on and on, no matter the rating. Phrases like "I could never please her" and "I never did it well enough" echo over and over. Grades easily become weighed down with parent hopes and disappointments, becoming a vehicle of censure of the young person. They also can serve as the basis for odious social comparisons. "Why aren't you more like … ?" "Why can't you get good grades like … [your brother, your cousin, the kid next door]?" The damage to self-esteem is obvious.

Getting an Education

> **"Here is why I want you to go to school."**
> "When I was 10 and my sister 15, Mother said, 'I want to teach you a lesson about hard work. I want you both to go to school, and I don't want you to get any ideas about boys.' She took us to the cotton fields on a hot day and put us to work picking cotton. I spent the whole day, and I think I made 15 cents. I never worked so hard in my whole life. She wouldn't let us take any more rests than anybody else. I will never forget it. When I walked out of there, I vowed 'I'll really work in school, never you worry!'"
>
> *—Bell*

In the families of most interviewees, study and education were stressed—you had to do your homework before you could play. Many parents want more for their children than they had and see education as the way up and out. Some yearn for their children to have the educational opportunities that they did not have. The messages are poignant and powerful:

- "My mother was a garment-factory worker, my father a machinist. They were adamant that I must continue my education and be more than they were."

- "The only message I really got from my father was not to go into the coal mines. 'I want you to get as much education as you can. I don't want you to have the life I have in order to support a family.' It was hard, dirty work. He would get up at 3 o'clock in the morning and go down into that coal mine for 6 or 8 hours. When he would come out, he was so black you couldn't even see him. He wound up with black lung disease."
- "Education was very much emphasized. 'If nothing else happens, you're going to go to school, to college. You will go to school. You will be more than we had the opportunity to be.' They insisted on it."
- "My father was well read, but had poor English—a very bright self-educated man. Books and education were very important to him. He regretted that he didn't have more."

Women received a few mixed messages about education. Susan's mother wanted her to go to college in order to marry "somebody with a lot of status." Melissa's father said he wanted her to graduate with a career in mind, but he actually expected she would get married. Education was secondary, a means to an end.

EXPECTATIONS ABOUT WORK AND CAREER

> ### *"Where are you going?"*
> *Carl grew up on a 160-acre cotton farm that required efforts of all family members and was directed by his mother.*
>
> "One day, I wasn't working very hard. My mother didn't say anything the whole day until almost sundown. Everybody picked up their sacks, tossed them across their shoulder, getting ready to quit. She just looked around and said, 'Where are you going?' I stayed out and picked cotton until about 9 or 10 that night. I was 5 or 6 years old. We lived right next to the woods; it was pretty scary with the owls hooting. Finally, she called and said to come on in. But she didn't have to spend a lot of time asking me to work on future days. Lessons like that stick with you."
>
> *—Carl*

Most of the people I've talked to received strong, motivating messages about excellence, striving, and hard work. Messages like:

- No goal is insurmountable. If you want it, you work for it, and you figure out ways to get it.
- Complete the job; don't do it halfway. Be thorough at what you do, do it well enough that you're proud of what you've done no matter what it is.
- Be the best you can be; don't accept less.
- Don't give up! See it through, and don't let it defeat you.

Career Direction and Gender Differences

Because most parents have strong expectations for their children regarding work and career, only a few people I talked to complained about too little direction and guidance. Instead, more people had complaints about excessive pushing in a direction that did not feel right.

Career expectations have traditionally fallen more heavily on men than on women. Parents and family "were pushing me to be" … a scholar, a doctor, a rabbi, a professor, or some other prestigious occupation. The type of work or career acceptable to parents for their sons had to do with stability, security, and prestige. A job where you can always make a living, are able to support your family, are treated fairly, can survive economic fall-outs, and know you're going to have a paycheck. Also, a job that is not based on political limitations. Furthermore, music and the arts are great as an avocation, but not suitable as a career.

Prior to the feminist movement of the 1970s, women tended to face two sets of career expectations. Work was expected to be a "fill in" unless working was necessary to help support the family. Traditional expectations directed the young woman to "until" and "in case" careers. Work "until you get married," or get an education and develop skills "in case something happens to the family."

Some parents still assume that the young woman will focus on family rather than career and steer the young woman to the type of work they feel would be compatible with family responsibilities. Others are concerned that their daughters not be left in the lurch in the event of a marriage going sour, illness, death, or some other unforeseen circumstance arises. Some mothers have urged daughters not to be "stuck" as the mothers were, and some of the young women see the negative example of their mother's life as something to avoid.

Some parents support career goals for their daughters but send strong messages about what they consider to be appropriate fields and levels of work. A few parents even want daughters to set career goals higher than the daughters do: Ann wanted to be a nurse; her father countered with, "If you want to be in the medical field, why not be a doctor?" Beatriz thought she wanted to be a veterinarian because she loved animals. But because she didn't want to be engulfed with all of the required education, she chose nursing. It took a while to convince her parents and grandparents, who were pushing her to become a doctor; they thought nurses were just handmaidens for doctors.

Other parents, and counselors too, have narrow views of what is socially acceptable for a young woman. Joan's father encouraged her to be a nurse or a teacher. A female physician was unheard of at the time. But Joan did pursue her own goals and became the physician manager of a multi-disciplinary research and treatment program.

Marisa's parents wanted her to be a scientist. Her father gave her a feeling that, intellectually, she could do anything she wanted within a certain realm. Yet, certain things weren't proper for a woman. She couldn't be a physician, because it wasn't fitting for a woman and would bring her too much pain. Journalism was much more acceptable. Marisa became the manager of a large hospital clinical laboratory.

Sally's mother had always told her that she'd better make do with what she had and not to aspire to much else. "They never expected a lot of me: maybe I would be a nurse or a secretary. I remember thinking about medical school but never daring to say it. When I finally decided it was what I wanted to do, they tried to talk me out of it—'That's too hard! That's too much work!' Many times, my mother's attitude was, 'Oh, poor Sally. You have too much to do.'" Sally became the physician in charge of a regional genetics program.

Growing numbers of parents now assume that their daughters will pursue a career and are supportive of all kinds of career possibilities. Faith's father said she could be anything she wanted to be and that he would send her to college anywhere. Laurie has always seen her mother work; she was allowed to stand next to the piano while Mom taught. "There was never this big dichotomy of work versus home and family," Laurie said. "She's always been affirming of my desires to be career-oriented."

EXPECTATIONS ABOUT RESPONSIBILITIES

Responsibility and self-reliance are frequent messages for young children. "Being given," "taking on," and "shouldering" responsibility carry different connotations, ranging from excitement to a sense of burden. A few families rejoice in having the children remain carefree during their younger years, but many families expect children to carry responsibilities suitable for their age and gender.

For some of us, "being given" responsibility heralds an important step toward independence and is an exciting accomplishment. As the oldest children, Ann and her twin were given responsibility early—chores in the barn with dairy cows, anything to do with planting and harvesting, and driving the tractor. "You got help if you needed it," Ann said, "but basically, this was your job, so get it done." Ann recalls the excitement she felt when they were given the responsibility of taking care of the farm while their parents took a weekend away. For the first time, they were going to be in charge without having a relative come and stay with them.

"Taking on" responsibility can provide important learning. Mel learned the responsibility of banking money for his father's store as a 12-year-old. Rachel learned in her Navy family that women and children in Navy families must take care of themselves and be totally independent for long periods of time.

Other young people are expected to "shoulder" additional responsibilities: to take care of younger children, to set an example, to help manage the household, and to do odd jobs and take paper routes to help support the family financially. Such messages and experiences can become a life pattern of heavy responsibilities and hard work, often coupled with some measure of regret and/or resentment.
- Alice was oldest of seven children: "I was a second mother. On certain days, you were to milk the goats, wash or dry the

dishes. Plus, there were certain things we had to do on my father's bakery truck, and we couldn't leave to catch the school bus until we did them. I was always halfway in charge of the house. I've always been old beyond my years."

- Wes grew up on a farm in Iowa: "We raised a lot of alfalfa, and you'd have three cuttings a summer. By time you finished the last field, you'd be ready to go over it all again. You'd keep going all summer long, putting up hay. In my entire life, I've never had the time to do things like read. I never had time to do something I wanted to do just for fun."

OTHER VALUES

We receive other messages that communicate values about honesty, dependability, consideration of others, money, social relations, and the like. Two of these stand out from interview data: the place of money and the importance of service to the community.

The Place of Money

The value of money and its use and place in the family and society carries different meanings for people. One type of message is the overriding importance of having money; the other is a realistic understanding of money and its function in family and society.

- "The measure of success was how much money I earned."
- "Education doesn't matter; the almighty dollar speaks."
- "My mother discussed financial situations very clearly with us. We knew how much money Father made when I was 8."
- "Mother was a CPA, so she was constantly saying that I needed to have a better understanding of business and finances."
- "We couldn't have a piano because it wasn't essential. Only the essentials in life are those you take time for or spend money on.

You spend money for shoes on the feet, food in the belly, a roof on the house, and you don't go on vacations."

Service to the Community

I am struck with the number of people who received messages about helping other people and paying back to the community. In a way, this should not be surprising, as many interviews were with people in the helping professions. "There wasn't anything more important than giving to other people," one interviewee said. "My father would do many things for people. That was what you were supposed to do," said another.

- Joan's parents had this feeling: "You owe back to the world if you're lucky to get something. They were always helping people, giving them money if they had it to give. There were many hobos around during the Depression, and they would feed them and be kind to them."
- Ross's parents were actively involved in volunteer work, and Ross saw them "give back" to the community. Expectations were set early in his life that he would pay back to the community when it was time.
- Ava's parents were always active helping in the community. Her father was active in the church and one of the founding members of the cooperative store. She attributes her decision to go into community nursing to her family's involvement in the community.

Cultural Messages

Many messages communicate the norms of a particular culture. For some cultures, a very powerful message that is repeatedly emphasized is, "Don't do anything that would bring shame on the family or that would harm our good name." Elvira came from a Filipino family, and the fact that her parents were divorced brought shame on the family. Her grandmother emphasized that, coming from a broken home,

Elvira and her sisters would have to do their very best in order to offset that stigma. This was a very powerful motivator for Elvira.

BRIDGE

In this chapter, we focused on the content of mentoring messages, looking at common themes, including messages about our worth as a person, love and attention, trust and independence, rules and authority, and other values and expectations. Messages are loaded with predictions and expectations about our abilities and possibilities, work and career, gender roles, education, and much more. In the next chapter, we will plow through the message thicket to understand the dynamics of mentoring messages, how they impact our lives, and how we deal with them.

Chapter 7

MAKING SENSE OF MESSAGES

How do we make sense out of the enormous number of messages we receive from so many different people? What makes messages so contradictory and confusing? How do we process messages? How do they accumulate power and have impact on our lives? These topics are addressed in this chapter.

We must make meaning of messages, even if it is to say "Nonsense!" and discard them. Just how we interpret messages is influenced by the frequency, consistency, and complexity of the messages; the variety, number, and influence of different senders; the context of the message; and the message content itself. Thus, the power of mentoring messages comes not just from the message that is sent, but, more importantly, from the meaning and importance we attach to it.

Interpreting the messages we receive is a complex process. We make meaning by connecting things together based on our experience and our awareness. In doing so, we might be influenced by various aspects of the message—its sender, the emphasis and choice of words, body language, or the situation. A message's forcefulness for a young person is particularly affected by the perceived influence and number of the senders.

Message Impact

Impact of the message on the young person depends on:	Influence of the message-sender on the young person depends on:
• message relevance (e.g., it "feels right") • the consistency and frequency of the message • the forcefulness of the sender(s)	• the closeness and comfort of the relationship • contact frequency • the perceived power and/or control of the sender(s)

Given the mix of subjective and objective factors involved in message interpretation, it is possible that we could give a message a very different meaning than intended. Or, we might interpret the message correctly. Or, we might get it right but apply it indiscriminately—even in circumstances calling for a more measured response.

Once we have given meaning to a received message, we have a variety of options for dealing with it. If the message feels right for us, we will accept it and use it as a guide for our behavior. If it does not feel right, we may reject it as well as the influence of the sending source.

The focus in this book is on received messages and the recall of those messages, especially those that became influencing and guiding—hence, the phrase "mentoring messages." In this discussion, what message-senders thought or intended to send is not our concern. The meaning and importance that each of us attaches to the messages—what we see, hear, and sense—are.

THE POWER OF MESSAGE REINFORCEMENT

As children, we are bombarded with messages from people who want to shape and guide us into being "good" people, leading a "good" life as defined by senders. The early process comes from immediate family members, especially parents, and then extends outward as we mature. A single message has limited power. We tend to respond to the pattern of messages. It is the pattern that is mentoring to us, guiding and influencing our behavior. Each of us has to find our way through a message thicket filled with messages from many different senders.

Message multipliers are particularly important in this sorting process. These are the same or similar messages sent by several senders. Such messages are reinforced through repetition, and they get our attention. For example, when parents are in agreement on their values and philosophy, we are likely to receive similar messages from both parents. The messages are clear, consistent, and straightforward. Consistency and reinforcement are enhanced further when similar messages come from older siblings, grandparents, and other extended family members. Here are two examples:

Message Consistency and Reinforcement

Positive

Cal was strongly influenced by his mother as well as his maternal grandfather, whom he admired greatly but saw infrequently. "I got from her the constancy that was lacking with my grandfather, whom I would see only every couple of years. There was a sustaining influence from her that made his influence have staying power as well. She, too, is fairly quiet, stoical, a listener rather than a sayer. A lot of their values were the same, a sense of place in the world, the human qualities and values."

Negative

When Jill was little, her mother, grandmother, and aunt all tried to curb her independence in order to make her fit their ideas of appropriate behavior. Long after their deaths, she still struggles with their powerful and crushing messages as well as her feelings of never measuring up to their expectations and never being understood—even though she has become highly successful in her field.

Most of us received positive, reinforcing messages that foster growth and development; however, others received a series of negative messages from the important people in their lives. When that happens, negative reinforcement sets in. Note the following contrasts:

You are experiencing a positive message multiplier when:
- your family tells you you're a "child of God," and your church community is also warm and accepting of you; or
- your mother sticks up for you against a teacher who unjustly accuses you of not writing a composition by yourself, and your grandmother reads and praises your essay.

You are experiencing a negative message multiplier when:
- your father tells you how deficient you are as a human being, and your older brother/sister adds more examples to hammer the message in; or
- your family says you are just "average," and your older sibling not only brings home better grades but shows off.

CONFLICTING MESSAGES FROM DIFFERENT SENDERS

Different senders send messages about various aspects of our behavior and our life. Sometimes, we can compartmentalize those messages and function all right. But when messages conflict, we are put in the position of having to decide how to handle them. Since many of these messages come when we are young and our decision-making apparatus isn't all that good, we can have problems.

This is particularly true of parent messages. When parents differ in their messages to the young child, it puts the child in a bind. One way out is to pay attention to messages with greater potency and from the more influential, powerful, or admired parent. Young children have to manage the dissonance in some way in order to keep their sanity. We have little to go on except our feelings, perceptions, and our need to find our way through this painful, contradictory message thicket. "Buying in" to the message from one parent can work if you bet on the right horse, but what if you're wrong?
- Mel handled the conflicts by buying his mother's messages and discounting his father. Only later did he understand how domineering and difficult she really was.

- Bruce saw that his powerful, domineering mother discounted the gentle father he loved and valued. He developed the gentle side of himself in his ministerial profession, but periodically, the demanding, relentless side came out under stress and in the privacy of his home. As he applied them, the messages operated in separate spheres.
- With her father, Brenda "always felt we had a grandchild kind of relationship, almost anything I did was fine, and he basically approved of me—a basic unconditional love. On the other hand, my mother was always into getting me to do things— learn Spanish, play the violin, practice. She was around me a lot more, because my father traveled. For her, I never did it well enough. If I got Bs, why weren't they As and, if they were As, well, something else could have been better. Things weren't ever quite right. She was very determined, and she really lived her entire life through me."

INCONSISTENT MESSAGES FROM THE SAME SENDER

Conflicting messages from the same sender usually say more about the message-sender than the young person. A parent can be unpredictable from one day to the next, applying rules in an erratic manner because of emotional or physical problems. The few people in my sample having such parents learned early to sense parental moods, and then stay out of the way and wait for moods to change.

In periods of transition and changing values, it is difficult for parents to hold to a consistent philosophy or posture in raising their children. In such circumstances, parents can be ambivalent or conflicted as to what they want for, and from, the young person. Most parents want their children to be safe, secure, and happy. But when the sands are shifting, it's hard to figure out how that can be done, and it is easy to be fearful or conflicted.

- Evie's mother wanted her to marry and have a good husband, but cautioned her to finish school. "'Don't end up like me, with only an 8th grade education and then a husband with three kids. But don't go too far, because then you'll be too smart.' Always that. 'Men don't like smart women,' and she still says that. 'You're too smart,' or 'You're too advanced.' She was happy with where I was with my husband—he was pleasant enough. After all, he didn't beat me, and we weren't broke; that was pretty good for her. Since my divorce, she does a number on me, 'Why aren't you married?' Or, 'Don't get yourself into something you can't handle. Be careful, you might regret it.' I don't believe it's a control issue; I think she's frightened more than anything."

- Laurie's parents were clear that they didn't want the children to be restricted by gender roles. Yet, in their struggles to move in new directions, they sent mixed messages to their daughters. "They allowed us to explore," Laurie said. "They allowed me to be a tomboy and allowed me to read whatever I wanted to. But they also expected more traditional career and life choices from me. As a result, they sent conflicted messages about career, about self, about identity—all that stuff."

DOUBLE-LEVEL MESSAGES FROM THE SAME SENDER

Sometimes, we get mixed messages from our parents or family that are difficult to deal with because they are loaded with so many different meanings. These double-level messages can be crazy making, and they can easily crumple feelings of self-worth. The words in the message say one thing but may be contradicted with non-verbal behavior. By inflection, tone of voice, and body posture, quite a different message is conveyed. Some of this might be beyond the level of consciousness of the sender as well as the receiver—except that to the young person, it doesn't feel right somehow. The support, encouragement, and approval in the message could sound real, but these positives are undercut by another, more hidden message.

Two examples are illustrative: half-hearted positive messages coupled with doubt and low expectations; and seemingly whole-hearted positives linked to another more ambitious goal for the young person to achieve:

- Laurie's mother was a very forceful person who said a lot of positive things. But when Laurie would achieve, she'd hear, "'Oh, you're going to Harvard. Oh, who'd have thought they'd ever accept you at Harvard.' It added a layer to the fear of success. It pushes all the self-destruct stuff. Well, Mom didn't expect it, so it must be okay not to do quite as well."
- For Trish, "With my father, it was always, 'Go to it, honey. You're wonderful, you're terrific, you can do anything.' But when I did it, there was more to do. Never enough. 'You won that race, but you can be in the big statewide one next week.' Just yesterday, I had to deal with the mixed-message thing. I was feeling like I should be able to do the task at hand, but I was blocked. The more I looked at it, I was hearing something inside. So I asked myself, Who are you listening to? You're listening to your mother say, 'Big deal! Who do you think you are?' Their messages were still there. That's what my parents were like. I never could satisfy them."

MESSAGE BACKFIRES

When we interpret messages and buy into them in an all-or-nothing manner, the message can backfire. Because mentoring messages have a great deal to do with our achievements, our career progress, and our job satisfaction, they are important motivators. Applied universally, however, under all sorts of conditions, messages can backfire and have unintended negative consequences.

— *"I was fired as a rate-buster."*

"When we hired out to chop cotton," Carl said, "we were always way ahead of everybody. Mother said, 'You don't slow down and work like they do. You hired on for this price for a good day's work, and you're going to give it whether they do or not.'" One summer, Carl worked for a furniture manufacturing company. In two weeks' time, he was fired as a rate-buster. "You had to lace chairs," Carl recalls. "I'd learn my chair, and pretty soon, I would be cranking them out. Then they'd switch me to another chair that I could learn to lace all over again, which would slow me down—but there are only so many chairs. The guys would tell me to slow down, and I didn't understand. It didn't matter what the others would do, you give the guy a good day's work. I couldn't understand why I was fired, and finally the foreman told me." Only after several similar experiences of this sort did Carl learn to be selective in applying this message to avoid further backfires.

— *"I learned I could bail out."*

Yvonne's father accused her of starting things strong but quitting in the stretch. She bought into that message. Later, when she ran into difficulties in college, she told her father that she wanted to leave school before they flunked her out. "My father said, 'All right.' I expected that he'd give me some sort of a fuss, but he didn't. I learned that I could bail out on things; nobody forced me to stick around and see things through."

HOW WE HANDLE CONFLICTING MESSAGES

All of us have received messages from separate senders that are different, sometimes even conflicting. Our sense of how to handle these conflicting messages is related to the power of the message senders and the options we feel we have. We tend to pay more attention to messages from the person we feel closest to, who has the greater power, or with whom we have the most contact. If parents strongly disagree on messages, we will listen to the powerful parent, provided that parent is around and is a significant force in the family. People to whom we feel close but who are absent or otherwise unavailable are not likely to have great impact on us through their messages unless those messages are reinforced by other people.

RESPONSE OPTIONS

Although it is obvious that one can theoretically accept a message or reject it, the power differential between parents and children, plus the desire of the young person to gain love and attention from parent figures, cause the young person to look at options. Here are some of the various strategies people use.

Accept the Message

When there is no conflict in the message or when it seems reasonable, and when relations with the message sender are good, the natural response of the young person is to accept the message and to follow it. We buy in; we conform. Usually that works for us, as it did for Peter and Hal, but sometimes, like Elizabeth, we buy in to messages that are not good for us.

- Peter's father didn't feel that smoking or drugs were appropriate. "He seemed to accept alcohol but in moderation. It was always things in moderation except for drugs and smoking. He strongly emphasized what his desires were and why, and they seemed so logical. He shared his thoughts. There were very few demands or directives. But if there were, they were obeyed, because there were so few."

- Hal's physician father had a very strong personality. He was very warm and loving of him as a boy, teaching him sports, directing his life. "As far back as I can remember, I was going to be a doctor. We had our conflicts later when I grew up, but we still practiced together for a number of years. I scrubbed in surgery with him, so we worked very closely. I think he was a good influence on me. There was never harshness or conflict."

- Elizabeth was so used to following the edicts of her domineering mother that she unconsciously transferred the power from her domineering mother to her dominating husband, only later taking it back.

Accede

As young children, we might see that there is no alternative but to yield to the powerful parent whose messages insist on certain behaviors. Some situations are more constructive than others. Helene learned to accept the present reality, but with reservations. Polly, on the other hand, saw no alternative and paid a price for acceding to her mother's demands.

- Helene's father was "a typical Frenchman who ruled the family." His only way of handling adolescents was to lay down the law and carry it through with physical punishment, despite a weeping mother. What he said, whether or not it was true, was the rule; that was it. Helene thinks her father's insistence on his own view was probably the reason she decided on her own to investigate the truth of things. This quest led to her becoming a scientist and to a long career in her field.

- Polly's domineering mother had them all fearful. "My sister rebelled. I think I ate. I was always known as 'Poor Pol, good old Pol, she'll do anything you say.' I didn't openly rebel; I didn't sass or shoot a look. I obeyed with a smile and a gnawing inside."

Withdraw

Some of us find a way to withdraw, to get away from the power source physically or psychologically. Young children usually don't have the option to leave home or avoid the situation, but they can withdraw in other ways. Diane would go hide in her under-the-porch retreat and bury herself in reading. Farveez was watchful and would keep out of the way of his father's emotional behavior.

Ignore

If there is little power involved, we can afford to ignore and turn a deaf ear to parent messages. Wil's parents were immigrants and had little influence over him. His goal in life was to surpass them. Brigitte looked down on her mother's family, who were from backwoods Tennessee, as "really uneducated, aggressive, obnoxious people. Maybe their influence on me was to make me be better than that."

Covert Rebellion

Teresa rebelled strongly against her father's controlling, domineering behavior, but it was too risky to do it openly. Instead, she covered up her real feelings and outwardly conformed. Even into her mid-20s, Teresa felt she had to behave this way:

> "There are some things I do with a great deal of trepidation in my life, because he might find out. I will continue lying to my father because he isn't able to accept things I do in my everyday life. I couldn't stand the aggravation it would cause and the terrible disappointment it would be for him. I can just see the look on his face."

Leave

Getting out and away from conflicts and domination is another option, but only for people old enough to leave home. This involves planning a strategic withdrawal: a move away from family that will give freedom, be acceptable, and not create a rift. Going away to college or a specialized training program and going into the military have been socially accepted ways to separate from burdensome parental constraints and messages.

Break Away

Sometimes, the young person has a severe enough rift with a parent's effort to dominate and control that a full-scale rebellion follows, and the young person leaves home abruptly.

Reexamine

For many of us, reexamination of messages occurs naturally with maturity. We gain an enlarged view of the world through reading, life experience, and education. The power of early messages is mediated or even countered by new environments, increased knowledge, and the increased ability to make decisions for ourselves.

BRIDGE

In this chapter, we have examined the dynamics of mentoring messages, why they have such importance in our lives, and how we deal with them. The influence of messages extends into the far corners of our lives and our mentoring process. Mentoring messages are a way for people to transmit values and expectations to the young in the society. Those values often are deep, abiding, overarching influences in our lives and affect all areas of our Mentoring Mosaic. Those messages that have had the most positive effect on us in terms of who and what we want to be influence the kinds of models we find mentoring. These are the people, figures, or images we admire, seek to emulate, or value for their example to us. Mentoring models is the topic of the next section.

Chapter 8

WHAT ARE MENTORING MODELS?

When I asked 36-year-old Sandy about the female role models for her age group, she thought for a minute and came up with a list that included Cher, Jane Fonda, Candice Bergen, Oprah Winfrey, and Whitney Houston. What did she admire about them? All of them have kept healthy, attractive bodies. All go against the stereotype of older women not being appealing. All are open and honest about being older. They are also bright, versatile, and multi-faceted—not to mention good businesswomen.

— — —

Several years ago, the *Los Angeles Times* reported on what the editors called a highly unscientific survey that the newspaper had taken via computer bulletin boards, asking people born after 1960 who their heroes were and why. On the list were familiar names that have come up in mentoring interviews, people like Gandhi, Martin Luther King, Jr., Madame Curie, and Albert Einstein. But they also included contemporary models like Stephen Hawking and Bill Gates, people with "values or morals or brains I can look up to." Heroes also included Captain Jean-Luc Picard of *Star Trek* (as a model of a manager) and Bart Simpson (as someone who finds freedom in a restricted world). One responder cited personal friends who had a caring attitude toward people rather than famous people or fictional characters.[10]

---

[10] The Next Los Angeles: Turning Ideas Into Action. *Los Angeles Times*, July 17, 1994. Part-S, p. 5.

In this chapter, we focus on what makes a mentoring model, what models look like, and how we are drawn to them.

Our mentor-bonding pattern influences the place that mentoring models have in our world. Those of us who have made positive connections with the people around us are likely to build personal relationships with models close at hand in our lives. These often become our mentors. Non-bonders are likely to focus on more distant models, where they can be observed and evaluated in a way that allows the non-bonders to remain apart, independent, and feeling "safe."

Recalling the previous discussion of mentoring messages, sometimes our message-senders are models of the behavior we are aspire to, and sometimes they are not. The messages that we accept give us a mindset to watch for models who exemplify these messages. We are drawn to people who are likely carriers of our message themes.

> Ruth's mother wanted her to "be a lady." Somehow, Ruth's mother made it clear that she herself was not a model of what she wanted for Ruth, but she provided little other guidance. Ruth started searching for women who might be "ladies" so that she would know what to do and how to behave. Journalist Dorothy Thompson, who was prominent at the time, was such a model. Her photo at the beginning of each column showed a well-groomed, poised, attractive woman with light hair coiffed neatly into a bun. At some unconscious level, Ruth said, "There's a lady." Here was an intersect between Ruth's interest in journalism and "a lady." Bingo! A model winner.

MENTORING MODELS: WHAT THEY ARE

Mentoring models come in various shapes and sizes. They can be towering figures or very approachable human beings. They can represent the ultimate, the very best, the epitome of perfection; or, they can provide practical examples of how to achieve a goal that's important to us. Mentoring models could be people in our lives or those more distant, such as celebrities or historical figures. They also could be fictional characters or other non-material representations that we have read or heard about or that come to us in our imagination, visions, or dreams.

Regardless of the model form, the essential ingredients of mentoring models are two: We are attracted to them, and their example is guiding to us. The model does not have to do anything for us; indeed, the model might not even know that we exist. It's the example of that person's life or action that provides direction for us. What makes a model mentoring is its guiding, influencing quality as we identify what we want to do or be and how we might best achieve that. A few tip-off words people use:

Nouns

"the epitome of ____"

"the ideal ___ [professional, etc.]"

"an inspiration to me"

"a superb example of ____"

"an exemplar"

"a model of perfection"

"someone to try to follow"

"an outstanding person"

"my idea of what a ____ should be"

Action Verbs

"try to emulate'

"want to follow"

"idolize"

"looked up to"

"awed by"

"inspired by"

"worshipped"

"attracted to"

"drawn to"

Exemplars and Examples

Models come in two major forms: exemplars and examples. The differentiation is a matter of degree.

- Exemplars are those exceptional cases we admire, find outstanding, and wish to emulate.

- Examples are those good illustrations of the kind of behavior we are interested in learning about or from.

Exemplars are those we would like to be like. Examples are those from which we can learn. There is an idealistic, larger-than-life aspect to exemplars. Examples are more down to earth and are simply a part of the collection of behaviors we assemble in order to choose the behaviors we want to incorporate in ourselves.

Model Themes

Most of us have model themes. We are attracted to people, characters, or figures that represent particular values, qualities, or futures to which we aspire. Other models are more functional, providing examples of specific competencies or positions we wish to attain. They show us, by their example, ways of performing specific roles, acting in certain circumstances, or handling specific situations or difficult problems.

WHERE THEY COME FROM

In our growing-up process, we have an ever-widening exposure to people. At first, we are surrounded by close family and friends. As we go to school, we are exposed to teachers, peers, and other adult figures; and then, we are exposed to even more people in our work and social lives. Unless we continue to live in a tightly knit, isolated community, these circles widen like ripples on a pond. Our exposure is broadened as we learn about other people—real or imaginary, past or present—through reading, interaction, and other experiences. These real people, historical figures, and fictional characters are all sources of mentoring models.

- People nearby: Our earliest sources of mentoring models are the people close to us, those who are around in our daily lives. Examples include immediate family, relatives, and friends.

- People more remote: These are people we possibly have never met, but we know about them, we hear about them, read about them, even see them—in person or via the media. We learn about them through biographies, news articles, movies, profiles, oral histories, performances, television, and the Internet. Examples include well-known or famous people and historical figures.
- People "made up," imagined, created, or "seen": We find heroes or other people we identify with and want to be like in fiction, myth, and even comic strips. We learn of them through stories, folk tales, and legends. Sometimes, we invent them, like imaginary playmates, or we find them as compelling figures appearing in dreams.

Models who are real people in our lives often become mentors to us. In this chapter, we will focus on functions served by models. The discussion of mentoring relationships with people who also are models to us will be addressed in Chapters 11 through 14.

TYPES OF MODELS

The following collection of mentoring models is drawn from interviews. We look first at real-people models we observe and with whom we interact. Then, we turn to historical, fictional, and other types of models.

Real-People Models

The real people we look up to are models:

- of excellence;
- of independence;
- for relating to people;
- for coping with adversity; and/or
- for learning and growing.

We will spend some time examining real-people models, because many models are of this type.

Models of Excellence

Many of us seek out and remember models who stand for rigor, high standards, competence—for doing your best.

— *"Excellence is the word."*
- To Cal, the chief of pediatrics had "a certain dignity, a certain presence, a certain established competence—excellence is the word. I've found it very difficult to accept in medicine anything less than the very best I can do."

— *"Rigorous, tough, and really made the mind work."*
- Kay admired teachers who were "rigorous, tough, and really made the mind work." She cites a number of such models, starting with a high school teacher who "didn't allow much space for flabby thinking." One college professor was "the epitome of excellence and a task-master." Another was a superb historian who focused on "bright students who seemed to be well informed about the past as well as having opinions of their own. Those are the folks that I gravitated to, enjoyed, and remember. They clearly had a lot to do with my intellectual formation, with how my mind works and my own standards. I learned that I didn't have to accept less. I don't suffer fools very well."

Models of Independence

We also seek out models who function independently.

— *"He was a person who could make it on his own."*
- Todd admired the outside contractor for the oil company where he was working on a summer job. "He had all of these maxims about life, and he shared his experiences. He valued his independence and would never work for a corporation. I always admired and respected him because he was the person who

could make it on his own. He wasn't beholden to anyone—all in contrast to another project engineer who was very much a company man, definitely focused on job security. Comparing and contrasting the two of them was a good experience for me."

—*"The value of being self-directed."*
- Raphael looks forward to having his own business someday. When he was a teenager, he lived with two highly motivated uncles who had emigrated from Colombia, set up a grocery store, and made a success of it. Raphael worked in the store when he could. He had a chance to observe his uncles and "learned to appreciate the value of being self-directed and having the discipline to accomplish things on your own."

—*"The first independent woman I had known."*
- Sally found the woman dean of students in medical school an inspiration. "She was the first independent woman I had known. She traveled a lot, was not married, and was involved in many activities. I had never seen independent women doing things on their own and enjoying themselves."

Models for Relating to People and Society
Interviewees gave many examples of models for relating to people— perhaps because so many of the people interviewed were in the helping professions. Some focused on caring, compassion, and helping people. Others focused on human qualities, such as practicing your faith, being a good person, understanding and valuing other cultures, and dedication to family and building strong ties.

—*Of caring, compassion, and helping people*
- Mel's father was very caring. If people were hurting in the community, he would very quietly do things that were supportive. "That was just what you were supposed to do."

- Jack idolized a thoracic surgeon who had both compassion and superb clinical skills. He was a tough guy, Jack remembers, but "he taught me a lot about the importance of compassion and caring for sick people. I just about worshipped the ground that man walked on."

—Of human qualities
- Ray decided he wanted to become a physician like the family doctor in his small town in South Dakota. "The only doctor in town, he took care of all of us. He was the epitome of the gentle, caring, and effective person. He gave us all red medicine for whatever ailed us. It tasted bad, and we all got well. Beyond that, he was just a soft-spoken and interested human being, and I admired him for the sort of person he was."
- As Owen talked about his parents, his admiration for his mother came through. He said his mother was quieter, but probably the stronger of the two. His father was always up front, vocal, and outspoken, while she was quiet and held back. Still, "She was the glue that held it together. She was a calming influence. I think if you took someone like my father and let him get out of control, he probably wouldn't be with us today. She knew when to say, 'Tommy, not now, next time.' I think she was the moderating influence on what could have been a hot-head run wild."
- Claire's chemistry professor was solid, but also a warm and sensitive human being who could relate well to students. "She didn't talk at you. She would keep questioning you until she understood what your problem was. I admired her for her human qualities as well as for her excellence. She was just a model of what a human being should be."

—Of being a good person
- Russ' maternal grandmother was his model of how to be a good person. "She was very rational, someone everybody

respected, and she had a very good social network. She wasn't educated but was very curious intellectually. She was always working to improve herself—for instance, reflecting on her anger in order to better manage it."

- Lara's grandmother "was a replica of my mother in many ways. She did factory work, but she would always be taking in stray people, providing shelter, giving them meals. First and foremost, she was a good person. Also a tremendous influence on me."

—Of understanding and valuing other cultures

- Andrea admired her father because of his interest in the world around him—in geology, communities, and cultures wherever his naval assignments took him and the family. Although not formally trained, he read a great deal and took correspondence courses. "Every place we moved to, he took me with him on long walks. We went to the fish market in Honolulu because he wanted me to see what that culture was like. He took me to Buddhist temples and different kinds of churches."

—Of practicing your faith

- Brenda talks with deep feeling about Jeanie, the missionary she knew in Mexico when she was 10 and Jeanie was about 30: "An outstanding human being who would go off into the hinterlands and walk days into the mountains for the purpose of converting people and spreading the word of God. What impressed me most was that she had the courage of her convictions, that her mission in life was so important and other things were irrelevant. Fears of being killed or mistreated were not as important as doing what she needed to do. I guess her determination was even more important than her courage. I don't understand the tears that I feel inside thinking about her. Maybe it's just a deep feeling of admiration for what she did."

- Elizabeth's mother was her first important mentoring model. She preached the importance of "practicing your faith." Elizabeth went into nursing as a way that she, too, could practice her faith; however, she became discouraged with organizational realities. As she investigated other ways to use her nursing, she discovered the books of Albert Schweitzer and Mother Teresa, two people who were truly practicing their faith. Using them as models, Elizabeth searched for humanitarian programs where she could fully contribute her skills. She joined the Tom Dooley Foundation in Nepal for a three-year stint. Although Elizabeth reluctantly returned home because her funds were depleted and her family needed her, she planned to return to Nepal.

—Of dedication to family and building strong, enduring ties
- Owen greatly admired his grandmother who raised three children by herself. "She was a lady of quiet strength who made her living by cleaning people's houses. She raised three girls by herself and gave them all a sense of worth. To this day, these ladies all come across as very dignified, refined people. It all came from her. She had no education at all; her mother had been a slave. She was always the strong figure who could do almost anything, and she held this family together by her own force."

Models for Living Your Life

Models for living life vary greatly from one person to another, reflecting as they do our individual interests and needs.

—Of coping with adversity
- Raphael's grandmother was a "pillar of moral fortitude and strength of character." She was born in Oklahoma, lived through the Depression, endured the deaths of three husbands, and had her fair share of life's hard knocks along the way. "Yet, the youth of her spirit and her charisma were such that everyone who met her immediately fell in love with her—they thought she was just

terrific, and she really was! All this gave her an amazing strength of character, lots of fortitude, and a taste for life. She was a tremendous influence on me. I like to think that despite what happens, you should be able to overcome it and excel."

—*Of learning and growing*
- Jim had been resistant to mentoring, rebelling from the control of his older sister when they were growing up. In his auditing job, he traveled in close quarters with his audit team all over the world. What impressed him was the learning and growth he saw in one of his colleagues. "That year, I had seen Lee growing as a person and developing in ways that were appealing to me. So I decided to stop fighting and do what I could to learn from the people and experiences around me. Lee was a good influence: His enthusiasm, energy, and desire to learn were contagious. I picked up on that and became committed to learning."
- Lucy was amazed when, at age 40, her mother went back to school to get her B.A. and then followed that up by completing two master's degrees. She had wanted to go to school so long and, in a sense, had lived through her daughters. Finally, after having reared her family, she could live for herself. "She took the risk and went back."

—*Of enthusiasm and energy*
- Ben had a string of models he gravitated toward, starting with his older brother who was "always enthusiastic about what he was doing." He also talks about a medical resident he worked with. "I admired his enthusiasm for things and learned a lot from him and his attitude. He just loved medicine! He was one of those people who always looked for the interesting side of the case he was taking care of. He never lost that spirit no matter how busy he was or how late at night it was. It was very stimulating to be around him. You sort of piggyback on someone like that."

Historical Figures and Famous People

Equally as important as models from the circle of people around us are more distant models we hear and read about but usually never meet. Virtually everyone I talked to could recall people they admired from having learned about them through biographies or other media: Eli Whitney, George Washington Carver, Madame Curie, Gandhi, Stephen Hawking, Oprah Winfrey—the range of models is astounding.

Books and television are sources of mentoring models for young people growing up in isolated communities where the breadth and diversity of real-people models is limited. Reliance on impersonal sources of models also is common for non-bonders because such models are far safer to admire and emulate. Here are a few examples:

From Men

Mentoring models for men are somewhat predictable, following cultural and historical patterns for life and career direction. As we see below, mentoring models for women are different.

—*"I found a lot of motivation from reading about her life."*

- All of Daniel's mentoring models have been historical or famous people whom he has never met. Most were people who impressed him with their creativity and appreciation of the things around them, people like Leonardo da Vinci, Isaac Newton, and Jacob Bronowski. Daniel was especially affected by reading about Madame Curie. For the first time, he appreciated how hard people study. He realized that he had never really applied himself. "So, I found a lot of motivation from reading about her life, her study techniques, and the way she worked. That was a very crucial book."

—*"They did something that had never been done before."*

- Reading biographies was important in Stan's growing up. He tends to identify strongly with individuals in everything he does. I asked him if any stood out. The inventors and political types: Thomas Jefferson, Alexander the Great, and similar figures. I asked about the attraction, the appeal. "In the case of the inventors and explorers, I suspect it was that they did something that had never been done before; the accomplishment. For the political figures, it was their influence on large numbers of people, their ability to help improve lives."

From Women

Mentoring models for women reflect the need women have felt to find models who provide options for living one's life in ways other than the traditional woman's role. In their interviews, they talk about the importance of women who were:

- ahead of their time, like Margaret Mead, who really added to scholarship and caused people to rethink their ideas about family and society;
- bold, adventurous, and unconventional, like Katharine Hepburn, Amelia Earhart, and Anaïs Nin;
- social activists and humanitarians, like Mother Teresa and Eleanor Roosevelt; and
- gutsy and non-traditional, like Ingrid Bergman, who actually had an affair. "I thought that was awful, but awesome!" one interviewee said.

Fictional Characters or Symbols

In addition to real people and historical figures, mentoring models can appear in fictional form via print, film—even comic strips.

> Charlayne Hunter-Gault's favorite comic strip growing up was "Brenda Starr." She was the center of attention in the newsroom and had all of the best assignments as well as wonderful romantic adventures. When Charlayne grew older, she still thought of Brenda. Charlayne knew there was a universe of experiences out there that was different from what most black people had who were college graduates—beyond being a teacher or working for the post office. Charlayne gained her University of Georgia journalism degree and became a featured reporter on *PBS News Hour* before moving on to other journalistic assignments.[11]

Captain Jean-Luc Picard of *Star Trek* and Bart Simpson were mentioned at the beginning of this chapter. Many of us imagine "trying on" different behaviors or career options via fiction. The source could be a book series for young readers, such as the old classics of the Hardy Boys, Nancy Drew, and Sherlock Holmes. Fictional Sue Barton influenced many women to become nurses. Comic strip characters like Wonder Woman and Brenda Starr have been important models for some women—but "never Betty Crocker!" as one woman exclaimed.

- From the age of 8 or 9, Wonder Woman was Gloria's ideal. Gloria loved the Greek myths and legends, and Wonder Woman tied into that tradition well. Gloria credits Wonder Woman as a significant influence on her becoming an over-achiever. "Wonder Woman can do anything!" On the flip side, Gloria has come to realize the negative impact of that model. As she said ruefully, "It's a pretty heavy ideal to carry around."

---

[11] Interview for Washington Press Club Foundation, June 15, 1993.

- Nancy Drew was a model for Jill. "She was a feminine figure, yet she followed the clues and figured it out. Plus, she didn't follow the boys around; she led them! I didn't realize how important that was to me at the time."
- Tarzan was important to young Mel. His model of what was right and what he might be capable of came from reading heroic series of any kind—Sherlock Holmes as well as the Tarzan stories. He would move some of those heroic pictures into his own life, asking himself, "If I had the strength and prowess of a Tarzan, where would I be in day-to-day life?"
- Often models can have a long-term influence on our lives. The statue of the pioneer woman that Ruth saw when she was growing up in Oregon has been a strong guiding image for her. To her, the pioneer woman was strong in coping with adversity, fearless in protecting her children, and determined in the face of an unknown future. Ruth's identification with the famous statue is related to her knowledge that her grandparents traveled by covered wagon to Oregon more than a century ago.

BRIDGE

We are constantly on the lookout for mentoring models that represent or exemplify values that are important to us. They point a way as to how we might be able to live those values. As we have seen, we draw models from a variety of sources: people in our lives or in history as well as fictional characters. But there is more: When do we seek models, what are the circumstances, why do we seek them, and how do they serve us? These are topics for the next chapter.

Chapter 9

WHEN MENTORING MODELS ARE NEEDED

Our need for mentoring models is not static. As our circumstances change and we pass through different phases of life, the nature of our models is likely to vary. This dynamic is only accentuated by the speed of change in our 21st century world. Many models exemplify values that are enduring, while other models we thought would endure have now become obsolete. As the world shifts, and as we shift to new occupational roles and life phases, new needs emerge, and new models are in demand. In this chapter, we look at the circumstances under which we need and seek out models.

MODELS FOR RELATING WORK/FAMILY/PERSONAL NEEDS

Old models of managing the work/family interface are obsolete for many of us. Because the two-career family has become common and many single parents are in the labor force, both men and women have had to experiment with ways to blend work, family, and personal life—women especially. Models for effectively managing these complex situations are highly valued. Here are some that have surfaced in interviews.

For Blending Work and Family

Jillian worked as a physical therapist in an interdisciplinary program. One of the women physicians had a small child, and her second baby was born soon after Jillian joined the program. Jillian's son was born the following spring.

> "I had a role model of a successful woman physician who was raising children, maintaining a career, and staying balanced.

She was a role model I hadn't had. She was a couple of years older, and I felt very collegial, very much on the same level."

The woman chair of the pediatric department in medical school was an inspiration for Sally.

"It's amazing to see her grasp of concepts and see her deal with clinical problems in such a methodical way. She was very sharing, too. I've always felt in awe of her, this amazing woman who had managed to build a department out of nothing, raise five kids, and do all of these others things. In some ways, I see her very much like a mother—this woman who takes care of everything so competently."

By contrast, Chu felt alone in medicine. The only women role models available to her were very much the classic, never-going-to-get-married kind who were going to be completely dedicated to medicine. Instead, Chu wanted to marry, have children, and also have a practice. She had to figure out how she was going to manage it. The women physicians she knew were of no help—they had the attitude that it doesn't work if you combine family with a career.

For Balance in One's Life

Finding balance between work and personal life has been of keen interest to a number of people I spoke to, particularly those in occupations with a tradition of excessively long hours that tend to crowd out personal time. This concern can lead to a search for alternative models.

- The internist John knew in medical school was someone "to look up to not only in the way he practiced medicine, but he also had a sound balance between work and play, so he was a model for me."
- Sam's father was a model for him in many ways. He had the self-discipline to do things in moderation and also had a long-range perspective. Starting at age 40, he began taking off a half-day each week from his orthodontics practice, gradually

increasing the amount over the years until, at age 75, he was still practicing, but only one day a week.

- Sandra admired her father, who lived out his belief in recreation and leisure time and "taking care of yourself." A maitre d' in a restaurant, he chose not to move up to management because of his own interests. He played classical guitar and didn't want the headaches of being a restaurant manager.

For Living Life to the Fullest

Occasionally, we find people who seem to be able to do it all, to live life to the fullest, people with remarkable energy and a zest for living. The models we choose for living life fully will understandably change with our own maturation. A number of people in their 30s and 40s had models such as these:

- Letitia found Fred an incredible model for living life fully. "He has more energy than most people. He's the kind of person who works hard, plays hard, and enjoys himself very much. He's a top-notch writer, an excellent editor, and a very articulate person with an incredible mind that picks up things right away."
- Carl's intern when he was a senior medical student was "a character who always generated a lot of awe in other people. He performed well, yet he was a lot of fun, very gregarious, and did everything outside of medicine to the nth degree. He had a robust social life. He could work three days in a row, stay up all night delivering babies, get off work, go ski for two days, and then come back, and do it all over again. He had unbelievable amounts of energy."

For New Ways of Being a Woman
I have been impressed with the deep interest that women express about how other women work out their various life roles.

<u>Multiple Options</u>
Clarisse, a well-regarded psychotherapist, has a whole collection of models for being a woman. She started her model collection in her 30s and was still doing so in her 70s.
- "Anne is in her early 40s. I admire her brilliance and her capacity for innovation. She has many sides and represents the hope of that generation of young women who have thrived on the women's movement and did not get caught in anger or rejection of men. She's warm and affectionate but also has a kind of toughness about her as well as brilliance. She represents all I would have liked to be at 40 and was not."
- "Leila seemed to have a totally different quality from any woman I'd ever met. She was sort of earthy, had been a therapist in Europe. Here was a woman with a lot of life experience, including her husband having been in a concentration camp. They had been in London during the World War II bombing, with one small child. She had professional training and, at the same time, she was a very good mother and wife—she was a good role model."
- "Lois is a feeling, intuitive person, very warm and expressive. I watched her operate with strength in a way that's different from what I'd seen before with some academic intellectual types. It's nice to see what's possible. I'm learning from young women."

<u>Trailblazers</u>
Glenda and Evie admired women who were pathfinders, who were "doing it first."
- Glenda saw her friend Clarisse as continually learning and growing. "Clarisse earned her doctorate at 56. She's been like a

big sister, doing it first." Glenda had been successful in organizational consulting but wanted to switch fields to psychotherapy. Following Clarisse's example, she enrolled in a doctoral program, received her Ph.D. in her 60s, and became a practicing clinical psychologist.

- Evie admired Ruth for being "a real person and ahead of her time for women." Ruth's drive for academic achievement proved to be a motivator for Evie, who said to herself, "If Ruth can get a Ph.D. when she's 50, there's no reason I can't get my B.A. degree when I'm only 30."

Different Models of Feminine Strength

Women I talked to want to live a life using more of their potential, including their strength; how others have done this is a matter of great interest.

- Tess' 8th grade music teacher was an example of the kind of teacher she admired. "She seemed to be a gentle individual, yet in command of herself and the students. She expected something from you and was a disciplinarian—a soft disciplinarian. She was fun to be around and enjoyed people."

- Marisa said, "I have sought out strong women—that's very clear. The principal of my high school had been a nun but had left the convent; in those years, that took tremendous guts. Another was a physician. My mother has been a tremendous influence in my life. A well-known journalist, she is a non-conformist female. My great-grandmother, whom my mother's talked about all her life, went into the jungles of Colombia and single-handedly 'slayed dragons,' so to speak. As I look back, the women who have truly fascinated me and have been important to me and my sense of identity were gutsy, non-traditional females."

- Kay admired Dixie Lee Ray who was a scientist, a popular educator, and later a governor. "Making her way at the time that she did, and having the courage of her convictions, it had to be pretty challenging getting ahead in a world where women weren't always valued. She was extraordinary from the point of view of popular education about science and technology. I have a lot of admiration for the common sense she possessed and the barriers she broke down."

MODELS FOR CAREER DIRECTION AND DEVELOPMENT

Early in our adult lives, we seek out options for work and career that are affordable and feasible—and then usually, we narrow down the choice to one. Models can be helpful in showing, by example, roads that are open, ways we might move, and goals to which we might aspire. They also are helpful throughout our work lives in illustrating ways to increase our competencies.

Finding an Accessible and Affordable Education

It is easy for us to feel limited in our career options. We might live in a small town, have very little money, or know of no others who have succeeded beyond a narrow avenue of career or work choice. In situations like these, models are particularly helpful. While famous figures or celebrities are too far out of reach, if we see someone else close to our age who shoots for the moon and makes it, we think, *Then so can I.* Such models are figuratively a step ahead of the younger person. They point a way or a direction and a means of carrying it out.

Examples
   — *"Leading the way."*
        Carl grew up on a family cotton farm in rural Arkansas. His older brother went to college, did well, and went on for his Ph.D. He was a model for Carl by leading the way. Carl didn't have to wonder about what he was doing there in college as "just a little boy from the farm." Carl adds, though, "He

wasn't my hero. He was a constant tease, overbearing, and bad-tempered. But as far as the trail he blazed, it was helpful."

— *"He was broke, and he could make it."*

Evie's cousin went to the university to be a teacher. "He didn't have any money, so he went out to the boonies to teach in one of these shacks of a school. He'd go back to summer school every year. He was about 40 when he got his Ph.D. I remember thinking that if he was broke, and he could make it, so could I. I didn't know that people could make it without money."

— *"You can move out to other places."*

For Don, the example of the high school student in his town who graduated with a full ride to Harvard on a scholarship caused him to think, "Gee, you *can* come from North Dakota and move out to some other places."

Choosing an Occupation or Career Path

We can struggle to find an occupational path that is right for us, especially if we are under- or over-directed or influenced by adult figures. Bruce found himself turning away from models imposed on him early in life; his most important models developed much later. Carl, in contrast, was without models.

- Bruce's mother insisted that her sons be professionals. One son was to be a doctor, and Bruce was to be a lawyer. Instead, preferring to follow the footsteps of his father, he entered engineering school but found the work unsatisfying. World War II intervened and provided a welcome time-out from parental pressure about his career future. It also provided him time when off duty to read and reflect. When his navy ship was anchored in a Chinese port, he chanced on the writings of Albert Camus. Camus became a model for Bruce of a humanistic existentialist and was a significant influence on his later pursuit of graduate work in philosophy.

- Carl didn't know what to take in college. Since his brother majored in biology, so did Carl. That was about the extent of his aspirations. There were no role models in those early years who could ever make him think he would become a physician. By taking the first steps of going to college and then majoring in life sciences, Carl found a new career direction.

Making it in a Man's World

People entering career fields previously closed to them have had difficulty finding relevant role models. This challenge has been particularly true for women: how to be an effective woman professional in roles traditionally held only by men; how to be assertive without assuming an aggressive masculine posture; how to behave in situations for which there is no historical experience—in short, how to make it in what has been a man's world. Fortunately, now that professions have opened up to women, many more models are available.

- Jill felt a great lack of role models when she was the first woman doctoral candidate in a graduate school of business. She was frustrated that the only woman on the faculty was taking a subservient role in the system. She didn't intend to be a woman like that.
- Claire first tried copying a male minister's style. She found it very dull, but she had no other model. Later, a few other women moved into similar ministerial roles and formed a colleague group to chart their way in this unknown territory.
- Jenna had to adapt to male models because no women were in law firm partner roles at the time. It was not easy, she said. "I've had to see the qualities these men have that work for them and what qualities I have that can be noticed. Finding your own style rather than using an accepted male style is hard."

Comparing Ability

Those of us who are breaking new ground in terms of family traditions have few guides by which to evaluate our ability. Models who have "done it" or "made it" and seem to have no more smarts or advantages than we do can stimulate us to raise our own expectations to another level.

- Ben's older brother was always enthusiastic about what he was doing and did well. "So I just said, 'I'm going to do what he's done, except I'm going to do it better!' That was my goal. So I worked hard, was valedictorian with a straight 4.0 record." This was sibling rivalry in a constructive way.
- Sally read Florence Nightingale and Clara Barton in junior high and thought caring for people was a wonderful thing. She thought about medical school but was afraid. In college, she managed to take all the pre-med courses, but thought of herself as a biology major. When she entered graduate school in anatomy and histology, she found she was taking classes with medical students and doing well. It was then that she said, "I can do just as well as they can; I'm going to go to medical school!"

MODELS FOR ENHANCING WORK COMPETENCIES

Many examples of models for enhancing work competencies are available. Here are a few drawn from different fields.

- Jim watched the commanding officer's style of management to see how effective it was. Jim noted, "He was excellent at getting away from his office rather than being chained to his desk. He would walk around the facility, gathering data, asking the pressmen why they were doing it this way. The division heads were more bogged down in administrative stuff. He knew more of what was actually going on. He was constantly surprising the staff by asking questions about things that seemed to be inconsistent, always being on top of the situation. His priority was seeing that things were running right."

- Terence listed an array of people at his company who he learned from and admired. Each was an exemplar for a specific aspect of the work. One person was an excellent model for gaining an appreciation of the precision and complexity of equipment, another for tact and tolerance with people, another for very forward thinking, and two others for exacting standards.
- Paula identified one model who was superb in articulating and putting concepts to use. Another was the best technical supervisor she'd had, providing very practical tips on how to deal with issues that came up.
- Alice listed a number of people she admired among nursing instructors and supervisors: the human qualities of one, the strictness and consistency of another, the manner of managing paperwork and supervisory responsibilities of another, and the willingness to test new theories of still another.
- Ray admired certain professors "for their fount of knowledge, wide clinical experience, and ability to make informed judgments by sorting out the important from the unimportant. They were people who had great empathy with their patients, who encouraged students to think for themselves, and corrected mistakes gently and with compassion." Ray aspired to be like that.
- Gloria remembers a psychologist who used to lead a session on motivation. "I said to myself that to be able to walk into a classroom for a whole day's session on motivation without one note the way he did—that would be the most wonderful thing in the world. He was so loose and relaxed. Nothing they threw at him was something he couldn't field. I saw that as the ultimate. Well, now I can do that. I like to have some notes handy just as a backup, but by and large, I go in and fly by the seat of my pants, and I do really well."

MODELS FOR MANAGING LIFE TRANSITIONS

In our mature years, life transitions become more frequent and upending, requiring new behaviors, new goals, and new expectations. By this time, we have outgrown old models or are entering new arenas that require new outlooks and skills. Earlier, we looked at models that people have found for undertaking higher education, for the transition from school to career, and for balancing work and family and personal time. We will explore other life transition needs in Chapter 20. Meanwhile, here are a few examples for growing older.

— *"Still growing and doing his work."*

As a new minister, Laurie admired a minister many years her senior. "He has a spring in his walk, he's willing to take on new stuff, and he's still growing and doing his work."

— *"Life doesn't end at 50."*

Kathy has many things to say about an older woman professional she's known for quite a while. "I guess I just like her professionalism and her attitude about life and the growth she's experienced. I see her as a model, not for me to copy but to learn from. She's older by 17 years, which tells me that life doesn't end at 50. There are so many things to do, think, and see. The way she's so vitally involved is exciting to me.

— *"They did their richest writing in their 80s."*

Off and on throughout the years, Clarisse has read a lot of books written about Carl Jung by women. Frances Wickes and Esther Harding did their richest writing in their 80s. "They became role models for me—women who continue to be productive, valued, and growing on into their later life. That was probably my first sense that life goes on increasing in complexity and depth as you get older. At that time, I was in my early 30s."

— *"She's a model for life, for living."*

Ned has had a long-time friendship with Bea, now in her 80s. She is a model to him of aging—of an approach to life that includes being prepared for death when it comes. "She believes in herself, in contributing to the growth of her community, and in leaving something behind. She isn't sitting in her room, being sorry for herself, and drinking alcohol from teacups like some of the women she knows. She's a model for living."

— *"She tries to be like Mrs. Butler."*

Connie talks about her mother, who is 70 and in a nursing home. Her mother's neighbor in the facility is 100. "Mom tells me that she tries to be like Mrs. Butler. She admires her qualities, and everybody loves her."

BRIDGE

In this chapter, we examined the nature of mentoring models and how we use them to learn from during various life stages and transitions. We have yet to ask how mentoring models appear, develop, and change. These topics are addressed in the next chapter.

Chapter 10

HOW MODELS APPEAR, DEVELOP, AND CHANGE

What is the process by which models occur in our lives, how does it develop, and how do models change? Are we passive agents in this process? What is our role? We turn to these questions in this final chapter on mentoring models.

PRESENTED AND DISCOVERED MODELS

Left to their own devices, young children naturally size up and connect to people, to some more than others. Those they admire and want to be like or emulate become models. Not all people we are drawn or attracted to are models. Many, we simply enjoy, want to be with, and want to bask in their presence — if we are so lucky. Those who become mentoring models are those we not only admire but also want to be like or learn from. Their example is guiding and influencing for us.

Parents and other close adult figures also have a hand in the process. Some parents influence the model-building process by exposing the young person to people they feel are good examples of the values and aspirations they want for their child. Some parents are more directive, both presenting the desirable models and urging their acceptance. Conversely, they might expose the child to negative examples as something to avoid. The key is the reaction of the young person: Is the model accepted and followed or rejected and ignored?

Some families have strong traditions as to the nature of work the young person should pursue and/or the type of person he or she should become. The family might actively program the child or simply assume that the young person will continue in the tradition of the family. Following in the footsteps of other family members is taken for granted.

We will refer to models chosen or selected by others as "presented models" and those that are self-chosen as "discovered models."

Presented Models

Presented models are communicated or conveyed by a parent figure to the young person, subtly or directly. Certain people are held up as examples. "Look how great ____ is?" Or, "Why don't you do what ____ is doing?" Such phrases are often tip-offs to presented models. Models are "held up," "handed down," "pointed out," or "set up" as models. Whether or not the young person accepts a presented model depends on how relevant the model is to the young person and the sense of having a choice in the matter.

Held-Up Models

These are people who epitomize the values of the parents and/or who illustrate possible career and life paths. They are held up to the young person as a positive possibility—not an edict or requirement.

> Ruth's mother and aunts held up the model of an older cousin who was an elementary school teacher. They would make admiring comments about her and her life. Teaching was something they felt Ruth could aspire to, but that career path did not appeal to Ruth.

Pointed-Out Models

Another way parents identify and communicate models is by pointing out negative models that are vivid and illustrative of an undesirable future.

> Eva recalls a restaurant, "a terrible greasy spoon" in her hometown that always had a sign in the window, "Waitress Wanted." "My mother used to say, 'If you aren't going to work in school, you're going to have to work at old Joe's place!'"

Vignettes such as this one usually are used as a motivator to encourage the young person to take education and learning seriously as a way out of a limited future.

Handed-Down Models

These models have a strong flavor of insistence. Such models are presented to the young person with an expectation that the person *will* follow the path of the model. The effect on the young person can be positive, negative, or neutral, depending on how close the model fits the person's own aspirations and the nature and amount of pressure applied. Men in our culture can have heavy doses of this type of modeling.

"Going along" is the path of least resistance for some young people faced with pressures from a strong parent figure.

> Kerry's mother wanted him to be a scholar like his grandfather, but he identified more with his contractor father who was a practical businessman. Kerry became a physician to please his mother but, unhappy with that decision, later left the practice of medicine to become an entrepreneur.

Occasionally, handed-down models are presented in a critical, competitive tone, more in the fashion of "Why can't you be like ____?" Such handed-down models usually don't work except in a negative way.

Inherited Models

Some handed-down models are based on family tradition, a point where mentoring messages and mentoring models intersect. The people I talked to were positive about their traditions. In their families, the exemplars were not only competent and successful in their fields, but several also were respected leaders in their community. These models can be very positive and powerful for the young person whose ability and interest in following the family tradition are clearly present. For a family member who is different, there could be problems.

- "Everyone significant in my life was a physician—I never considered anything else." Cal came from a family of physicians and educators; he combined the two fields by going into academic medicine.
- "I come from a long line of school teachers," said Lila, a high school vice-principal.
- "All the women in my family were professionals" and were held up as models for pediatrician Brooke.

Discovered Models

Many of us find our own models. While we are influenced by the values of the family, *we* are the ones who find the models, *we* are the agents of discovery. Some of us are model collectors, finding ourselves drawn to many models through our interactions with people, our reading, and exposure to the media. We might do this fairly automatically, or we could study people and handle the process more deliberately.

When we are choosing our models, we can decide whether to move toward or away from those presented by parents. Wil chose to move away because he didn't approve of his immigrant parents and set a deliberate course to surpass them and their values, particularly those of his father. In contrast to Wil, those of us who have bonded to parent figures are likely to be attracted to models with similar values and/or characteristics.

To a large degree, the process of finding models is unconscious. Yet, if we examine the process, it goes something like this: exposure, attraction, and selection. We are exposed to people or representations of people from our personal experiences, stories we are told, things we hear or see, and what we read. Out of this mélange, we find figures we are especially drawn to; some sort of magnetic quality is present. Such figures often become mentoring models. We identify what we like or admire in the model.

We could view the model as an example of something specific we would like to be able to do or be. Or we could see the model more broadly, representing an outstanding example, an exemplar—the ideal, the ultimate, the epitome of something we value and would like to emulate and to become like as much as possible. The range is vast: It could be a skill or talent we might develop, a way of coping with a life problem, the work we might choose to do, or the way we live our life.

HOW MODELS ARE USED

Once we have spotted one or more models, how do we use them? Do we jump in and copy the model's behavior? Do we study the model's behavior and note it as something to learn from? Or do we internalize what the model represents to us by digesting those aspects that are important and making them ours?

Copy/Mimic

Children are tremendous mimics, often to the chagrin of the adults around. It is natural for children to copy the attractive, admired model. We mimic the model as completely as we can and try to behave like that person. In copying, we are practicing the new behavior, trying it on for size. As small children, we are not very selective. Later, we are more likely to copy certain behaviors and not others. We can identify some of our models by looking at our pattern of mentoring interests or mentoring play (see Chapter 17).

> In high school, Janet found herself tutoring the kids in her geometry class who were having trouble understanding the problems. Janet did this daily at lunchtime. She would stand at the blackboard holding chalk in one hand—just like their teacher, Mrs. Kurosawa—but with a sandwich in the other. She would try to be as enthusiastic and systematic as the teacher was as she walked her classmates through the theorems and exercises they had earlier in the day. In the

process, Janet was building experience and confidence in teaching and speaking.

Learn From

Although most of us as small children automatically copy models, those of us who had models pushed on us are more reluctant to do so. We might consider certain behaviors that look as though they could work for us, but we are very clear, even adamant, that we use them in a selective way to learn from and not to copy.

As we become older and have more exposure to people and a wider variety of potential models, "learning from" rather than direct copying happens quite naturally. We pick and choose behaviors we want to emulate as we build our own collection of mentoring models.

Internalize

Internalizing occurs when some aspect of the model becomes a part of us. The model stimulates or generates an internal thought process that is guiding and influencing.

Some of us start this process in childhood. We noted Mel and his Tarzan model in the previous chapter. As a young boy, Mel would move some of the heroic images of Tarzan into his own life and ask himself, *If I had the strength and prowess of a Tarzan, where would I be in my day-to-day life?* Then, he would try to act more in accordance with the picture in his head.

But for most of us, internalization occurs later, as we gain more experience and maturity. Don, the manager of an architectural firm, illustrates the process. He was 40 when I talked to him. At that point in his life, he said:

> "I still look for role models, but I think they need not be personified with an individual now. I can look at concepts or pieces here or there. I'm getting to the point where I know what I'm doing as much as many of the people around me. I can now

use that creative skill to size up my ideas and other people's thinking, and then put the two together. I've also grown clearer about my basic values and my comfort level with the decisions I make. I have more perspective about those decisions. When you're in a decision-making position early in life, it can seem terribly traumatic, like it's going to change your whole life. Then, as you're involved in many decisions, you realize the temporal nature of decisions and that their importance over time varies with the kind of decision. So at this stage in my career, although I think people need role models throughout life, it need not be a singular person. I have been in situations where I'd sit down and think, *I wonder how Jeff would have reacted in that situation.* Not only Jeff, but others I know."

HOW MODELS CHANGE

Some of our models stay in our memories forever as lifelong model companions. For others, the passage of time might topple our model off the pedestal of our own making. We become newly aware of the model's deficiencies and no longer admire the person as much as we did, or we develop a new interest or a different standard of excellence. The model is no longer relevant—there is no longer a fit.

Diminished Admiration of the Model

There are several reasons why some models come to be valued less over time: with maturity and experience we may become more aware and more discriminating about what we value and about the ability of the previous model(s) to fit new model concepts or standards.

Admiration Gap Narrows

As we learn more about ourselves and our surroundings, our self-awareness causes us to value ourselves more and to value the model less, thus reducing the admiration gap. The person we had placed on a pedestal is no long held in such high regard. Jack's reminiscence many years later about an experience as a pre-med student illustrates this point well:

> "I admired the ways various professors did things and interacted with students. Professor McGraw taught comparative anatomy. He explained that if all the pre-meds did well in his course, they would have a good chance of getting into med school; if not, they wouldn't get in anywhere. Looking back, I recognize he had no more power than the man in the moon, but I remember that pompous guy walking back and forth. He had us terrified! He used to draw pictures with two hands and students would take notes in teams to keep up with him. He used obscure textbooks. He had the power because we gave it to him. At the time, I thought that the sun rose and set with him."

Awareness of Model Deficiencies

Often, we connect to models based on limited data. We see some things we admire, and the halo effect takes over—we then admire all aspects of the person's behavior, such as we know it. We don't see the warts. With increased knowledge about the person, deficiencies become apparent, and our admiration can wane. This process either leads us to abandon the person as a model or to see the model more conditionally.

Changed-Model Concept

As we become more experienced, our conceptions of the occupational field we're in often change. Quite naturally, what we consider exemplary behavior changes, too. This is particularly true with the accelerating pace of social, economic, and technological changes affecting many occupations and professions.

> Lara remembers thinking that her teacher in her diploma nursing school was "an absolutely wonderful nurse, everything I thought a professional nurse should be in terms of starched white uniform, white cap, and a professional manner." She pauses for a moment and adds, "I would not hold that same esteem for her today."

Needs Filled

The original need for our model might no longer be present. The model is valued, but the time has passed. This is particularly true when our own skills and abilities increase, or when the transition we have been coping with has been completed successfully.

Needs Change

Needs change for various reasons, ranging from changing interests, to changing life or career stages, to unexpected events or happenings.

Changing Interests

A model could no longer be relevant in light of where we are in our career and/or life interests. We might not be aware of these changes, however, and be stuck with old models. From time to time, we need to reexamine old models to check their relevance for us today. Clarisse's experience is a case in point:

> Clarisse had thought to continue her psychotherapy practice and professional work into her 80s because of the women role models she had when she was young. Instead, she has new, more personally satisfying projects under way that involve life cycle changes. She has reflected about these models from the past. "It's as if those women I only read about became internalized at a point in time long ago. They are still there in me as images that are now outdated. It feels as if I was stuck in old challenges."

Unexpected Events or Happenings

As we move through the life cycle and are confronted with change and crisis, our models are bound to change at least somewhat. They become less useful to us in the light of:

- the downsizing, closing, or expansion of businesses;
- phasing out of older technologies and opening up of new ones;
- the opening of occupational doors previously closed because of gender or racial barriers;

- changes in health and well-being; and/or
- changes in personal life or economic status.

Changing Life/Career Stages

"Although once we needed, now … " is a fruitful phrase for us to think through. Times change, and so do we. Models for parenting are put aside for models of aging. Models for career advancement are put aside for models of a balanced life or retirement.

- Although once we needed models for learning a profession or occupation, we now need models for management, for handling political processes, and for balancing work and career.
- Although once we needed models for managing marriage and career, we now need models for how to pull ourselves together after a death or a messy divorce.
- Although once we needed models for becoming a competent worker in one occupational field, we now need models of transitioning to other lines of work.
- Although once we needed models for managing an education and then a career, we now need models for phasing down work and eventual retirement.

Surveying Your Mentoring Models

The guides in Chapter 19 can be used to survey your mentoring models and identify those that continue to be guiding and influencing in a positive way, those that once had a place but are no longer relevant, and the gap where mentoring models are needed but do not yet exist.

BRIDGE

In this section, we examined the relationship of mentoring messages to the models that we choose or are presented to us, and how models develop and change. Some models become mentors; most do not. The subject of mentoring relationships is the focus of the next section. Attraction—so obvious in our choice of models—is one key in developing mentoring relationships. Also important is our experience with adults in our lives and our mentor-bonding pattern. Just how this all comes together in forming mentoring relationships is a subject to which we now turn.

Chapter 11

WHAT MAKES A MENTORING RELATIONSHIP WORK?

What *is* a mentoring relationship—and what does it take to make it work? What is the mysterious glue that holds together the relationship of mentor and mentee and makes it effective?

I pondered this question one afternoon at the beach, fresh from a swim and surrounded by yellow pads with data from my research. Suddenly it became clear: Like a stool, a major mentoring relationship is supported by three legs—*attraction, action,* and *affect.*

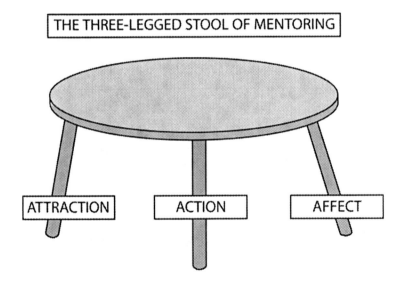

Figure 2. The Three-Legged Stool of Mentoring

Another image also is useful: Attraction and affect serve as bookends to support the action a mentor takes on behalf of a mentee.

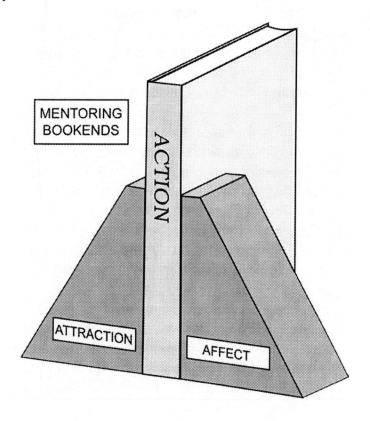

Figure 3. Mentoring Bookends

Action on behalf of the mentee is at the center of all mentoring relationships. For a major mentoring relationship to take place, however, the two bookends of attraction and affect must be present. Attraction and affect are the two feeling components of a mentoring relationship. They support and validate the actions that the mentor takes on behalf of the mentee. Attraction is the positive emotional pull drawing the mentee to the mentor: those things the mentee admires, values, and wishes to emulate. Affect is the positive feeling tone of the mentor toward the mentee: the respecting, valuing, liking, and taking pride in the mentee. A full, or major, mentoring relationship has all three basic supports. It also extends over time, is comprehensive, intensive, and formative in the mentee's growth. If the attraction–affect bookends are weak or non-existent, or if the action is not central, the relationship will be limited or short-lived.

What differentiates a mentoring relationship from a mentoring model is interaction—the dialogue between the two people. Interpersonal communication is present, and it moves in both directions. Whether that happens and how much it happens is very much related to our mentor-bonding history. Where mentor bonding is absent or limited, the scope and depth of a mentoring relationship will be limited as well. Furthermore, the nature of the relationship will parallel early bonding patterns in important ways.

In this chapter, we examine mentor–mentee[12] interactions closely. What is it in the interaction between two people that fosters the development in the mentee? What does the mentor do that makes it work? We focus on the role of the mentor in each of the three elements of a major mentoring relationship: How are mentees attracted to mentors (attraction)? How do mentors demonstrate their positive regard toward the mentee (affect)? And what are the many action roles mentors play to help the mentee (action)?

---

[12] I have chosen the power-neutral word "mentee" to describe the receiver in a mentoring relationship. Occasionally for clarity, "junior," "younger person," or "protégé" is used. "Mentee" seems more appropriate, because mentoring relationships of one form or another exist throughout our lives, and because mentoring relationships naturally shift to increasing parity over time.

ATTRACTION

Something about the mentor attracts or appeals to the junior person; the mentee is drawn to the mentor. We talk about the "chemistry" between people. Sometimes that chemistry exists because of similarities to important mentor-bonding people in the past. No interaction is required for attraction to be present. However, for a mentoring relationship to develop, interaction must take place—either in the action the mentor takes on the behalf of the junior person, or in the affect demonstrated by the mentor toward that person—usually both.

In our discussion of attraction in Chapters 8, 9, and 10, we saw that the two most common attraction roles are exemplar/example and energizer. Usually, the mentor is a model—an exemplar or example of something the mentee aspires to be like. Mentors can energize people through ideas and vision, through human qualities, or through exceptional talents and skills. They have positive qualities that the mentee admires. The mentor could be likeable, fun to be with, charismatic, comfortable, or trustworthy—or be a crusty but brilliant star. A model is not necessarily a mentor, but a major mentor is always a model who is attractive and appealing on some dimension, if not several.

Because attraction to a potential mentor is related to our mentor bonding—specifically our experience with the respect/trust/relevance triad—non-bonders or limited bonders might well keep a potential mentor at arm's length for one of the following reasons:
- You admire the person but doubt that the person values or respects you as a person.
- You admire the person but don't feel safe in trusting him or her with data about your inadequacies or needs.
- You might have had bad experiences with people like the potential mentor that cause you to be unwilling to trust.

- You admire and respect a person very much but don't see that what he or she could do is really relevant to your needs and goals.

AFFECT

Affect is the other emotional component of a major mentor relationship. The direction of the positive feelings is reversed. In attraction, the mentee is drawn to the mentor; in affect, the mentor is drawn to the mentee. A major mentor connects with the mentee, has positive feelings *for* the mentee—likes, confirms, respects, and sees value in the mentee. Also, the mentor cares enough to share information, provide instruction, or give advice to the mentee. Trust, as well as respect, often is present and mutual. Believing in the mentee is an important ingredient. In describing their mentors, people use words like "believed in me," "had faith in me," "saw potential in me," "knew I could do it," "saw something in me," and "had such confidence in me."

"Encouragement and support" is the phrase that mentees often use to refer to this dimension of their mentor relationship; these words are so intertwined that they usually are expressed as one phrase. Just what does the mentor *do* to be perceived as supportive and encouraging? People say "My mentor … "
- "understood me."
- "listened and cared."
- "took an interest in me."
- "was open and receptive."
- "helped me overcome doubts about making it."
- "had faith in me and made me feel confidence in myself."
- "opened my eyes to my capabilities."
- "kept telling me I could do much more than I realized."

Support and encouragement influence the extent to which the mentee feels understood, accepted, and valued. Mentors can provide us with positive feedback about our talents and capabilities and can help us see ourselves in a new light. As one person's mentor told him, "You have abilities; all it means is hard work."

Some of us felt *encouraged* to do different things: "to use my talents and enter contests," "to take a job where I could exert leadership," and "to go to college when others said, 'Well, you can be a typist.'" Others felt *supported* by their mentor who "helped me survive the situation," "reassured me that it's okay to be a girl and go into science," "helped me get financial assistance," and "supported me when I had doubts about making it in engineering school."

Supportive and encouraging behaviors are important especially when the young person has doubts about self and abilities, is floundering, is having difficulty being understood, or needs reassurance in seeking an important goal.

Inferred Affect

Although affect is an emotional tone, some mentors—often men—have difficulty expressing or showing feelings. In such situations, affect can be inferred only by action that the mentor takes on behalf of the mentee. This was Jane's realization.

"My father's display of emotion, other than anger or humor, was minimal and hard to read. It wasn't until a recent time that I could understand how very much he valued me. The tip-off came from thinking through what it meant for him to buy me a portable typewriter when I was in high school and then later, a desk to put it on. In our post-Depression household, all home improvements were bought 'on time,' on the installment plan. Only when one major item, like a refrigerator, was paid off could another purchase be considered. These were not casual decisions, and the backlog of desired purchases was great.

Given that context, I now can see the pride he must have had in
me to support me as he did. His feelings were manifest only
through his actions. I couldn't see that at the time."

Gender Differences

The data support a slightly different take on affect for men and
women. Men tend to have doubts about such things as coming from "a
rinky-dink town," being black and coping, coming from another
culture, and doubting one's capabilities. Women, too, have doubts
about their abilities, but also about themselves as women, about
moving into non-traditional roles and having the support to succeed,
and about managing or balancing family and career.

One of John's mentors "saw that I was cared for properly, nourished
me. He saw me through some rough times as a student when I was
having feelings of uncertainty about myself." Men use phrases like "he
tucked me under his wing" more than the words "support" or
"encouragement." For men, the wing-tucker provides a safe,
protective learning environment that is needed without any question
of appropriateness.

Affect Plus Action

In major relationships, *affect* is always combined with *action*. The
mentor might combine giving feedback with caring, provide
opportunities with respect, and find resources with encouragement.
Here are two examples:
- Sam described his mentor as "tough—he would come into a
conference and start quizzing you on stuff, but he always
treated me with great respect. I had a great affection for him."
- John told his mentor that he had to buy a microscope for medical
school but that he didn't have the money. "He said, 'No
problem. I'll lend one to you.' I never took him up on his offer,
but it was nice that he would do it. He was really supportive."

ACTION

All mentors take some sort of action on behalf of the mentee: The mentor *does* something for the mentee. Actions are the most visible part of mentoring. The nature of the action varies greatly according to the position and resources of the mentor, the mentor's inclinations and style, and the mentee's needs and interests. The number and range of action-taking roles is almost limitless, depending on the interest, creativity, and resources of the mentor as well as the receptivity of the mentee. The greater the number of action roles, the deeper or more comprehensive the relationship is likely to be. Obviously, the longer the duration of the relationship, the increased likelihood of the mentor taking many types of action.

Action-taking roles never operate in a vacuum. They vary with societal changes, including changes in organizations and technology and trends in professions—topics we will discuss in Chapter 23. Although many of these changes put a new slant on mentoring relationships and the types of action roles needed, we can get an idea of the range of mentor action-taking roles from the following illustrations, drawn from interviews. In major mentoring relationships, these action roles are always supported, like bookends, by attraction and affect.

Action Roles in Mentoring

Teacher/Coach

Most of us have had skill developers, teachers, or coaches who have been important in our lives. They help us develop our physical, artistic, intellectual, and mechanical abilities as well as our social and leadership skills. They are schoolteachers at all levels, athletic coaches, music teachers, scout leaders, and pastors as well as parents, siblings, and friends. We remember them fondly.

"I learned a lot from him," and "she taught me a lot" speak to the importance of the teaching/learning function of a mentor. The teaching could be via formal class situations or internships, or informal passing on of knowledge, such as demonstrating or sharpening skills. Teaching might be on a basic level, or it could extend to highly complex cognitive concepts or technical skills. Although a coach is more focused on individual development, the roles of teacher/coach overlap to the degree that it is difficult to separate them.

The teacher/coach is of almost any age or status and in all walks of life: "My yoga teacher guided my reading into Tolstoy, Russell, and others," "my karate teacher taught me self-discipline," "the conductor of the symphony taught me to bring out the soul in music," or "the crew chief taught me how to improvise regardless of the circumstances." We also find mentors in surprising places: Nurses learn a great deal from their patients, manufacturing supervisors from production workers and parents from their children, particularly their adolescent children!

Examples

"I was 18 years old in the Navy and figured these big machines didn't need close tolerances. My warrant officer taught me that those things run within

.002-4 clearance and that precision really mattered. He really taught me to respect the power that these things were capable of generating."

• • •

"My neighbor knew all about babies, from crying to diaper rashes. She knew what to get excited about and what not. She never gave me advice, but, by example, she showed me that being a mother was so natural that it would just come to me. I ended up with a good feeling about my mothering capabilities."

• • •

"My mentor in management pulled me out of my straight, rigid jacket and showed me a way of doing things differently with people—and getting the work done just the same. I learned a lot from him in using tact with people. Before, I was renowned for being a despot."

• • •

"My marketing professor taught me to evaluate the entirety of a given situation and to be able to speak concretely about it."

Technical Guide

Obviously, there is an overlap of the technical guide with the teacher/coach role. I separate these roles simply to emphasize the importance of this action-taking mentor role in the complex, fast pace of our changing technology.

For most of us, the need for technical guides comes from our work. Often, it is crucial to have a mentor who will teach us skills at the appropriate career time. In academic medicine, that time is soon after medical school. The physician whose experience is quoted (at right) received excellent training, but she was some years out of medical school. She said, "I should have had a research mentor long before I did. I really resent my time in my post-graduate years. Neither of the other researchers were mentors, and I was left too much on my own without anyone saying, 'This is how you do it' and 'These are the short-cuts.' If I hadn't had a mentor, I'd never be able to function in academic medicine."

It's important to note the difference between a mentoring *relationship* and mentoring *information*. For many of us, our technical needs are short term and simpler. I'm thinking of the periodic needs many of us have for computer consultants. When I call a software company, I get one-time information from a voice on the phone. No relationship is established; it's simply question-and-answer troubleshooting for a particular difficulty.

Example

"I studied circadian rhythms and the effect of exercise or bed rest. I had to write this up into a presentation for a major conference, and I'd never put together this kind of talk before. I didn't know the first thing about it. Luckily, a very senior colleague coached me in a one-on-one process.

"The first time I gave the talk, he said, 'Oh, God, a crash course in public speaking.' Then he said, 'You want a minute or so of introduction. You'll cover these points, and then you have a minute for your conclusion. You'll need three typewritten pages triple-spaced and four copies of it, and you'll want duplicates of your slides. You can't have more than eight slides.'

"He told me all the ground rules that make life simple. 'This is how much information you can get on a slide,' And he'd say, 'Yes!' or 'No, this won't fly, and this is why it won't fly.'

"After I gave my presentation before the big antibiotic expert, my mentor said, 'You're so lucky having the Harvard professor of pharmacology and antibiotic studies here for your talk. It really went well.'"

Challengers/Prodders

Many mentors push the mentee to go beyond the person's present reach, whether this has to do with goals, effort, level of performance, skill utilization, development of potential, or career aspiration. They are mentors who insist that students work at their top performance. They are exacting, have very high standards, and demand that mentees meet them.

Abby's high school drama teacher was "a holy terror" but knew her craft. She taught her students precisely what they were doing that was not working. Abby "nearly went insane" trying to make her Lady Macbeth monologue better, but she did succeed in reaching the finals in the competition.

Other mentors are softer—nudgers—helping young people see their potential, venture into new areas, and take risks. Dean's psychologist mentor pushed him out of the nest, nudging him toward professional autonomy. "*You* go evaluate them; I don't want to see them."

The mentor who holds high standards could be distant, remote, angry, or demanding—or kind, compassionate, and helpful to the young person. The success of this mentor role depends on the "fit" with the mentee. Some of us respond well to the "exacters;" others of us do much better with "evokers." Some of us thrive on being pushed, prodded, and challenged; others of us need to be drawn out and nurtured more.

Examples

"My economics instructor kept prodding me. If I allowed myself to slack off, she would come up with 'Are you satisfied with being less than best?' She knew how to press my buttons to get me to move!"

• • •

After finishing her stint as chair of the ethics committee of the state dietetic association, Laura planned to take it easy for a year. But she didn't reckon with her mentor/colleague, who kept insisting that she was capable of doing more. Laura knew she could do it, but just needed "a little prodding." The pushing paid off, and Laura later became president of the association.

• • •

When Al was administrator of a clinical laboratory, his pathologist boss pushed him to get his master's degree and to try being entrepreneurial. "One time, he said, 'I want you to be supervisor of serology.' I said, 'We don't have a serology department,' and he said, 'Create one.' That's a challenge I couldn't turn down!"

Exposer

This action role ranges in intensity from providing opportunities for the junior person to actively fostering and pushing the person. The extent depends on power, influence, access, and interest of the mentor as well as the receptiveness of the mentee.

The "exposer" role is a familiar one. We do this with children when we introduce them to paintings in an art museum, have a young boy talk to an Eagle Scout, include children in conversations with other adults, and make it possible for young people to listen in on meetings. We take it a step further when we discuss the experience later—"debrief" the experience to gain additional meanings and understanding. As adults, we value mentors who help enlarge, expand, and broaden our knowledge, our awareness, and our ability to make contacts and network.

Examples

"My cousin Edward didn't want us to be 'common women,' so he took it upon himself to teach my sister and me some 'class.' He would spend Saturday nights with us, improving our vocabulary, listening to classical music, and playing bridge."

• • •

"It was my first professional job in personnel. My boss took me with him on industry-wide labor negotiations. I was to watch him, assist in negotiation preparations, and be a gofer."

• • •

"My boss exposed me to aspects of the business world, like industrial espionage, that I never knew existed, as I had come from a technical mechanical-engineering background."

Allower/Entruster

Some mentors allow an unusual degree of freedom because of confidence and trust in the mentee's ability to perform.

In research or creative fields, being free to develop your own work and your own role is the expected mode. For most of us, however, the degrees of freedom are more limited, and delegated responsibility comes when trust and confidence in the junior person builds.

Allowing and entrusting are viewed as a matter of great privilege. Mentees highly value this evidence of trust from the senior person. Kay's mentor was a high-level state executive who allowed Kay a great deal of freedom. Kay learned to keep her mentor informed about things without being at her door every day. "She gave me enough rope to hang myself. It was a good experience all around."

This mentor role is not the same as the supervisor who abdicates leadership responsibility; for the allower/entruster, this is a conscious mentoring strategy.

Examples

Raphael expressed interest in administration at the time he applied for a pharmacy position. Once he was hired, he took it upon himself to implement new things. Before long, his mentor/boss saw that Raphael had a good ability for systems analysis and creative problem-solving, so he made opportunities available to Raphael. In one such project, Raphael was set loose to create a totally new pharmacist position for the clinic and make it work.

• • •

When he was an administrative intern, Cory was allowed to do all the buying, close the general ledger at the end of the month, and also do special studies that were to be presented to the board.

Door-Opener/Sponsor

As adults we value mentors who help enlarge, expand, and broaden our knowledge and our ability to make contacts and to network. Mentors who occupy influential positions in organizations are in a position to open doors, provide resources, and even sponsor mentees.

Kerry was invited to attend an international orthopedic conference by his physician mentor. Elise's fellowship director arranged for her to present a paper at a conference. Tom's personnel boss took Tom with him on industry-wide labor negotiations to watch and assist in negotiation preparations. Rachel's dietetics mentor was influential in her being appointed to the commission on accreditation as well as other appointments at the national level.

We are not surprised when we see a mentor provide special opportunities in business and the professions, but this can occur in childhood as well, as the second example (below) demonstrates.

Examples

Deb's director of research and development had Deb sit in on high-level meetings to see how the director dealt with political situations. After each meeting, the director debriefed with Deb to explain the political scene. The director also put Deb in charge whenever he was gone. "I functioned independently. I had to deal with the researchers by myself, or be in committee meetings by myself, and I needed to represent and speak up for the R&D perspective."

• • •

Jillian was elected student body president when she was in 5th grade. Her principal arranged for Jillian to attend interscholastic meetings where boards of officers from elementary schools met bi-monthly and had her participate in planning for athletic events. Jillian was exposed to a sophisticated process not just as an observer but also as a planner and idea-generator.

Career Guide

A career guide combines some aspects of a counselor, consultant, director, and groomer. The mentor can discuss philosophy about the profession or can outline specific action steps. Some teachers are talent spotters and will suggest fields or avenues to explore. High school teachers and college instructors are helpful in terms of introducing careers, what you can expect, what training is like, and where to apply to a school. Later on, mentors can be useful consultants about the appropriateness of positions when contemplating a career change. They also can help the mentee clarify professional goals and philosophy. Some mentors are directive and advice giving; others use more of a listening and thinking-things-through approach.

The mentor can provide a practical perspective on careers by sharing knowledge of career trends, of fields that are opening up or closing down. He or she also can advise the junior person on the routes to advance career status, what "tickets" the person needs to punch.

Example

Jack was certain he wanted to be an oncologist. "My physician mentor discouraged me by saying, 'It's fine if you don't mind living at the end of a dead-end street.'

"He told me to go work with another doctor in a research area that was really hot. 'If you're still unhappy and want more surgery, then come back and talk to me,' he told me. I had become a sharp young surgeon. What I didn't realize was, so was everybody else.

"It turned out that radio-immunoassay taught me scientific discipline and lab methods. His advice showed immense foresight and wisdom."

Culture Guide

In many situations, a mentor guide to culture can speed the process of "fitting in" for a newcomer and can make the difference between success and failure in that setting. Some organizations assign an older employee to a new hire specifically to "show him the ropes." This can be done formally through preceptorships or informally with the "old hand" guiding the novice. Mentees remember the person "who taught me what to do and not to do," and "how to make it in that culture."

Culture guides are important for the new worker moving into an organization: the novice high school teacher moving to a new school, a business graduate joining the treasury department of city government, a mechanic in a first job building airplanes, or the new rabbi whose formal education stressed academic preparation rather than temple operations. They are especially important to the outsider now transplanted to, living in, or working in a different racial, ethnic, or other cultural setting.

For the person promoted to an organizational level requiring political skills, where a misstep could easily damage one's career, a mentor can make a real difference. The mentor can provide insight on political interactions that appear to be going on, identify coalitions, show how decisions are made and communicated by higher-ups, and advise on how to make a negative recommendation. The mentor also can be instructive in dealing with power and politics in the organization.

Examples

Lois remembers joining an organization in the 1960s when the issue of civil rights was very much present. "This big black man took me under his wing and showed this nice little white Irish Catholic girl what the big old world out there was like in terms of race relations. He taught me everything I needed to know in order to do the job. He also opened up vistas for me—the whole panorama of other people and minority and ethnic matters."

• • •

Gloria had worked for Scott several years earlier in their health maintenance organization, and they trusted each other. This was vital in her new administrative role, because, she said, it was a "very political environment. I had no idea what I was getting into. The politics are so complicated because the physicians are partners and cannot be fired. You don't have a straight-line hierarchy. You have to get things done by virtue of your ability to influence, keep yourself clean, and avoid being crushed or taking an arrow in the back. He showed me the ropes and how to survive."

Protector

Mentors in power positions are known for their ability to stand up for, go to bat for, or work on behalf of mentees. These actions can take the form of the protective mother defending her child, the corporate manager storming the battlements, or even the executive of an international aid organization in a foreign country defending the staff from the affronts of that country's bureaucrats.

Sometimes, kids growing up have a family member who serves as protector or advocate. Similarly, mentors in key positions in organizations can exercise their clout to back up their mentees when they get into difficulties, either because of errors by the mentee or because of power or political reactions to behavior.

Examples

Barry's dissertation chairman came through for him in tight political situations. "During my oral exam, when other people started nit-picking me, he was good at thumping the other professors, whipping them into line so they didn't give me too bad of a time."

• • •

When Brooke was a new physician, she turned to an older woman physician who told her, "I'll make a tough old broad out of you, so you won't accept the usual putdowns that women allow themselves to accept."

• • •

Evan was on the verge of leaving college because of trouble with several administrators in his department. "I was likely to be drafted and sent to Vietnam. My professor urged me to stay and get a degree. He then arranged a transfer for me to the psych department."

Problem-Solver/Mental Stimulator

This action role emphasizes the development and use of the analytical and creative powers of the mind—the ability to evaluate a situation, find meaning, or understand the logic. Mentees credit such mentors for "teaching me to reach a higher order of thinking."

Mentors also are sounding boards: They listen, make comments, give perspectives, offer opinions, and help the mentee think through problems.

Tip-off phrases include "helped me define my own philosophy," "talked things over with me," "played with concepts and ideas," "bounced ideas around," "lots of talks," "philosophized with," "clarify my thinking," and "a sounding board."

Examples

"My internship supervisor cracked the whip: 'You have a brain; you can think this out. You have to make these kinds of operational decisions, and you can do it.' I kept wanting people to tell me what to do because that's what I'd learned in parochial schools."

• • •

"The chief neonatologist had a real impact on my intellectual growth. It was his style of brainstorming, encouraging you to come up with ideas, to have an opinion. I hadn't thought nurses could be in creative roles. But he offered instant trust: 'Here's what I want to do for outreach in terms of neonatal problems, but I don't know how to do it. I want you to work on it.' "

• • •

Elise's physician mentor gave her "the best tools for continuing clinical education. He demanded an extensive textbook review. Then he had me ask myself three questions about the patient unrelated to the main diagnosis, then research it, and write it up. The approach was systematic and involved pinpointing some research, relating it to the patient's needs, and stretching to go beyond the immediate to other implications."

BRIDGE

This chapter examined the basics of what makes a mentoring relationship work: attraction, action, and affect. Mentors take actions on our behalf. When those actions are supported by attraction and affect, a major mentoring relationship is at work. Such mentoring relationships have a richness and comprehensiveness that is impressive. Additional factors that affect mentoring relationships are described in the three chapters that follow. Chapter 12 examines the three basic mentor forms of mentor–mentee relationships: the traditional mentor, the step-ahead mentor, and the co-mentor. Understanding these mentor–mentee forms is important. As we move along in life and career, we move away from traditional mentors toward more level mentor relationships.

Chapter 12

THE THREE BASIC MENTOR FORMS

When people talk of mentors, they usually are thinking of the classical form of mentoring that dates back to the ancient Greeks. As the legend goes, Athena, in the guise of Mentor, became the tutor of Odysseus' son, Telemachus. Mentor was an older wise person whose role was to guide and form the young man. In that sense, Mentor functioned as a traditional mentor.

But two additional mentor forms are highly relevant for our modern day life: the step-ahead mentor and the co-mentor. In this chapter, we will examine the three basic mentor forms, what they are, what they look like, and how they affect mentor–mentee relationships.

Each of these roles describes the power difference between the mentor and mentee relative to status, age, and experience. The difference is greatest between the traditional mentor and the mentee, and least between co-mentors who have equal status and power. Each of these forms can be compared to social roles as defined in anthropology:

- The traditional mentor can be likened to an elder.
- The step-ahead mentor can be likened to an older sibling.
- The co-mentor can be likened to a peer.

THE TRADITIONAL MENTOR

In the classic tradition of mentoring, the mentor is a generation older than the mentee and has considerable experience and status. Status could be in terms of titles, degrees, and accomplishments, or it could be by respect, admiration, or recognition—whatever is valued by the family and/or the community. The mentor, symbolically the Wise Man or Elder of the tribe, hands down or passes on the knowledge and wisdom of the culture to the naive young person.

The role of the mentee or protégé is to study, learn, and accept. The power difference between the mentor and mentee is great. The mentee looks up to the mentor. The relationship tends to have broad scope and is fairly intense and long lasting during the youth and early adult years of the mentee.

The old apprentice–master indenture in colonial America was based on the classic mentor relationship, although this was a limited, instrumental role in learning a trade. In the practice of "sending out" the young child, the master was often legally bound to give the child a basic education as well as a trade. Power was strong and legally enforced, but since the young person usually had no choice in the decision-making, respect and admiration often were missing. The three-legged stool of attraction/action/affect was missing a leg or two. The best master-apprentice relationships, however, would fit the classic mentor model.

Those of us who had parent figures or other adults as early traditional mentors usually find the relationship changing over time. As the junior person matures and gains more knowledge and skill, the power difference gradually diminishes. The younger person speaks up and assumes more responsibility, and more authority. Several things could happen, all leading to a transformation and gradual leveling out of the power difference—or a break or drifting apart in the relationship

THE STEP-AHEAD MENTOR

Young people often turn to others slightly older than themselves as models or guides. For those of us who are younger members of the family or have older cousins or other relatives nearby, step-ahead mentors appear early in life. Usually, all of the characteristics are there. We look up to these older brothers, sisters, or cousins: They are stronger, more skillful, or more talented. They show us what we can be, what we can shoot for—or, in a negative way, they can show us how deficient we are. Our mentoring relationships with them can carry through life, though they tend to level out with maturity and become more co-mentoring in nature. They can set the pattern for relating to other older and more-experienced peers.

The step-ahead mentor is several years older and more experienced than the mentee, yet close enough in age for the two to relate comfortably and informally with each other. A step-ahead mentor is viewed as more approachable than the traditional mentor, as there is less power and status differential. The relationship can be long-lasting or related to a specific phase in a person's life. It can be narrow in scope, as in learning a specific skill, or it can be broad. Mentor–mentee relations in adult life often assume this pattern. Not infrequently in adult relationships, the age difference can be reversed. The mentor might be much younger than the mentee, which is particularly true in learning new technology.

It should be noted that if you are the older child in your family, you might have been thrust into a step-ahead mentor role for younger siblings whether you wanted to or not. If that is the case, *being* a step-ahead mentor rather than *having* one is a more familiar role for you.

Also, if you have been unable to relate well to adult figures in your early life, you might skip the traditional mentoring step altogether and go directly to the step-ahead place, seeing these relationships as less threatening and more acceptable to you.

Whatever our personal mentoring history, most of us will need step-ahead mentors during some phase of our lives, particularly in times of personal life transition or technological change.

THE PEER OR CO-MENTOR

Often overlooked, peer or co-mentoring is an important form of mentoring. Peer mentoring rarely appears in early life, but it assumes greater prominence with each passing year. Sometimes, the relationship starts with the more experienced person serving as a step-ahead mentor. Then, with the junior person's growing experience, it could transform naturally into a peer relationship. Or, it could start as a peer friendship and gain multiple connections. But always in co-mentoring, there is a "give and take," a level playing field, and a comfort with and respect for each other. Should that change, the co-mentoring ends.

Look at the words people use to describe this form of mentoring relationship: "we dovetailed," "colleague mentoring," "cooperative not competitive," "collaborative," "complementary," "sharing," and "sounding board."

Co-mentoring comes into its own when you and your peers have developed enough knowledge, skill, and experience to be able to offer something of value to each other. The communication and interchange are easy, because power, experience, age, and status are fairly similar. In the early years, the co-mentoring role of peers is limited. As we gain more life experience, this often becomes the major mentor form.

Co-mentoring usually has considerable attraction and/or affect—that's what usually brings the two people together and helps form the relationship. You discover a commonality of interests with a friend. Or, you admire an acquaintance who can do something you can't do—or who can do it better, or who has had different life experiences and offers a new perspective. Sometimes, you discover someone who seems to look at things the same way you do, even seems to know what you're thinking.

Co-mentoring can be reciprocal or mutual. In reciprocal mentoring, each brings to the partnership some distinct and complementary talent, insight, or skill that enriches the other. One could have a particular niche or expertise that the other does not have. If the need is in the area of one person's competence, that person is the step-ahead mentor for the moment. Because the roles shift frequently, there is reciprocity and balance. Each adds to or gives to the other in the relationship, and each receives in turn.

In mutual mentoring, the partners have sufficient common interests and connections that the ball bounces back and forth almost without notice. A discussion flips from reciprocal to mutual mentoring and back again. The lines between the two forms of mentoring are blurred.

I think of several areas of adult life where co-mentoring is of value. One is colleague mentoring, particularly where colleagues come from different but connecting disciplines, such as in urban planning, environmental management, interdisciplinary clinical treatment, and medical research. Another is coping with life transitions and crises. Still another is the independent entrepreneur role and lifestyle where exchange of information and development of networking relationships are vital.

It is important to note that networking can lead to two kinds of peer relationships. First is a one-on-one relationship where information-sharing and/or emotional support is reciprocated. Second is a pattern where the giving and receiving is balanced *within* a network but not necessarily between the same two people. For more information on networking, see Chapter 24.

In later adult years, our desire for the mutuality of peer exchange becomes more pressing. It is in this stage of life that both reciprocal and mutual co-mentors are important. Most of us will still be able to find step-ahead mentors from younger cohort groups when we need guidance in some aspect of new societal, economic, or technology trends, but the importance of peers for the mutual later-life journey far overshadows that need.

MENTOR EXAMPLES

Traditional Mentors

Our first and most significant mentors are usually our parents or parent surrogates. Certainly, their influence can be comprehensive and molding, particularly in shaping life goals and values. Where this positive influence is missing, the young person often turns to other sources if they are available. Teachers or other adults in the community frequently fill this role. Often, this is a natural transition as the circle of people around the young person widens.

Evie's piano teacher was the dominant force in her life from the time she was 6 until she married at 19 and intermittently thereafter. The relationship was comprehensive and long lasting. She was a far more important mentor than anyone Evie met through her profession.

> "She was an outstanding piano teacher, but that wasn't what I was after. The support she gave me in my studies encouraged me to reach farther. Her faith in me and her teaching me a sound value system that I wasn't getting from my family—all of this was more meaningful than the technical aspects of the piano. I was confused growing up in a home where there was a lot of alcohol but no money for further schooling. I was disillusioned with my parents' marital life. Yet, I was able to talk to her about things very openly and never was punished. I admired her and was very

close to her. She was happy in what she was doing. I liked the peaceful environment she provided."

The purest examples of the traditional mentor at work came from interviews with physicians in academic medicine. This is the one field in my sample that had well-established mentoring patterns. Young physicians in fellowship programs expect to have mentors. Those I talked to were resentful when this did not happen and were painfully aware of their loss and the handicap to their research and to their careers. On the other hand, physicians who went into private practice reported no mentoring traditions of the classic mentor type, nor any expectations thereof.

> Stan's long-term mentor was a leading figure in medical genetics. Although Stan originally came to work with him for a two-year period, the relationship has been ongoing for decades. "He boosted me to lots of opportunities and has taken great pride in what I have done. He is very generous, with an extraordinary record of selecting promising people and supporting them. He is interested in the broader aspects of science as well as the arts and literature—just a remarkable all-round person." Over the years, Stan said, my mentor has served as a "supplementary father."

Our mentors can be very significant in either professional or personal matters, rarely on both.

> Lucy's English professor was an important mentor to her in many ways, and she saw him as a very wise person. But once, when she tried to reach him on an emotional level when she was breaking up with a boyfriend, she said, "He was just bewildered."

Step-Ahead Mentors

Sometimes, our pattern of mentoring relationships tends toward the predominant use of one mentor form. Ben's pattern of step-ahead mentors began in childhood with his uncle who was just a few years older. The pattern was repeated after high school in a youth group, and then again in medical education.

> "One guy in my high school youth group was four or five years older. I'm still in awe of him. He was incredible: spoke English brilliantly, spoke and wrote Hebrew fluently, was fantastic in sports, was into culture. He had a mind like a whipsaw and could play intellectual games. He opened my eyes to human capabilities. I found myself transported from a situation in high school with the 'Hey, how-you-doing' type of thing to the most intellectual world. It was mind-boggling.

> "In medical school, I met a physician from Yugoslavia a few years older, and he took me under his wing. He taught me virology. I loved it, and I thrived. He was very approachable at my level, and we could joke around. I spent the summer in his lab, plus time in my third and fourth years. The research captured my heart. I think that kept me sane during medical school."

The use of step-ahead mentors has been the historical practice in several professional fields. The nursing profession uses preceptors widely. The physicians I interviewed considered much of medical graduate education a process of residents teaching residents. As Joan recalls:

> "The residents put their rotation together. The lab instructor only came in to do lab teaching; he wasn't on site more than that. Residents organized everything. When necessary, they went to a staff member for an opinion. Fortunately or unfortunately, most of medical graduate education was a process of senior residents teaching residents. The two fourth-year residents were very capable, marvelous, and very supportive."

Co-Mentors

Co-mentoring is a relatively unrecognized mentor form. Those who view the traditional mentor relationship as the only true mentor pattern do not see co-mentoring as a mentoring form at all. They refer to such relationships merely as "friends." Yet, many of these connections are far more extensive than friendships. If we look at the formative, guiding influences that shape our lives, some of these peer relationships command our attention. A synergy comes from co-mentoring: Together, the two individuals are able to cope with or adjust to situations and to accomplish things far better than either one could alone. As our world becomes more complex, the ability to connect, interact with, learn from, and work collaboratively toward mutual goals is a valuable skill.

Also of immeasurable value is the mutual help and support we can give each other as we cope with stressful periods of life. Co-mentoring arises not only out of common interests, but also out of strong needs. The relationship is active so long as the need continues. For example, those in rigorous training programs—from firefighters to Peace Corps volunteers to doctors and nurses—often draw together for warmth and succor to get through a difficult training situation.

- Each time Catherine's family was transferred to a new military base, she and her brothers drew very close and helped each other through the transition. Once settled in, they each went their own way.
- During the year that Val and a friend were living and working in England, they formed a co-mentoring partnership to encourage each other to learn and grow. They went to the opera, traveled in Europe, and ventured forth on many new experiences.
- Sue and her co-worker had both suffered a recent personal trauma; Sue had given birth to a "preemie," and her friend's child had drowned. Plus, both women were experiencing marital difficulties. Their co-mentoring, formed out of acute need, transformed and continued on many levels.

Here are other examples of co-mentoring, both reciprocal and mutual mentors. I've arranged them by occupational field.

Reciprocal Mentors

—In Interdisciplinary Practice

- Lucy was the psychologist member of an adolescent medicine teaching team when she connected with a woman pediatrician on the team. "Lana sought me out. She was one of the first physicians who really valued my expertise and insights and wanted to learn more. Because Lana valued what I said, other physicians did, too. She opened some doors. She would say, 'Do you want to come up on the ward and do rounds?' Afterward, she might say, 'If you could make this more pointed and present it in this way, the interns and residents are going to pay more attention.' Until then, I just couldn't find a place for myself when it came to teaching. I learned that I had to structure things differently for physicians. I hadn't learned the system. So Lana and I had a kind of mutualness, a mutual mentoring maybe—a very non-competitive kind of relationship.

  "That was also the first collaborative relationship I had in terms of writing papers. Lana was the doer: She'd write the proposal, and I would review it. She would meet with the research committee—I still felt a lot of intimidation and was out of my element when talking to doctors. It's been the most complementary working relationship I've had. We could be critical with each other, but the criticism would be muted. There's a special teaming that maybe will happen once in a lifetime. Later, I faced one of the most difficult separations when she moved to Texas."

—In Engineering

- Rob's most recent mentors have been complementary rather than competitive. He talks about his mentoring with a co-worker: "I have specialized depth that he lacks in certain areas. We fill in each other's voids very nicely, and we're not competing. He is an excellent theoretician, and, with my hardware capability, we have pulled off a lot. We would brainstorm, shoot holes in each other's ideas, and come up with solutions. We complement each other."

—In the Ministry

- Bruce recalls the reciprocal relationship he had with the new woman director of religious education at his church: "She has particular skills in group leadership and group dynamics. She is able to listen carefully and discern what is going on in a group situation, in board meetings, in committee meetings. Her sensitivities were far beyond my own perceptions. I could teach her in the world of concepts, books, and ideas—that has always been my forte. She had skills in other areas that I have needed and depended upon. So we traded off our different strong points and made a good team."

- When Claire went into the ministry, she knew she was in the first generation of women in the profession. "There were no previous guides for women in the ministry, so we women learned to be in constant touch. We have very different styles and abilities, so we use each other for clarification in our work and our lives. It's very reciprocal. We need each other. And since we're the older women in the district, there is no one else to turn to."

—In Social Work

- Pat and her classmate in social work graduate school provided counseling for each other. "We talked about all the things we were going through with our field work experiences and our classes. We discussed various concepts. She had more clinical experience coming into the program, so she was a good sounding board for me, and I helped her think about things less emotionally."

—In Nursing

- Mary and another nurse of the same age were working with the same job description. Here is Mary's description of her co-mentor and their relationship: "Barb has had experience in organizations, setting up programs, working on committees. She's been my mentor as far as leadership abilities and skills. She's into research and is very resourceful. She's put me on to some good articles, and we have had long discussions about the whole transition to leadership. Plus, she builds up my self-confidence: She sees me as more capable, organized, and self-confident than I see myself.

  "But Barb doesn't have the clinical expertise that I have. Often, she will ask me how I would teach something at the bedside, what kinds of difficulties I have run into, and how I handled them. We share a lot of information. I also help her in her personal life. I went through the death of her mother, her fears about getting married, her subsequent disillusionment with marriage, her frustration with working with women, and her decision to go back to school.

  "She and I complement each other and work well together. She's a good sounding board and is as supportive as I am of her. The relationship started from common work interests, and now it's turning into a friendship."

—In Medicine

- Brian talks about Carl, his physician colleague: "Carl is a real influence on me because he has a serious interest in becoming knowledgeable about management. I can pick things up easily, but I don't pursue reading like he does. I just enjoy discussing management topics with him. We've always co-mentored each other and have a good back-and-forth relationship on issues regarding our group practice. We have some different viewpoints, but they don't clash; they dovetail more. So I think I've had a lot of growth through my association with him.

"He's better at assessing situations and looking at political consequences. He's helped me be more alert to political ramifications of decisions and actions than I might have been otherwise. He's still way ahead of me in that area, without question.

"I'm always looking for innovative ways of doing things. Finance is one of my primary interests, so I will come up with various ideas and present them to Carl for an assessment of their political implications. Then, I make modifications and come back with something improved."

Mutual Mentors

In mutual mentoring, the partners have sufficient common interests and connections that the ball bounces back and forth almost without notice. A discussion might flip from reciprocal to mutual mentoring and back again. The lines are blurred.

> When Lacey was 21, she and her brother were thrown together on a family trip to Europe. Neither wanted to go because they shared a mutual aversion to being uprooted from their friends. "Suddenly," Lacey said, "we discovered each other as human beings."

> "We see that as a turning point in both of our lives: He was no longer baby brother, and I was no longer older sister wanting to boss him around. We started talking to each other, finding out about each other and what we wanted from life, really caring for each other. That's when I began to get some really good feedback and a lot of support from someone else in the family. My parents were supportive in their own way, especially with respect to the values they wanted for us. But my brother is different. He has always looked on me as knowing exactly what I need to do for myself. Even if he thinks I'm off track, he has confidence that I'll eventually

figure it out. He supports my essence whether or not he agrees with my technique.

"Now, we both have this mutual assistance thing in that we're always there for each other. He really cares about me, knows what I am capable of, and says, 'This is who you are, be proud of that.' I discovered my first mentor, I think, when my brother became a human being to me. The one person I could always come home to, no matter how much I messed up my life, who wouldn't say, 'I told you so.' It's a very free feeling to have someone like that."

I was fortunate enough to be able to interview Lacey's brother and hear his side of this remarkable story.

"We were all we had. We did not want to go on that trip; we were not ready to leave our friends. We established a bond that was just amazing. To this day, she's one of my closest friends. A mind that connects. The understanding she has for my emotion-packed life and drama.

"It was a survival relationship at first. She is a tremendous source of support and nurturing. She knows what this [entertainment] industry can do. I can talk very openly with her about what is going on for me—the upsets, the joys, the frustrations that come with this industry—and also get her view about the jobs I've taken to supplement my income. She's been there to remind me not to sell out on my dream."

Here are a few examples of mutual mentoring in careers:

- Joanne speaks of a relationship that started as a childhood friendship in British Columbia and has continued as both women pursued education and entered the same career field: "Erica has been my friend since 7th grade. She is like a sister. She's a health professional as well, and we made the decision about the same time. It was something we both talked about, were interested in, and went in together. She is a sounding board, a support person for me, and has been all my life. She is in Victoria and I am in Vancouver, so we hop the ferry for a visit and sometimes get on the phone."

- Two women have been Ruth's friends and co-mentors since graduate school. Over the past 25 years, all three obtained doctorates and worked in professional fields. "We've shared our values, goals, interests, and knowledge; our trials and tribulations; and our struggles and delights in our life journeys. Since we no longer live in the same community, our connections are usually limited to telephone, e-mail, and occasional visits. Despite the great physical distances, we are somehow there for each other. We've helped each other clarify career goals and dilemmas, write books, and deal with health problems and difficult personal life transitions."

- Mutual mentoring relationships don't always come easily. Many have to be cultivated and worked on. Joan had the same role as another male physician. They learned to get along together after some negative beginnings. "We got to the point where we knew each other well enough that we could just toss things back and forth in a clinical or teaching situation and supplement each other. At times, it was a very stimulating experience."

The Special Case of Spouse/Partner Mentoring

When we think about mentors in our lives, we don't immediately think of spouses or partners. Yet, for some of us, they play a very important role in our mentoring. Most partner mentors are of the step-ahead or co-mentoring forms. Not all spouses or partners are mentors, but where they are, they are a rich source of mentoring that should not be overlooked.

Few men I interviewed saw their partners as mentors, other than noting their encouragement and support. Terence's wife is "steady," and she backs him up. Dick's wife has "given and given and given." Bruce was aware that his wife opened up for him the world of relationships: She taught him about the deep emotional dimensions of life.

Most of the reports of spouse/partner mentoring come from women. In recent decades, when so many women entered the workforce, it is not surprising that they would first turn to the men in their lives for mentoring counsel, guidance, and support.

<u>Step-Ahead Partner Mentoring</u>
- "My spiritual and intellectual self was constantly being stimulated by his sermons and the people we met. He opened doors by introducing people."
- "I rely on him a lot; he's been through it all. I respect his judgment, though I wouldn't want to work with him—he's very authoritarian."
- "I've learned much more from him in personal growth and management. You focus your energies on those things over which you have control."

<u>Reciprocal Partner Mentoring</u>
An increasing number of women and men acknowledge the contribution of their partners, and how they, in turn, provide mentoring to their mates.

Reciprocal Partner Mentoring

One partner on "What my partner does for me":	"And what I do for my partner":
"He's logical, objective."	"I show him the feeling part, the people aspect."
"She holds me down."	"I push her up."
"He was the systems analyst and guided me in logical thinking."	"He did a lot of teaching in his job, and I would help him with lesson plans."
"He doesn't let me get away with this self-sacrificing thing."	"I don't let him get away with retreating."
"He brings in reading materials."	"I help him in getting along with people and making it in the corporate jungle."
"She's learned more about priorities and being patient."	"I've learned to be more aware of details and to be more powerful about things I feel."
"He would hear me on the talks I was giving."	"I started his bookkeeping system."

BRIDGE

In the previous chapter, we looked at the basic requirements for a major mentoring relationship and then examined more carefully the variety of action roles that a mentor can take on behalf of a mentee. In this chapter, we went further to identify three common role structures of mentoring relationships: traditional, step-ahead, and co-mentors. Next, we will examine more closely three elements of the interaction between mentor and mentee that make the relationship have significant impact on the life of the mentee: the scope, intensity, and duration of the relationship. Recognizing that major mentors are not universal, we also will look at the value of minor mentors and examine "the strength of weak ties."

Chapter 13

THE IMPACT OF MENTOR–MENTEE RELATIONSHIPS

Thus far, we have reviewed the behaviors and attitudes that define a mentoring relationship. A major relationship has the three basic requirements of attraction, affect, and action. A minor mentor relationship has only one or two. We need to add more to the model if we are to understand the impact of such relationships.

Attraction, affect, and action relate to the attitudes and behavior of the mentor and mentee, as discussed in Chapter 11. Three additional factors—scope, intensity, and duration—describe the nature of the interaction between the mentor and the mentee as well as the impact of the relationship on the mentee.

Impact of a Mentor-Mentee Relationship

Low Impact— — — — — — — →— — — — — — — →High Impact

Scope: Comprehensiveness ranges from narrow to broad
Intensity: Energy/activity ranges from low to high
Duration: Time span ranges from short to long

How broad is the scope of the relationship? How intense is the energy? How long does the relationship last? The significance of the relationship depends on the tilt. If the tilt is toward the high end of the scale on two of the dimensions, it is likely to be a high-impact relationship. Rarely is a mentoring relationship high on all three variables. Scope and duration are often linked: If the relationship is long and enduring, the scope usually will be broad. High-intensity relationships are seldom maintained over long periods of time. If the tilt is toward the low end on all three factors, the relationship is likely to be limited and the impact minor.

SCOPE

How broad and comprehensive is the mentor–mentee relationship? Does it encompass both personal and professional concerns, or is it limited to one? Does it extend to most aspects of mastering a professional field, or is it limited to a specific situation or skill? Within that one area, is it broad and all-encompassing, or is it more narrowly focused?

Our mentors can be very significant in either professional or personal matters but rarely in both. That is not surprising when you consider that mentoring relationships often start with a fairly single-minded purpose, a special niche: "A mentor for _____." We want to develop certain skills or understand certain subjects. We want help in solving a problem or making a decision. Interviewees talk about having a mentor "for fishing," "for the African years," "for a research problem," "for the discipline of scientific writing," "for the twilight years," "for my spiritual journey." This is particularly true in later life, as we will learn in Chapter 22.

Niche mentoring usually starts in the short-term with a special focus, although it can apply to broader vistas. A mentor "for fishing" suggests a more limited relationship than a mentor "for my spiritual journey." Niche relationships can have high or low impact, depending on the scope, intensity, and duration of the relationship. We could even chance to find a mentor to fill a highly significant but missing niche, as did Ned: Originally, Bea was his mentor "for writing," but in time, she became his mentor "for the twilight years" and "the mother I never had."

Many long and enduring relationships have a broad scope. Sometimes, they encompass both developing one's career interests and living one's life. Or, the scope is very broad within one professional field. Ned developed a relationship with a traditional mentor, the chairman of pediatrics in medical school. The relationship was comprehensive and intensive in career and professional matters. Although it was rich and long-lasting, it did not extend to the personal realm. At the time I talked to Ned, he said the relationship had been ongoing for 20 years, a long time for a mentoring relationship. The relationship has now shifted to the wise counselor and the experienced clinician/researcher with the status and power difference understandably narrowing over time. I asked Ned how he would describe this special mentor relationship.

> "I found an idol while I was in medical school. He really imprinted on me. I thought he walked on water. He's been my academic boss continuously. We'll soon be going into our third decade. We've gone to meetings together, and he's gotten me on committees. I've shared a motel room with him, and I've had my car break down and needed him to give me a ride. When things trouble me on professional issues, I call him and say, 'I need to talk to you,' and he sets my head straight. … He can't handle personal issues, which is okay. But what's medically sound, what's a good program, what will be good for me in my own growth—he's always been available to me on these issues."

INTENSITY

The intensity of a mentor–mentee connection is hard to define but obvious to the persons involved. It has to do with the frequency and depth of contact and particularly the energy expended in the interaction. Given the super-heated nature of a high-intensity contact, such relationships are usually of limited duration. Indeed, it could be the expectation of a time-limited relationship that allows it to burn so strongly.

> Another of Ned's mentors was an attending physician when Ned was an intern. The scope of the relationship was broad, including both personal and professional issues. The intensity

was great: "He got into one's bones" is the way Ned describes it, but the duration was time-limited. When Ned tried to get close to him later, the physician wasn't available; he had a different agenda.

DURATION

Short–Term Relationships: *"During ... "* or *"Until ... "*

Much of mentoring is time-bound. When you think of mentor relationships you have had, some can come to mind that were active during a specific time period and then ended. The senior person helps you during this phase or stage. The words people use to describe the relationship are tip-offs: "During," "while," and "until" suggest a time-limited relationship. *During*—a training program, the time you worked in the organization, lived in the community, were going to school. Or, the relationship lasted *until*—I finished the program, she left, I was transferred. We talk about a distinct time period during which the mentoring was active. At the conclusion, the relationship ended or changed.

These connections can be quite intense during the life of the relationship and highly significant to growth and development. Relationships ebb and flow. Some mentors are aware that their mentoring will last a finite period of time. Louise counseled students in a graduate school of management. She knew there would be a distinct end at graduation when mentoring would conclude, and any ongoing connection would be more on a social basis. Mentors we meet "during" or "until" can be either major or minor mentors, depending on the nature of the connection.

Long-Term Relationships: *"Enduring ... "* and *"Still ... "*

By contrast, enduring relationships can span years, even decades, as noted before with Ned. The frequency and nature of the contact changes, but the value of the relationship does not. The mentor "was always there for me." "It lasted a long time." "We still meet." "We keep in touch." "It has been an enduring relationship." Look at the tip-off words of "enduring," "still," and "lasting."

Enduring relationships that span years or decades often are broad and deep. Many are major mentoring relationships that have transformed over time from a traditional or step-ahead form to a colleague or co-mentoring basis with reciprocal benefits for both people.

Long-Term High-Impact Mentoring Examples

The following examples have the three requirements of attraction, affect, and action. In addition, they are high on scope, intensity, and/or duration. They further illustrate that high-impact relationships can come from any of the three mentor forms. We saw several examples of traditional mentors earlier. Here are two examples of high-impact mentoring, one step-ahead and one co-mentoring.

- Lois' older brothers were always looking out for her: "It had to do with being the baby and a girl. They taught me to be an athlete, to do boy things. They took great pride in my abilities and always set up situations for me to achieve in. They taught me to throw a baseball so I didn't throw it like a girl. I ended up playing softball into high school very competently. They used to pole vault, and they saw to it that I learned how to pole vault. I adopted swimming as my sport and swam competitively for a number of years. "My brothers also emerged as spiritual or emotional mentors, especially Josh. When I was a teen-ager, I went to him with most of my teen problems rather than my parents. It was very important that he approve of my behavior and that he set the standards for me. I told him things I would never have brought to my parents. Josh would say, 'Just be yourself, you're terrific!' While he wanted me to do all these wonderful things and was teaching me how, he was also saying, 'You're just fine the way you are.' "

- For 25 years, Ruth has known a couple—Mel and Brenda—from the time when they were first in a professional association together. They would meet for lunch periodically and discuss professional problems and issues, meetings that proved mutually beneficial. Several years after they met, Ruth's hospital suffered a severe financial crisis. In the massive personnel cutbacks that ensued, her position was eliminated. Despite her years of service, she was suddenly without a job. It was a time when there were no exit strategies or support. Ruth was devastated. Her friends insisted on meeting with her immediately and talked of career options. Their support and practical strategies helped her weather the storm and forge a new career direction.

CULTIVATING MINOR MENTORS: THE STRENGTH OF WEAK TIES

Up to this point, we've focused on major mentoring relationships that have strong impact on our lives. These high-impact relationships can be of any of the three mentor forms we discussed in the Chapter 12: traditional, step-ahead, or co-mentor forms. Since few, if any, relationships start out in a high-impact way, it is in our best interest to see what other mentor forms can work for us. If we search for only one type of mentor, we can fail to recognize other potential relationships close at hand and later regret letting those opportunities pass us by. That happened to Louisa:

"Now I know enough about my mentor-bonding pattern to understand why I never had a mentor in grad school. My mentor-bonding pattern with men, starting with my father, is zero. Yet, in my doctoral program, all the potential mentors were men. The style of these male professors was not the warm, personal relationship to which I naturally gravitated. I didn't see the possibilities as I do now. There were openings where I could have developed a relationship, but I passed them by."

It is easy to overlook relationships that are more limited but accessible, useful, and practical: minor mentors, who can fill the bill of a mentoring relationship on some, but not all three of the attraction/affect/action legs of the three-legged stool. They might never score high on scope, intensity, or duration. Yet, multiple "minor" relationships can enrich our mentoring life. For that very reason, we will benefit from understanding and utilizing the "strength of weak ties."

Most mentor–mentee relationships start small, with a degree of exploration and testing involved. Although a few develop into major mentoring relationships, most stay small and remain minor. However, there is much to attend to in "the strength of weak ties," a concept developed by M.S. Granovetter.[13] He points out that having a number of weak ties can be very strengthening to an individual. My research supports his concept and convinces me that we stand to profit by cultivating minor, as well as major, mentors. A cascade of minor relationships can mount up to something very meaningful and substantial. These days, the strength of weak ties also is emphasized in mentoring connections made via networking and the Internet.

One exercise I have used with groups to help them examine their personal support systems is suggestive. The exercise identifies six different supportive functions—intimacy, sharing, self-worth, assistance, guidance, and challenge[14]—and asks people to list names of those who fill each particular function for them. It is not uncommon for women to list the same few people, usually family members or

---

[13] M.S. Granovetter, The strength of weak ties. *J Sociol* 1973;58:1360–1380; M.S. Granovetter, "The Strength of Weak Ties: A Network Theory Revisited," in Peter V. Marsden and N. Lin (Eds.) *Social Structure and Network Analysis*, Sage Publications 1982.

[14] Adapted from Sondra J. Herman, *Becoming Assertive: A Guide for Nurses*. New York: D. Van Nostrand & Co., 1978:74–76.

close friends, in most of the boxes, suggesting strong ties. Although I do not have sufficient similar data on men, the existence of many "old boys' networks" suggests that men are more accustomed to establishing "weak ties" than are women.

Networking as a Mentoring Strategy

Interaction flourishes with people you know and with whom you are comfortable. Our whole culture, as Sinclair Lewis once so astutely observed in Babbitt, has been based on informal groups and formal associations, from civic clubs and professional associations to business lunches and golf cronies. A commonality of interests and experiences can, over time, lead to broader and deeper relationships. That is the basis of "old boys' networks."

Women and various racial and ethnic minorities, who were in the vanguard as they moved into corporate jobs and professions historically dominated by men, often found that they were excluded from the "old boys' networks." Gradually, they formed their own ways of making connections. Networking rituals for women in the entertainment industry developed to include "power (baby) showers" and "job showers." Women executives in that industry say they owe some of their most critical career opportunities to women they met through the women's network.[15]

Through increased awareness and networking, minor mentor relationships are now flourishing for both men and women. Out of these limited contacts can come opportunities and beginnings of significant mentoring relationships. In today's world, networking and mentoring via the Internet, as well as face-to-face meetings, are expanding exponentially. Networking has become such an important mentoring strategy that I have devoted Chapter 24 to the topic.

---

[15] Lacher, Irene. "A New Kind of Networking," *Los Angeles Times*, Calendar Section, March 2, 1997:8.

Serial or Relay Mentoring

Another form of brief-encounter mentoring has a multiplier effect: a chain of mentoring encounters that results in serial mentoring. The value of this form of mentoring became clear in a mentoring program that I was engaged in for a state dietetic association. An equal number of mentors and mentees had been identified and paired, and we envisioned on-going relationships between each mentor, the more experienced person in the profession, and the early-career mentee.

But we quickly discovered that distances in the state often made on-going relationships impractical. Instead, what developed spontaneously was the practice of the assigned mentor making an initial contact with the mentee, exploring needs, and then usually referring the mentee to another person in the mentoring program who could be more helpful—either because of the specialty or proximity. As time went on, a chain of these mentoring contacts developed that mentees found very helpful. All the mentors in the chain were leaders in the field and were strongly committed to the mentoring program and to the development of new entrants into the profession. A single link in the mentor–mentee chain might not be profound, but the series of contacts developed in a way to multiply the value of the experience. Since most mentors kept tabs on mentees throughout the chain, the multiplier power made the mentoring chain a high-impact relationship.

Mentoring Moments

One other bite-size form of mentoring should be included in discussing the strength of weak ties: the brief but significant encounter with another person that is life-changing in importance. The encounter that changed one's life "came at a defining moment and turned my life around," one interviewee said. The encounter includes an insight, an opinion, or a bit of advice that fit the person and the situation deeply. The suggestion could provide the missing key to a person's career puzzle. Or, it could be the singular experience that points the person in a new direction. Regardless, it is a profound moment or experience that stays with you. That person stays in your mind as a significant person in your life. We might say the person is a minor mentor providing a major moment. Examples here will help:

- Louisa remembers: "When I was in graduate school, we were required to keep a personal journal as part of a behavioral science course I was taking. These were turned in to the professor and handed back with marginal notes. I will never forget what was written on mine: 'When will you take responsibility for your own competence?' I never had the opportunity to clarify this with the professor, but it has stayed with me. Over the years, I came to see the profound message he was sending me."

- Lyle was a wounded veteran who went to college on the GI Bill. This was a new social experiment, letting anyone go to college, even people with a poor high school record like Lyle. A requirement of the program was to be tested and interviewed by a group of academics and psychologists to see if the veterans were aiming themselves in a reasonable direction. When Lyle came in for the interview, the academic team had all the test data in front of them and asked him what he wanted to study in college. He told them he wanted to be an electrical engineer. "Well," Lyle recalls, "they all laughed spontaneously—it was a gift to me, because they laughed good-heartedly and told me that it was probably the last field I ought to put myself into. In fact, it wasn't clear exactly what I ought to do. They said I was an artist of some kind, but it wasn't clear what kind, so why didn't I just go into arts and science and see where I came out. Well, that gift of straight judgment was a godsend. That was first-class mentoring. It was just a single day's encounter but a real turning point." Lyle went on to become a writer and a minister known for his writing. He has never forgotten that moment.

- Rachel told the counselor she wanted to go into dietetics but believed that she couldn't make it through chemistry. "The counselor said, 'I made it through chemistry, so why can't you?' I only saw her for a few moments twice, but her words were the turning point for me."

What we see in these examples is evidence of action in the way of informed advice. The mentor source had sufficient regard for the person—affect—to offer the advice. The mentoring source was sufficiently valued—attraction—for the recipient to listen and to act on the counsel. Just a whiff or wisp of mentoring as strictly defined, but most valuable—demonstrating, once again, the "strength of weak ties."

BRIDGE

Thus far, we have looked at mentoring relationships as if they were static and unchanging. We've looked at the ingredients required for a mentoring relationship to exist as well as the basic mentor forms or structures. But change is the only constant in our lives, and it is at those intersecting points of change when we most feel the need for mentors. The next chapter on the dynamics of mentoring relationships examines mentor relationships in movement: the life cycle of relationships and how mentoring relationships change over time. We will catch a glimpse of how relationships connect, continue, and conclude. Finally, we look at the sequence of beginning, maintaining, and ending mentoring relationships as well as the convolutions that can take place during the process.

Chapter 14

THE DYNAMICS OF MENTORING RELATIONSHIPS

Thus far, we have looked at the "what" of major and minor mentoring relationships—the requirements and the basic mentor forms. Now, we turn to the how: the very dynamic process involved in mentoring. This chapter deals with change in the mentor–mentee relationship over time, from its beginning to its end.

A mentoring relationship is a two-person social system, operating in a specific environment. We start, in systems terms, with the inputs to the relationship—what the mentor and the mentee "bring to the table." Each brings personal goals, needs, and aspirations to the relationship. Each also brings personal preferences and style differences that may impinge on the dynamics, and each is affected by the constraints and opportunities in the environment. Their interaction produces outcomes in terms of learning, growth, and mastery for the mentee— and pride, satisfaction, and often learning for the mentor. Since it is an open system, the outcomes of the mentoring experience feed back into the system at all points and influence its direction and change.

We know something of action behaviors that the mentor takes on behalf of the mentee as well as the emotional tone (attraction/affect) that connects the two people. Now we turn to the dynamic, changing aspects of a mentor relationship over time: the connecting, continuing, and concluding of mentor relationships. To understand what is possible in a mentoring relationship, we need to look at two key factors: the readiness of the mentor and receptiveness of the mentee.

WHAT THE MENTOR BRINGS TO THE RELATIONSHIP

Readiness of the Mentor

The readiness of one person to mentor another flows most heavily from the mentor's maturity level and ego needs. Awareness of and interest in mentoring also enter into the equation. Mentoring cannot be faked; either the prospective mentor is developmentally oriented or not. Ability to communicate is another essential.

Mentors must have reached a certain level of maturity and worked out many of their own ego needs in order to work effectively on behalf of a mentee. Many relationship difficulties can be traced to problems in this stage. Here are several examples:

> Jack, a young and brilliant medical researcher, was new in the role of principal investigator in charge of a small research group. When I met him, he was going through a painful process of learning to mentor others. He was familiar with being a mentee and was very trusting and believing in his mentors—particularly his chief, who was still in the picture.

> Being a mentor was new for Jack, and he knew he was not doing well with at least one promising young physician in his group. Jack was very open and eager to understand what wasn't working and why. As we talked about a recent incident, he said he realized that he had accorded "excessive" weight to the viewpoint of his chief and did not adequately "look after" and support his mentees. In the process, he lost his group's trust and was still paying for it. A friend also had told Jack that he was too insecure to be a good mentor yet— that he was so preoccupied with what his group thought about him that he didn't pay attention to what was going on inside the group members as individuals.

Jack's experience is a common one for younger people. Effective mentors are far enough along in their careers and have had sufficient validation so that their ego needs do not get in the way. Usually, traditional mentors have gone through the mid-life transition and are motivated by generativity: the desire to share and to pass along knowledge to the next generation.[16] However, age alone is not enough, as the following example of Jerry's grandfather shows.

> *Poor Jerry,* I thought when I saw him struggling. Jerry, about 11, and his grandfather were paired in a compass-orienting exercise in an intergenerational summer camp I was attending. Grandfather's voice became raised, and several of us turned around. Jerry was having trouble following the instructions, and Grandfather was insisting that Jerry do things *his* way. No matter that Jerry's self-esteem was crumbling; no matter that he was holding back tears. I was busy in my own grandparent role and didn't notice what happened then. But the next time I looked, Jerry's grandmother, a really together person, was walking through the exercise with him, pausing to ask him questions, listening, giving him some information—all was well again. Grandfather's ego was too much involved in the task for him to be a helpful mentor. You'd think Grandfather was beyond that, but not so.

Elise has had experience with both good and bad mentors. She still rankles at the memory of an experience in her post-graduate traineeship.

> Her official mentor started her on a "wheel-spinning" research project that she later learned experts had worked on for a long time with no solution. Elise felt that her mentor must have been aware of that, and she resented having her time wasted on this totally inappropriate assignment. From this experience, Elise is convinced that "people can't mentor if they are not secure, because then, they can't give."

Mentoring another person is a generous act. The mentor must be able to reach out and to share. To be an effective mentor, you must be willing to

---

[16] See Daniel J. Levinson, *The Season's of a Man's Life,* Knopf, New York, 1985.

sublimate yourself, allow the spotlight to be focused on the mentee, be willing to take a back seat when rewards are handed out. Yours is the internal satisfaction of knowing that you helped make it all happen. If you are competitive and secretive, you are not likely to open up your bag of resources for others. Misers don't make good mentors.

Impact of "Parenting" vs. "Mentoring" Postures

Another trap mentors can fall into is "mothering" or "fathering" instead of mentoring. We can confuse personal caring with mentoring, treating the mentee like a son or a daughter, or wanting close social ties not of the mentee's choosing. "Smothering" or "hovering" are words people use to describe a mentoring approach that fosters continuing dependence. Suzanne's mentor "mothered" her instead of encouraging her to be independent: "She preferred a kind of mother/daughter relationship that wasn't healthy for my career advancement," Suzanne explains. Caring, supporting, and encouraging are all part of the affect of mentoring, but believing in and helping the mentee develop also means having a realistic view of what's appropriate and the ability to let go.

Impact of Biases

Many an otherwise good mentor can be limited because of conscious or unconscious biases. This is particularly so of men who do not know how to work with women, actively dislike them, or see them only as sexual objects.

- During her stint on a fellowship, Kay obtained assignment to a well-regarded and highly competent executive. She relates: "I have huge respect for him. He's smart, quick, and has very good political judgment. I learned from him the whole concept of interweaving public service with private sector experiences and the different challenges of management and leadership in the public and private sectors. But he didn't seem to put as much of a premium on women on his staff and didn't give you as substantively rich projects. As a result, my talents were not fully used."

- Andrea's architectural drafting instructor in college "put the screws on me. He didn't want women in the class and said, 'Look, there's no place for women in architecture. You'd be much better off if you got out.' He would fail me for any miniscule mistake. I became discouraged, dropped out of school, and shifted my career goals—but I would have been good in architecture."

Gender bias can be coupled with age and other biases.

- Fran's professor in fine arts was quite frank: He told her he'd give her priority if she were a man. "He said, 'Certainly, as a married, older woman, you'd be at the bottom of my list.' It's hard to paint productively," Fran observes, "when you feel unsupported."
- When Glenda applied to graduate school, one professor was cold and cutting, "Why should we waste money on someone who only has 15 years to work?" His assumption was erroneous. Now in her 70s, Glenda has had a long and successful career in psychotherapy.

Then there are the sexual hazards, as pediatrician Nora discovered in her medical training.

- Nora's primary mentor had urged her to spend a fellowship year with a researcher at Stanford. She said, "He's a very bright man, but he wasn't that much of a mentor. He was about 45 and a big flirt, not someone you could talk to. He's older now, and he's dropped that role with me. But at that time, he would make such off-the-wall comments that some days when I'd see him coming down the hall, I'd jump into a closet, because I didn't feel like dealing with his comments. He could be a very effective mentor in terms of academics, but because I never knew which guy I was going to get, I avoided him."

Impact of Non-Mentor-Bonding Patterns

In addition to maturity stage and ego development, people vary in their ability to mentor because of differences in their mentor-bonding patterns. Non-bonders can be oblivious to the need for, and value of, mentors, and they can appear unwelcoming to people who turn to them for help. "Why can't they do it themselves as I did?" they wonder, some with a fair degree of irritation. Carl admits he is not a good mentor of others. He is even impatient with his young daughters when they come to him for help. A non-bonder, Carl developed an array of self-mentoring strategies, and he expects others to go figure things out for themselves. Co-mentoring is the only kind of mentor relationship that interests him.

Non-bonders do not have to be stuck there, however. Mentoring might not come easily, but there are strategies by which mentoring skills can be consciously developed, as described in Chapter 26.

Mentor Style

Mentors differ in how they see their role. In part, these differences are a reflection of the personal style of the mentor and, in part, of organizational relationships. A mentor who has supervisory responsibilities for the junior person often takes a more active and assertive role. Some mentors believe in a strongly directive approach to all aspects of the mentoring relationship; others offer a mix of directive and reflective guidance.

Ned and Stan are both physician directors. They regularly deal with young people and have developed their own styles and philosophies about mentoring. Ned believes:

> "… a mentor should be less directive and more nonjudgmental, a provider of alternatives, a mirror of ways of looking at things that the mentee might not have seen. When a decision has been made, a mentor should follow up with his

support, whichever way the person chooses to go." Yet, his support can be very directive in terms of process: "I want to be a catalyst—to be a facilitator and cut through the red tape in the institution. I told a young man with a research project that I considered worthwhile, 'You need to have this in by a certain day to the research committee. I'm on the research committee. I'll get it through for you. This is who you go to. I want to meet with you four times in the next three months, and you'll have a paper out of it.' The research project had spark, and it hadn't been done before; it had merit."

Stan approaches mentoring differently. One of his own mentors believed in a strongly directive mentoring process, and in many of his mentoring relationships, Stan follows that path.

"I'm a very aggressive teacher and on the lookout for people who will respond to me. I'd like some intelligent response, preferably with a tinge of originality in their thinking as well as some evidence of diligence."

When Leo was an intern in hospital administration, his mentor was the CEO of a large medical center. The CEO's style was one of the most subtle ever described to me. Leo found it very effective and uses it now when he, too, is in a mentor role.

"It was almost as though he had a blind sense of confidence in the outcome. He never gave me instructions, but he communicated an expectation level without words, a sense of, 'This is what I expect of you. Just go do it, don't worry about it, I know you'll find a way.' It's like fighting your way out of a paper bag. It was such nondirective counseling. Still, somehow behind the scenes, it felt like he had orchestrated the end result. "Now I try to do the same: I give someone an assignment, but I don't tell them how to do it. If I can project that sense of confidence in them, then somehow, something comes out of the ionosphere that causes them to get the thing done. [With my mentor,] I was amazed that I was allowed to operate with as much freedom as I had, but behind the scenes, I'm sure he was reading reports and monitoring the system very closely."

None of her mentees had a reporting relationship to Louise, the graduate school counselor. Here is how she describes her role:

"I see mentoring as interaction, helping the students elicit clearer statements of focus and then developing a pathway through the system. My role is to encourage independence, arraying choices and helping the person realistically assess them."

Mentor Preferences

Mentors have personal preferences as to the kinds of people they like to mentor. The variations are many. Here are a few:

- "I prefer people as mentees who are conscientious and really dedicated to developing themselves. I had no use for one guy who was glib, not willing to work hard at any level—and a real leech."
- "I look for people skilled in the academic discipline, not prima donnas, people who are honest, can get along with others, are self-starters, and who have respect for people with ideas other than their own."
- "I'm attracted to mavericks who don't fit the mold, who need somebody to channel them. There's a lot of sparkle. It's exciting to work with people like that, seeing promise in the person."
- "I've been interested in young women who want to get an education. Girls have always had very poor counseling in school."

Mentor Satisfaction

What do mentors get out of mentoring? Many mentors are developmentally oriented, and helping people grow is satisfying. Being a mentor is not a limelight role; mentors take pride in being in the background, watching their mentee's progress. They report high satisfaction in helping mentees develop their potential, work through problems, consider options, and look at things differently. In addition, they have a sense of contributing to society and gaining a certain sense of immortality:

- "You owe back the world if you have enjoyed success. If you had the luck, you need to share it."
- "I have a sense I'm replicating myself by the people I'm training."

Mentors also gain a special satisfaction in working with groups that have traditionally been underserved—whether for reasons of geography, socioeconomic status, race, ethnicity, or gender—whose members really value the special attention of mentoring. One woman in the information technology field receives a real appreciation from women for what she has given them. From men, she senses more a feeling that it is expected.

WHAT THE MENTEE BRINGS TO THE RELATIONSHIP

Receptiveness of the Mentee

Many of us connect with mentors early in our lives and continue to make mentor connections from then on—in other words, we become "mentor collectors." People who have had trusting, helpful relationships with others early will reach out almost automatically whenever they have a need. But others go a different route, only becoming aware of and receptive to mentors at a later time in life. And some never do.

Late Bloomers

For some of us, our recognition of and receptiveness to a mentor is a late-blooming phenomenon, what I call the "not until … " phenomenon.

- Pat didn't connect with women mentors until her mid-life shift to spiritual growth and participation in women's growth groups.

- Russ didn't connect with men until he experienced unconditional positive regard from his male therapist when he was in his 30s.
- Glenda said mentors didn't come into her awareness and her life until after her husband left her, when she was forced to be on her own.

Other late-bloomers, like Kathy, weren't aware that women could be mentors or that there were models of mentors other than the harsh, aggressive, authoritarian types like many of the men she knew. Kathy's sudden change came when she finally had a woman boss who had the gentleness of her mother and the competence and no-nonsense attitude of her father.

Missed Opportunities

The "if only … " phenomenon occurs when the mentor is available but the mentee is not receptive. This later realization of missed opportunities is usually tinged with regret. There can be a variety of reasons for the misses, the "becauses":

- Because of her own rigidities, Brooke could not appreciate the tremendous social mentoring that Dr. Sandoval offered. She was receptive only to his technical guidance.
- Because Elise was bored with the routine lab tests, she looked at the research work more as a job instead of an opportunity and didn't think to ask questions.
- Because Jim sent out signals that he wanted to prove himself and not be told how to do it, he passed up many opportunities to have a mentor.
- Because Gary was in the middle of a divorce, he couldn't see the mentor for what he had to give.

Assertiveness of the Mentee vs. Dependence

Mentees vary, too, in their active or passive stance toward finding mentors, or developing relationships that might become mentoring.

- Jenna developed an effective way to know and be known by her law professors. During her undergraduate work, she lacked direction, and wasn't open enough to seek out people who could help her. She resolved that when she entered law school, things would be different. Jenna knew the program was going to be tough and that she would have to be more assertive. So she formulated some questions to open up a conversation with her professors, saying "This is what I like. What do you suggest? How do you see the alternatives?" Not only did this work for Jenna, but she also was noticed by some of the more junior law students who turned to her for advice.

- While Jenna learned to take the initiative in building relationships with potential mentors, Nora was more passive and mentor-dependent. Her maternal aunts were highly educated and a strong influence on her. Three of them were Ph.D.s, and one was an M.D. They were her closest mentors, and she rather took them for granted. Her physician aunt was Nora's booster, supporter, and mentor in the trials and tribulations of being a female doctor. The aunt advised Nora on how to further her career. After Nora moved from her home state and her aunt's strong guidance, she floundered. She had no strategies by which to find a mentor substitute.

Mentee Preferences

As mentees, we vary greatly in what we want in a mentoring relationship. Many preferences stem from our mentor-bonding experiences, others from the particular circumstances at the time and the availability of prospective mentors. Here is a sampling of mentees' thoughts on choosing a mentor.

- "I grew up pretty independently, and it takes a special kind of person for me to bond with—someone willing to have an equal relationship."
- "When I look at an organization or a leader to hook up with, I always want to be the tail of a lion rather than the head of a donkey."
- "I've been told my genius was in picking good mentors. That's one of my best skills. I have a terrific set of mentors, all of whom were very mature emotionally. I wouldn't touch somebody whose emotional integrity I questioned."
- "I won't establish a relationship if they want dependency from me. I'll try some things out with a tentative relationship—I check them out."
- "I have sought out mentors who would give me unconditional acceptance and good information. I wanted the mothering and the information. I consciously find someone who will help me in what I'm trying to do and help me articulate it."
- "I look for someone who takes a leap of faith with me and gives me an opportunity to show that I can do something I haven't been able to show before."
- "If the potential mentor is a man, I look out to see that no sexual expectations are attached. Too many women have had horizontal offers in exchange for vertical favors."

What a mélange of things mentees look for! Amazing that the two people manage to connect at all, and not surprising that many connections fail. But now, let's look at the connecting process.

THE LIFE CYCLE OF A MENTORING RELATIONSHIP: CONNECTING, CONTINUING, AND CONCLUDING

Connecting

Mentor Initiated

The initial mentoring contact can be initiated either by the mentor or mentee. One factor is the organizational role of the mentor. If there is a reporting relationship and the mentor is responsible for the staff member or student, the mentor usually initiates the relationship. Some examples:

—*From a Researcher*

- "I have always felt a responsibility to help people who work in my group to grow and develop to their highest potential. I select people carefully, and I expect that when they leave the project, they will go on to something better in their careers."

—*From an Information Technologist*

- "I'm responsible for 37 people. I consciously mentor those I feel an affinity for and make sure they get opportunities, especially women. I look for women who are bright and express an interest in going into management and systems."

—*From a Health Professional*

- "Either I've identified a problem and have been meeting with the person, or they have come to me because it's a problem."

Mentee Initiated

If the mentor is outside the organizational system or there is no reporting relationship, the initial contact often comes from the mentee. Mentors respond to overtures:

—*From an Editor*

- "You meet people along the way who turn to you, and you do what you can for them. Sometimes, you mentor someone you wouldn't choose to mentor. But when this person comes and asks you for some help, you don't turn the kid away."

—*From a Professor*
- "Students in some of my classes come up on a regular basis to ask questions or pursue a topic. They realize I'm approachable and not a censoring individual. Sometimes, things develop from there."

—*From a Psychologist*
- "The relationship might start very casually over lunch where the mentee says, 'I'm stuck, and I don't know how to proceed.' "

Some mentees have very clear, practiced, assertive styles to make connections. "You have to demonstrate your potential," as one person put it. Another said, "I go in with my homework ready. I discussed things I was interested in with a woman in kinesthesiology. She liked my ideas, and we worked them out." Trish had yet another approach:

"My parents always told me, 'You smile first, and people will smile back. You make the first approach, and you'll always get a response.' That was inbred with me. I used to go by and talk to the new administrator and say 'Hi,' and 'Hey, have you thought about doing something different here?' So she and I started talking, I would make suggestions, and she was a very good listener."

Mentor–mentee relationships usually start small. We might not even realize what's happening until long after a connection is established. Or, we deliberately take small steps to see if this is a relationship we want to pursue. Most likely, we do what comes naturally, influenced by our mentor-bonding pattern and our previous mentoring experience. Some of us feel comfortable seeking information and resources from others of whatever status or walk of life: "I know how to tap into people," Cheryl said. Because of the nature of her approach, people invariably respond positively. Others of us have consciously developed a style of seeking information and using that as a base for connection.

The Matter of Fit

Starting off in a limited way is sometimes a deliberate strategy to test the waters. If the chemistry and the fit are good, the area of mentoring can expand. This is a way for both parties to test the usefulness of the relationship and make it easy to contain or end it if it does not appear fruitful. The relationship could remain limited. Your tennis coach is a superb trainer, and you've mastered what you wanted in that one area or niche. That's what you contracted for, and that's what you got—an excellent mentor, albeit a minor one. On the other hand, the niche relationship might develop into something more, as it did for Evie, who realized that her piano teacher was truly a life guide.

Whether minor mentoring relationships blossom into something more depends on the needs and interests of each person, the emotional connection, their receptiveness, readiness, availability—and the fit with mentor-bonding patterns. This process I call "The Goldilocks Theory of Mentor Matching."

The Goldilocks Theory of Mentor Matching

Remember Goldilocks trying out all of the bears' beds and how dismayed she was to find this one "too hard," and that one "too soft"? But finally, the little bear's bed was "just right!" We seem to function like Goldilocks in connecting with mentors.

We might find one mentor too hard, another too soft, but this one—if fortune smiles upon us, and we are managing our mentoring process appropriately—just right.

When it comes to mentor matching, it really is a matter of fit.

That hit me early on in my research when two different people mentioned the same university dean as important in their mentoring process. One woman identified the dean as a major positive force in her life, while the other woman found the relationship toxic. Since then, I've found other examples confirming the old adage that it takes "different strokes for different folks." Look at the following matches and mismatches:

Matches and Mismatches

The Dean and Two Students

Match	Mismatch
Liz found the dean always "had something to offer in how you approach situations, what you do when you're in a meeting and how to handle yourself, what you hope to achieve and how you are going to get there, and the politics you'll find. She could talk about them as a woman."	Sara found the dean to be "a very controlling woman. I just could not accept that if I kept my mouth shut, I could have anything I wanted. I challenged her on principle all the time. I was in constant trouble, but I just had to do it. She stifled growth through fear rather than facilitating it.

The Assistant Hospital Administrator
and Two Department Heads

Jillian and Susan reported to the same assistant hospital administrator, Lisa. All three were bright young women of a similar age. Jillian could have been a little older, as she seemed more mature. She was the head of occupational and physical therapy; Susan was the head of a new quality assurance program.

Match

Jillian was able to establish a colleague relationship with Lisa. "I've learned a lot of organizational things from her, and she's learned some softening things from me." Most of the time, they could communicate on a peer basis, although occasionally, Lisa would pull rank. Such shifts were noticeable but not bothersome to Jillian.

Mismatch

At first, Susan had a positive relationship with Lisa, but then she said it changed. At the time I talked to her, Susan said, "Either I've outgrown her, or I've become a threat. She's more controlling— my hands are tied—I can't push things through without a lot of fight on her part. I can't share information on physician things, because she'll overreact."

Situational factors contributed to this being a mentoring mismatch for Susan. Her role was new, highly political, and required considerable physician interaction. Both Susan and Lisa were ambitious and eager to succeed in their new roles. Both had vulnerabilities as far as physician influence in the hospital. In such an unstable situation, Susan needed a mentor more experienced and skilled in dealing with physicians and political issues than Lisa was able to provide at this stage of her development. The fit worked fine for Jillian, because her domain was more stable, and she was more experienced in her role. The two mentees were in different situations: a new vs. an established position, a politically charged vs. a non-politicized position. Further complications had to do with the level of experience of the people involved.

The Department Head and Two Division Heads

Terence was in charge of technical maintenance, and Dick was in charge of housekeeping. Both reported to the department head of hospital maintenance. Their styles and backgrounds were different. Dick had been a professional musician, and this was a second career for him; Terence had grown up with machinery—it was his life.

Match	Mismatch
Terence was very positive about his boss and said that he influenced Terence's thinking "to stay current with technology and not to get mired in the past just because it's working well. He encouraged me to have some foresight about the changing needs of medical centers."	Dick found his boss to be a negative force and saw him playing games. "He'd call us in and ask for our opinions, get us to think deeply, and then we'd find out he already had his mind made up."

Terence made no mention of game-playing behavior in our interview. If it bothered him at all, it was probably offset with the mentoring he was getting in the technical arena.

Our experiences with early authority figures tend to influence our bonding with mentors, and we continue in our lives finding—or avoiding—mentors with many of the same characteristics. This makes mentor-matching a highly individualized process. What works well for one person might not work well for another. In the previous examples, two of the mentees had greater difficulty relating to the authority figure, which did not factor into the other relationships. In the discussion of mentor bonding in Chapter 2, we noted the power and influence of our mentor-bonding patterns: the amazing similarity of our mentors to the characteristics of the people with whom we first bonded, and the kinds of people with whom we did not bond. Our mentor-bonding patterns *do* affect our mentor connections.

Our mentor-bonding patterns draw us naturally to certain mentor forms—traditional, step-ahead, and co-mentoring—and away from others. We turn to what we are familiar with and trust. Some of us reject all traditional mentors because we are uncomfortable with the power and status differences and authority issues. That was true of Lyle when he was doing fieldwork for his training in the ministry:

"The minister would take me into his office, draw diagrams, and explain things. I found myself responding negatively. It was the overweening sense of his own importance that kept coming through, both in the teaching and our relationship.

"He had a thriving church, so it could have been an idiosyncrasy of my own about authority figures. As I discovered in military service, I had a tendency to fight or flee in the presence of authority. He just assumed I was eager to adopt his leadership style, and I typically did not make clear what my thoughts and feelings were. Instead, I kept to myself because of my background relationships with parents and siblings. I found myself backing off. It could have been owing to his readiness to assume the mentor role and my reluctance to be engaged in that kind of structure."

For similar reasons, we might reject, or simply not see, the possibilities of mentors of a different race or gender.

Our stage of professional development also affects the mentor-matching process. If we are neophytes, we are more likely to see a need for guidance and be receptive to mentoring than later on in our careers. As we gain experience, we want to try our wings, and that affects the mentor form that appeals to us—if any does. Throughout our life and career, our changing needs combine with our awareness and our increased ability to manage our own mentoring to influence the kinds of mentor matches that work for us.

CONTINUING:
PROGRESS AND SATISFACTION—OR PROBLEMS AND PLATEAUS

In a smooth mentor–mentee relationship, the two people gradually learn to blend their styles and needs with each others'. The nature and frequency of communication tend to become a blend as well. The relationship builds and moves on an even keel where needs and expectations mesh.

But there is an ebb and flow in mentoring relationships, as we have seen from previous examples. Things go smoothly for a while, and then there can be problems, if not crises. At this stage, the concern is dealing with problems and plateaus in the relationship.

Mentoring Thwarted or Aborted
You can have a promising mentoring relationship just getting started and all of a sudden, the rug is pulled out from under you—the mentor unexpectedly is transferred, laid-off, leaves, dies, or otherwise is no longer available. Your hopes grind to a halt as the mentoring relationship is thwarted or aborted. Paradise is lost.

The more complex the mentor search, the more difficult it is to find the "right" one. Although some of us do find paradise for a while at least, Eric searched endlessly for an appropriate mentor, almost like Jason and the Golden Fleece. He wanted to develop his skills both in clinical pathology and in management so that he could ultimately head a pathology department. In his searching, he could find mentors for the clinical side of his work, but not for management. His is a story of frustration, disillusionment, and defeat. When I met him, Eric had achieved his career goal as a head of pathology department, but he did so the hard way. Here is his story:

> Because he was eager to become a top-notch clinical pathologist and go into management in that field, Eric was looking for both clinical and management models. His fellowship year was a positive experience clinically but otherwise negative. To him, the department head mentor was "anti-organization and had some destructive managerial attitudes and practices—although in terms of science, he was a nice person and a great guy to work with."
>
> Even so, Eric decided to move with him to another university for two additional years of clinical pathology. In the new setting, the mentor had even more managerial responsibility, and, as Eric saw it, more of the mentor's bad characteristics came out. "It was all negative," he said of his time there.
>
> Eric reasoned that in order to find a good management model, he would have to look for a department head who had greater management responsibilities. He went on to two other university medical centers, but his search was futile. Eric found one head not only inept in management, but also a poor teacher. The other was "so much into the process of retiring that he let his secretary run the department."

We can understand Eric's disappointment. At the time he was searching, effective mentors and models in medical management were few and far between. Over the years, professionals in many fields have increasingly had to reach beyond their disciplines to gain needed knowledge and skills. Engineers, lawyers, and various health professionals have turned to M.B.A. programs. Journalists, dietitians, and a variety of others whose work involves a significant communications component have turned to experts outside their field in order to become skilled in computer graphics and publishing.

Disillusionment

It is easy to project onto mentors excessive attributes and expectations—the halo effect at work. We rationalize away the disappointments and tell ourselves that things will be better later. Given the attraction we have for the mentor, we want to see the person as larger than life. However, sooner or later, if the halo effect has been operating, disillusionment is bound to set in.

Several people I spoke to had mentors who they discovered were seriously flawed. How to handle that discovery, as well as the relationship, can become a real problem. By totally believing in and following the mentor, the mentee can land in hot water. In the examples that follow, Matt had such great admiration for his mentor that his disillusionment was great and traumatic. Jack and Hugh, on the other hand, pinned fewer expectations on their mentors and were able to find ways to work with and learn from them. Here are their stories:

- Matt was very impressed with his mentor in neonatology. He was well-versed in pulmonary diseases, knew the clinical work, and gave a lot to the babies. "He was always taking me here and there, showing me this and that. ... But he was terribly disorganized, never went to a conference on time, and would keep people waiting. Even then, I thought he was very good, and I took a fellowship with him. I was totally loyal to him, and I became polarized against other members in the division who he said were not good researchers. I was naive and believed what he said completely. Finally, I realized he didn't know much more about research than I did. He was just winging it."

- Jack's mentor had developed a new radioimmunoassay to measure small amounts of hormones in blood. "He had a great deal of genius, but incredible paranoia. He was totally unselfish with me. But in order to get along with him, I had to verbally share his delusions sometimes. He was afraid people would steal his formulas, and he'd fly off like a comet. Still, he was one of my important mentors."

- Hugh was realistic in his assessment of his mentor. "Walt was a stuffy, egotistical, very accomplished person who didn't relate well to others because he would anger them. I took him for what he was and accepted it. I was sort of a disciple. I acknowledged his intelligence, didn't fight him on it, wasn't jealous, just thought he was a very accomplished person. I said to him, 'Teach me the way.' I learned a great deal."

If we can appraise the whole of the mentor and determine what the person has that is admirable and worth learning, we often can shift the relationship to a conditional or limited mentoring that will work for both parties. This could constitute shifting from a major to a minor mentor relationship, something that might or might not work.

Shift in Values
Sometimes, the mentoring relationship will be highly positive for a period of time, and then there is a shift in either the mentor's values or the mentee's awareness that causes the junior person to withdraw respect. The behavior is no longer admirable or even acceptable.

- Bob's political mentor at a large commercial laboratory taught him a great deal. "He was such a skilled politician, so smooth. After watching him operate for a couple of years, I decided I was going to try to learn from him, and I blossomed under his guidance. He had more influence on me than any single

213

individual I've ever known. He would push me into the limelight to gain visibility; he would push like hell to get me out of my shell. Others would have given up on me long before that. As a result, I found that I could communicate well with other people and enjoy it! I'm now a people person, and that has not always been the case. I blossomed in those last 10 years. … Our relationship is strained right now. I don't agree with some of his tactics and some of his recent actions. I still revere the man I knew in those early years, but he's an incredible manipulator. I won't cut him off at the knees, but I can't go along with [what he's doing]."

- The administrator who trained Cory in hospital administration was a strong influence in both a positive and negative way. Cory said, "He gave me the opportunity to get involved and was very generous in his support. I was eventually given charge of certain departments so I could learn whatever I wanted. His goal was to make me successful. But he was very anti-doctor, and that led to his downfall. He had a chip on his shoulder and couldn't deal with doctors. Initially, I fell into that trap as well."

- Lucy's psychotherapist mentor was very helpful at a time when Lucy was depressed. "She gave me a kick in the pants and said, 'You teach summer school every year. Why do you do that? The world is out there. Why don't you go travel?' That was a challenge, and so I thought, All right, I'll show you! I got a ticket and was off to Europe for the summer. That experience broadened my scope tremendously and allowed me to take advantage of more of what the world has to offer. Her support and advice helped me get out of my depression, to break loose from the grip of my family, and then to question if I wanted to teach 40 kids each hour." Lucy left her mentor as the mentor began "to get into non-conventional psychotherapeutic methods and develop cults around her."

Shift in Accessibility or Availability of Mentor

Organizational changes can dramatically affect the ability of the senior person to mentor. In some cases, the mentor is no longer in an organizational role that supports mentoring. Or, the mentor loses political support and is preoccupied with organizational survival. Or, the mentor's personal career goals and interests have shifted.

Peg reported to the director of nursing in her hospital during a time when the organization was stable and the nursing director was secure and strongly supported by administration. Later, Amy joined the staff and also benefited from the director's guidance before organizational changes altered the situation.

- "As the nursing director went up in the hierarchy," Peg recalls, "I was always the one right behind her, her fair-haired child. She was my teacher, confidante, and alter ego, many times over. She had charisma. She was the one who set standards of care in that hospital. She is great to sit around and philosophize with, particularly in terms of managing people. She is probably one of the most nurturing, caring, loving, giving people I've ever known."

- When Amy became another mentee of the nursing director, she also received many positives. "She'd let us try new things, was enthusiastic, supportive, and helped us figure it out. When I was burned out and thinking, If I have one more kid with a nice wonderful family come in with cancer, I'm going to croak, she asked what I'd want to do to stay. We talked about my strengths and created a way to use them for the benefit of the patients and the hospital. "All that changed when we had a big shake up and the chief administrative officer, who was the director's support base, left. When that happened, everything went crazy for a while."

When Lynn's mentor, the director of finance, was promoted out of the department, their four-year mentoring relationship stopped abruptly.

- In the previous years, Lynn went through rapid stages of growth and became the assistant director of finance with her mentor always in the background helping her along the way. Then, because of business expansion, the director moved into a strategic planning position, and another person moved to the directorship. Not only did Lynn lose her mentor, but the new director to whom she reported criticized her for the shortcomings in the program. Lynn felt like a total failure. Finally, in desperation, Lynn went to the former mentor and told her how she was feeling about the loss of their relationship. "She said I'd have to stand on my own. In a way, it was a relief, because I finally knew where I stood. It cleared the air, and I no longer had hurt and angry feelings."

Mentors are not available for other reasons as well. The mentor could be dealing with political problems in the organization, health matters, marital difficulties, or family crises that shift time and energies away from mentoring.

Toxic Mentoring

Every field has its "bad" mentors. Some we mislabel as poor mentors because they fail to assume a mentoring role in a situation where we expect or assume mentoring would be present. Although it is true that some people abdicate their mentor responsibilities, far more are either not aware of the need to develop people, don't have the skills, or are not supported by the organization for doing so.

Some relationships are detrimental to the mentee, or they can become so. Although I have come to refer to these negative relationships as "toxic," it's not all that simple to pin on a label. We have talked about the importance of fit in mentor matching and how we all differ in what we personally find nourishing or toxic. This is important to remember as we visit "The Gallery of Toxic Mentors," developed from interviews. Although I've caricatured toxic mentors somewhat humorously, it is certainly not funny if the toxic mentor is yours. The several portrait types in our "gallery" are meant to be suggestive.

The Gallery of Toxic Mentors

Avoiders

Avoiders are not available or accessible. They either ignore requests or just don't respond. They can seem to do a disappearing act: "When she saw me coming, she'd seem to vanish into thin air, and I was left on my own once more."

Dumpers

Dumpers throw people into a new role or situation and let them flounder, either to sink or swim. For some Dumpers, this is a deliberate philosophy; on the other hand, others seem to be caught in an unexpected dilemma not of their choosing. Whatever the reason and whether purposeful or inadvertent, the Dumper's behavior causes a transition trauma that can leave lasting scars on the junior person.

- "I felt misled about my new job. I was promised orientation and was looking forward to learning from someone more experienced. Not only was there no orientation, but I was immediately expected to lead others."
- "My supervisor had a laissez-faire attitude. I was told that this was my unit, sink or swim. I didn't know how to present a budget. 'Never mind: Just sit there and develop on for the next month.'"

Dumpers can ruin potentially good leaders. Nancy was put in a leadership position, and then left totally alone. It was a painful period.

- "I had terrible doubts whether I should be in supervision. I didn't know what I was supposed to be doing, I didn't have a job description, and I wasn't getting enough direction. I was absolutely floundering. I started looking for another job completely out of management."

Blockers

Blockers actively avoid meeting the junior person's needs either by outright refusal of requests, by withholding information, or by blocking the person's development through too close supervision. When Yvonne started to succeed in her job, she noticed a change in her supervisor. "There was a lot of not including me in on things and whittling away my responsibilities."

Exploiters

Exploiters abuse their power position and treat junior people like personal flunkeys. Kerry knows that behavior well.

- "As the orthopedic resident, I was low man on the totem pole and errand boy for the chief. I was back to doing histories and physicals all day long for him or other attendings. They didn't care about teaching. It was almost an abusive situation: If you wrote orders that conflicted with what the attendings had to say, they'd raise holy hell. There were a lot of prima donnas there."

Criticizers and Underminers

Even more toxic are people who tear down the junior person in some way. Underminers are particularly subtle, and it takes awhile to realize what you're experiencing. Kirsten had a nursing instructor who undermined her confidence in her clinical skills by throwing her into impossible situations for her skill level and then giving her very poor evaluations. Others are more overt, tearing down the person or group publicly. Also, with a constant criticizer, the mentee can never do anything right.

- During Sylvia's internship, one instructor constantly drummed into her that she wasn't assertive enough and wouldn't ever be successful. "I did need to develop more assertiveness, but I needed more support in working on that. Her ragging me about it constantly made it worse rather than better."

- Claire's doctoral advisor gave her no direction or advice. "I floundered for a long time on my own. When you slipped up, he made sure you understood that he had seen it. His attitude seemed to be, 'I'm just going to let you try what you want, and, when you fall down, I'll criticize you.' There was not any real positive direction. I gained tremendous factual knowledge, but I still don't feel confident about the whole research process. At least I feel confident enough in myself that I can learn it on my own."

- As Dusty remembers, "One head nurse in coronary would line up the nursing students in the morning and tell us that we basically weren't ready to graduate, that we were not nursing material."

When looking at these toxic mentoring behaviors, it becomes clear that some occur because the supervisor or instructor does not have the attitude, skills, and/or maturity to be an effective mentor. Unclear responsibilities for mentoring and coaching also can be causal factors, as can stress and burnout.

Outgrown Mentor Mode

Camila's experience is a dramatic description of mentoring that was prized for its time but, when outgrown, became toxic. Her mentor was the director of a nephrology program who had developed a small inpatient dialysis into a 122-bed unit, plus a large home dialysis program for a Canadian province. The director had an incredible amount of drive, and her whole life was the unit. She helped to develop Camila's charge nurse role, particularly in interpersonal skills, interviewing, and managing conflict.

> "She was very good and guided me along. But after 10 months, I wanted to try my own wings, and I resented her hovering over me. In retrospect, she's not the type of person who would let go. The reason her unit runs so well is that she's constantly everywhere maintaining very strict standards. Things came to a head when she was sick for two months and chose me to be her replacement. It was then that I realized I could do the job. Unfortunately, when she came back, she started with the hovering business again. Because I had grown beyond that role, things were strained at work. Still, we were best of friends outside, and she finally did step back and allowed me to handle the work, even though she was uncomfortable."

When this point is reached, it's questionable whether the mentee still has anything to learn or gain from the relationship. The answer depends on what the mentee looked to and valued the mentor for. If it is protection and the mentee has now developed sufficient inner confidence and assertiveness, then the need for a protector is gone. If the mentee has developed the level of skill desired and maybe even surpassed the mentor, the need for a teacher disappears and the base will collapse. The question is, what is left? This is the time when the relationship must transform, or it will inevitably end, either by rift or by drift. Unfortunately, some mentors do not see this—they hang on. They may even see the mentee as ungrateful and feel used. It's the "after all I've done for you" syndrome. This is not too dissimilar from parents who find it difficult to allow the young person to cut the symbolic umbilical cord.

MENTOR ENDINGS:
CONCLUDING A MENTORING RELATIONSHIP

How mentor–mentee relationships end is partly influenced by the way the relationship was structured originally. Formal mentoring programs usually include a beginning, continuing, and a timed and structured ending. Less formal relationships conclude less predictably and may involve transformation, rift, or drift.

Mentor Endings: By Formal Conclusion

We are all aware of formal endings in educational programs. Although they are called by various names, the ending is noted by a ceremony during which the leaving person "graduates," "culminates," "commences," or otherwise completes a specified program. Whatever reservations the parties have had about the relationship are masked by the formal, laudatory ceremony, often marked by some written certificate of completion.

Mentor Endings: By Transformation, Rift, or Drift

In informal relationships, there is less clarity and certainty about the ending, and several patterns can occur. Instead of a specific time frame, the ending might occur when the work is finished or one person in the relationship moves on. The ending can be clear and clean, or even transformed into a friendship mode. The ending is explicit, the feelings warm or cordial. Often, however, mentor endings are more ragged and end either by a rift or drift.

Rift

"There is a season … " and when the same pattern of mentoring continues beyond its appropriate time, trouble starts brewing. The mentoring style that once served both parties well in the early period of the relationship can become intolerable. If the mentor's stance remains unbending, or if the mentee continues to cling, a final rift is almost inevitable.

With a rift comes an unpleasant happening or confrontation, and a residue of bad feelings can carry over and prejudice future relationships. There may be hurt, anger, bitterness, suspicion, and even cynicism and betrayal. "After all I've done for you!" "How could she?!" "Now I know ... " "I should have known better than to believe ... " "I used to think he was so great." "Things were so good and then ... " "Early on, I knew it was a mistake." These are comments similar to a failed marriage or love affair. After all, a major mentor relationship can be quite intimate: Emotions are involved, and both parties have invested a great deal. To have one turn on, or against, the other is immensely painful.

Often power and control issues dominate the interaction, regardless of the initiator of the split. One party is hanging on, while the other is trying to break out. Often, one of the parties is locked into the way things were while the other wants change. Marisa's experience with her mentor illustrates this well. Dr. Sandoval was the pathologist in charge of a hospital clinical lab when Marisa was a fresh laboratory technician, just 19 years old. She worked there until she was 37. Here is her story of a mentor locked into the traditional mentor role with no recognition of the growth and development of the mentee over an 18-year span or the mentee's need to change the power differential in the relationship.

A Traumatic Mentoring Ending

"Early on, Dr. Sandoval began giving me the job of teaching students, saying 'You can teach students because you're good at teaching.' My feeling about being special started from that very positive message.

"Over the years, the relationship became toxic because she didn't allow me to grow except according to her rules. She was very loving to me, provided that I would do exactly what she wanted: Always be on time; always work as hard as you can; if you see something to be done, do it; don't ask questions; be a handmaiden to physicians.

"Mentoring stopped when I started questioning her, and my beliefs started contradicting some of hers in terms of dealing with people. She was very authoritarian in her approach: "Don't question me." I talked to her about it, and she was angry with me. In the end, I needed to separate, and we did under the most toxic of circumstances. She had hurt me, and I had hurt her, too. She had placed a lot of trust in me. I wanted to please her very much, to have her be really proud of me, which was a child-like approach of dependency—I wanted her approval immensely.

"Years later, we met in San Francisco, went out to dinner, and talked as human beings. It was like coming home again. She told me how hurt she was because she was totally dedicated to her work, and at the time of our split, her husband was insisting that she retire the next year. She was like an oak tree—big and strong—but she cried, for the first time. 'Marisa, you know me. I'd die without work.' It was almost like I was able to talk to my mother as a human being. I started really feeling love for her and seeing how wonderful she had been for me and how much I had grown through her mentoring. Most of my technical skills were formed through her, also the ability to do hard work, to question technically, to feel I can do a test well, and to read a book and translate it.

"I was 19 when I went there, and I left at 37. At the beginning, I needed a mother. I was a kid, and I needed strong direction. Then later on, I started questioning, and she couldn't let go—and we made the break. The anger subsided when we were able to see each other as adults. I was truly able to tell her how much I had not only loved her, but also how much I had grown through her, even though it was very toxic for the last five years."

Just think of the situation of Marisa and Dr. Sandoval in the clinical laboratory: Of Marisa's 18 years in the relationship, 13 were good. However, five frustrating years were increasingly constrictive for Marisa, and Dr. Sandoval could not see it. The attachment had been so tight, there was no way to simply let the relationship drift. A stormy scene with recriminations was inevitable. What is unusual—and very satisfying—is that the two women could reconnect in later years, savor what they offered to each other in that golden time, and let the other memories fall away. Not many of us are that fortunate.

Marisa's breakaway experience with Dr. Sandoval is a sad conclusion to a mentoring relationship. But it is not always so, nor does it need to be. The most popular mentors I spoke to rarely encountered a rift in the ending of a mentoring relationship. Although a few transformed to friendship or colleagueship, most simply drift. The question is not *if* a mentoring relationship will end, but when and how, and whether the ending will be by transformation, rift, or drift.

Drift

It's easy to see why drift is the most common mentor ending. Many mentoring relationships are episodic by their very nature and have an anticipated termination. You finish your training program, you graduate, or you go off to a job placement. You both understand that there is an implied ending at the outset, a natural chronological progression and ending, often with cordial farewells.

Even if the relationship wasn't the best, it pays to have a friendly ending. After all, you might need a referral later, or you could meet again. Or, as a mentee, you've done what you set out to do, learned what you wanted, and gained all you could from the relationship. Now, you have a changed focus, seek different skills and knowledge, and want a different mentor style. You're ready to move on.

Sometimes, your mentor is ready to see you go. Ned mentors many undergraduates. When he finds them resistant, excessively dependent, impulsive, passive, or wimpy, he makes himself selectively unavailable. Marisa, who mentors clinical technologists who report to her, has her moments, too, when she lets relationships drift, as in the following example:

> "I put all my eggs in one basket with Libby. It worked for a while, and then it didn't. I saw behaviors I dislike—blaming others, being a victim. I was disillusioned, and I let it drift. There was no anger, I didn't feel betrayed, she didn't turn against me. She was neutral. If she had tried to sink my boat, I'd have tried heartily to sink hers."

So "drift" is a benign way to end a mentoring relationship when it has served its purpose, when it has met some but not all expectations, when either party is ready to move on. There may be no explicit discussion of the ending. Most likely, there is gradually lessened communication between the two people, indicating that the episode is finished.

Transformation

When transformation takes place, there is a leveling of the relationship, a more equal interchange between the two parties. Ned said his relationship with his mentor of 20-plus years has now shifted to the "wise counselor and the mature, experienced clinician/researcher."

Don went through a remarkable transformation in his relationship with his mentor, Kent, one of the three principals of the architectural firm that Don joined. Kent taught him the practical aspects of the profession of architecture. Here is how Don describes the transformation:

> "Kent was an extremely strong thinker, hugely knowledgeable and dedicated to the work. I learned by being around him how to respond to certain situations, sitting in meetings, watching him work. Honolulu is quite Asian in the way things are done: Be quiet, sit on the sidelines, and watch the elder person operate.

> "There was a project in Tahiti. I was very young to be the project designer, so he paid a lot of attention to it. One day, he wanted the design to be a certain way, and I knew it was wrong. I argued and argued, but I couldn't convince him. I was sufficiently dissatisfied that I went to one of the other partners and said, 'He doesn't know what the hell he's doing. The design ought to be this way.' The partner looked at it and said, 'You're right.' He helped Kent see the project from my viewpoint. That was the breakthrough. Our relationship really started to grow from that point on. I was able to present my opinions, and we started to bounce ideas off of each other.

> "Then it began to be much more reciprocal. He would look to me for the design input. During the course of another project in Maui, I moved from being an associate to a principal. Kent

slowly backed off and became involved only in the little pieces. I quickly took the stronger role to the point that at the conclusion of the project, and I was the principal in charge. That was a real transition and growth for me."

BRIDGE

We have spent considerable time delving into mentoring relationships, since people mentors are the most familiar source of mentoring. In these four chapters, we have looked at the requirements for a mentoring relationship, various mentor forms, and the dynamics of mentor–mentee relationships. You will find guides for surveying your own mentoring relationships in Chapter 19. In the next section, we turn to non-people mentoring—those very important and often unrecognized influences on us that have occurred as a result of the experiences we have had and certain environments we've found ourselves in. First, we turn to mentoring experiences and examine what makes an experience mentoring, the forms such experiences take, and their significance. Then, in the following chapter, we examine the rare but special case of mentoring environments.

Chapter 15

MENTORING EXPERIENCES

"The things that have the most impact on decisions I've
made have not been people, but situations and
environments."
—*Todd*

"Then, of course, a great mentor came along: the U.S. Navy."
—*Wil*

Todd, Wil, and others have helped me see that mentoring goes beyond
people relationships.

I met Todd when he was in his late 20s and in a junior management
position with a major oil company. Early in our discussion, he said he
would define a mentor not only as a person, but also "as a set of
circumstances." What were some of the circumstances that impacted his
decisions? Living in several different environments, he said, taught him
about people, class, and culture.

> The first major eye-opening shift occurred when the family
> moved from a middle class neighborhood in a rural Oklahoma
> town to an affluent suburb of Houston. There, the value
> system was "pretty amoral, and there were protection rackets
> in the junior high gym."

> One summer, when he was in his early 20s, Todd worked as a
> roustabout in the Texas oil fields and lived in a barrio "in a
> town that made money off of smuggling." He found it
> distressing and shocking, coming fresh as he had from the
> culture of the Harvard Business School. "It was a community
> that was culturally and economically in *The Twilight Zone*."

The sum total of these experiences vastly broadened Todd's outlook: "No matter where a person is coming from, I usually can find some common point to relate to. I don't have a preconception about what he or she should think."

Wil told me that he saw the U.S. Navy "as a mentor." Thanks to the Navy, he said, he had the opportunity to get in on the ground floor of radar development.

"The war [World War II] solidified and crystallized all my skills because the Navy put me in school. I spent years in and out of Navy schools of various kinds all over the country. When the war ended, I had four years of intensive electronics training that I didn't have when I started.

"When I went in, I was an amateur, a tinkerer, and a hobbyist. I had gone to engineering school but didn't have a degree or practical skills in the field, and I didn't have any experience. I volunteered and asked to be sent to radio school, and I was.

"The Navy moved me into radar—that was the best place to be for someone of my interests. It was a very exciting field during those years; it was just blossoming. I progressed very quickly and became an officer with rapid promotions.

"Radar was so new that I was on the frontier. I got into the Navy just in time to be present when the first radar set arrived in America. It came over from England, a primitive little funny box of junk. The excitement surrounding that box of hardware was incredible."

These are examples of mentoring experiences—those experiences that are formative and influencing in our lives. It is the experience itself that is mentoring. In this chapter, we look at the characteristics of mentoring experiences that make them so important. Then, we'll turn to three major forms of mentoring experiences: broadening experiences, maturing experiences, and unexpected opportunities (also known as "lucky breaks").

Mentoring influences come in all shapes, forms, and guises. A sizeable number of us are mentored more by events, situations, and circumstances than by our relationships with people. In the last section, we concentrated on interactional forms of mentoring, but as we can begin to see, mentoring is far broader. Focusing on people mentors to the exclusion of other mentoring forms is too limiting.

HOW DO WE IDENTIFY MENTORING EXPERIENCES?

Mentoring experiences can be the result of, or take the form of, an event, an ongoing situation, or a set of circumstances. Experiences happen. Some we seek, and others we do not. They can be traumatic or benign. Even the most traumatic experiences can be the stimulus for learning and growth, although perhaps not recognized at the time. Experiences generate change.

Mentoring events are those happenings that stand out, that are not part of the regular flow of life but are formative in some significant way. Such events are occurrences that take place with meaningful impact on our lives. They are occurrences that we learn from, that we grow as a result of, or that change our feelings about our lives and ourselves. Such events include moving to a new community, going into the military, leaving home for school or a job, or having a death in the family.

Mentoring situations are less dramatic than events. They have established themselves over a period of time without our realizing they were happening, and now they are present as facts of our lives. One example is being the eldest child in the family and, therefore, expected to take on greater responsibilities. Or, being born blind in one eye and having to cope with two-dimensional vision in a three-dimensional world.

According to Webster, a "circumstance" is a fact or an event accompanying another event. Mentoring circumstances, though brought about by factors external to us, provide the context for important parts of our life experience. Circumstances can be such things as coping with military assignments requiring periodic family moves, changed financial conditions, or having a dysfunctional family member or a chronically ill parent or child.

Since the distinctions between events, situations, and circumstances are slight, we can look at them together as mentoring experiences. Whether we are talking about a dramatic event, an ongoing situation, or a set of circumstances, what matters is the mentoring nature of the overall experience and the extent to which it is immediately or ultimately formative and guiding in one's life.

As with people mentors, it is our perception of mentoring experiences that governs their importance as mentoring influences. I agree with psychologist Ira Progoff that outer events have inner importance and can have strong emotional impact on us as we experience them.[17] Significant events or crises in people's lives can inspire growth or be traumatic, depending on how they are experienced. I am reminded that the Chinese ideograph for "crisis" is a combination of the symbol for "danger" and the symbol for "opportunity." For the people who see an experience as positive, the opportunity in the situation outweighs the danger. At the time it is happening, others of us might see only the danger, with the opportunity becoming clear to us only in retrospect. This has been true for me as I look back at traumatic events in my life that really pushed me in new directions and from which I ultimately grew as a person. We will examine this "Phoenix Factor" phenomenon later in this chapter.

---

[17] Ira Progoff, *At a Journal Workshop*, NY: Dialogue House Library, 1992, 167ff.

Clues to Mentoring Experiences

The following words and phrases from interviews give clues to possible mentoring experiences. Certainly they suggest experiences, but whether or not they are mentoring depends on the extent to which they are formative, guiding, and influencing.

There are *changed* circumstances, events, or situations:
- "It so happened that … "
- "The situation changed and … "
- "Then _____ happened, and I discovered that … "
- "No longer … "
- "I was surprised to find myself … "
- "My parents divorced and … "
- "My sister died … "

Then there are *givens*—the cards you were dealt:
- "I was the oldest, and I was expected to … "
- "I was tall for my age, and people gave me responsibility."
- "In a military family, you move around a lot."
- "It was expected that a girl … "
- "My father always … "
- "I was a twin and always searching for a separate identity."
- "We lived on a farm, and I had to help with the chores."
- "I lived with my grandmother."
- "My mother worked."
- "My mother was an invalid."
- "My father was ill."
- "We traveled a lot."

These are more or less enduring facts for a period of time that can have impact on the young person. What we want to understand is how events, situations, and circumstances are mentoring to us—what forms they take and what it is about the experience that changes us.

MAJOR FORMS OF MENTORING EXPERIENCES

A mentoring experience can be:

- eye-opening, broadening your perspective on life, society, and people;
- a maturing experience that catapults you to future responsibilities on a fast track;
- an opportunity to break away from something burdensome or constraining, or to move toward something important; or
- a turning point that is dramatic and life-changing.

Broadening Experiences

Broadening experiences are those that lead to understanding and valuing more of the world and its people, leaving behind a narrow outlook for an enlarged world view. Such experiences play a significant part in loosening the grip of cultural imprinting. The more diverse our experiences, the broader our view of the world and reality and the more options we see. Broadening experiences are a form of cultural consciousness-raising. They enlarge our view and move us beyond traditionally defined roles, perspectives, and behaviors. When these events work for our growth, they are mentoring experiences.

Mentoring experiences extend, reinforce, and/or contradict our early cultural imprinting. We need to remember, however, that although they influence us in how we look at the world and ourselves, they are not the *only* influence—earlier mentor-bonding patterns and family messages form much of the base for cultural imprinting.

At the beginning of this chapter, we saw the broadening effect of Todd's experience in the Texas oil fields. We add to that Val's experience in seeing the world. Val grew up in a small Texas town. Her family, particularly her father, expected her to go to college and get married. Val *did* go to college, but she had other post-college goals.

233

After completing nursing training, she worked as a nurse's aide to save money, with the intention of then heading for Europe. She felt "the whole world was out there waiting for me."

> "I just had to rebel. I was going to see the world, and nothing was going to stop me. I went to Europe with a small amount of money in my pocket and without my father's blessing. I attended an educational program in Paris, but by the end of summer, I had run out of money. So, I wrote to a London hospital for a job, and they said, 'Come on.' I ended up staying there for 14 months. This was a period of really trying my wings. There was nothing I couldn't do, nothing I couldn't achieve. It was the most marvelous feeling."

Val returned home when her father became ill and was hospitalized. Once her father was better, she joined the Air Force as a way of combining her profession and her fascination with the rest of the world. Soon she had orders for Japan.

> "I was against the [Vietnam] war, but I figured I could use my skills to patch up things. There were 25 of us just out of basic training who were going directly overseas. We were selected on the basis that we'd each been outside the United States, living on our own, and would adapt to the environment. All of us—nurses, physicians, and dentists—had traveled abroad hitchhiking or working."

Val is a good example of the "multiplier effect" of mentoring experiences. First, breaking away from family, then moving toward seeing the world, and then an unexpected opportunity, because of her maturity and experience, to go directly overseas with the military. We will see other examples where the build-up of mentoring experiences can have a multiplier effect, catapulting the person onto a fast track.

Eye-Opening Experiences

Some broadening experiences are particularly notable for their eye-opening quality. They give the person a different view of the world and of reality. They provide informal education and completely new learning. During college, Owen heard Martin Luther King, Jr., speak in Huntsville, Alabama. He sees it as one of the most important experiences of his life:

> "If you can envision a black child in the South who, from birth to adulthood, lived in the highly segregated society that existed before 1964, that's the way it was. You accepted and dealt with the reality. Then, all of a sudden, somebody comes along and says it's going to change. All of a sudden, you awake to the fact that, 'Hey, this is not the way it ought to be.' You can imagine the impact on me. At 19 or 20 years old, I had this bomb explode inside my head. It made an impact and has to this day.

> "I can remember becoming very bitter. [King's] vision, his 'dream' of things being different, made a whole generation of people suddenly aware of the injustice. It certainly angered me. My parents, my family, and friends had lived with segregation all their lives—I was a very angry young man for quite a while."

A few years later, Owen went to Nebraska for the last two years of college. There, he had a completely different experience:

> "I hadn't had any relationship at all with white people. It was like a foreign country to me. These people I worked for at the dairy company in Nebraska were another kind of education for me. I got the first clue that all white people weren't like the ones I had grown up to despise in the South. They were good to me, and I had excellent relationships. In a lot of these small Nebraska towns, there were no other black people at all. My informal education took place while working during those summers. I learned quite a bit about life, people, and myself."

Around the same time that Owen was growing up in the South, Don was a white kid growing up in a small corner of North Dakota—"not knowing any kids from the big city, not to mention minorities." Going to Boys' State made a big impact on him: He realized then that there was a much bigger world than he had experienced in his small corner of the state:

> "The kids from the big city were real go-getters, very intense and competitive. There was never open competitiveness in my hometown. It was an eye-opener. On the way back home from Boys' State, I took the train, and there was a group from West Virginia going to the Seattle World's Fair. That's the first time I'd ever talked with people from a long ways away. It was the first time I'd seen a black person. It was a real learning experience."

During their growing-up years, both men had additional mentoring experiences that have led them, in their respective worlds, to function in broader cultural settings. Owen learned to work effectively in management in both black and white cultural settings and in both government and the private sector. Don attended graduate school where half of the architectural students were foreign students. Later, he became associated with an architectural firm doing business in Hawaii and the Pacific islands.

Nassrin's eye-opening experience occurred with her move from her native Iran to go to college in western Illinois, where she lived in a dorm.

> "Seeing people from other countries really amazed me, because back home, everybody was Persian, and that's it. A lot of Asian students attended the same English class as I did. We spent a time together talking about the differences in all our countries—how they treated their fathers and boyfriends and girlfriends. I was amazed—what a good opportunity!"

Eloise's experiences were eye-opening in a different way. Her father, a miner in a little mining town in northern Ontario, died when she was 13, and Eloise had to work part-time. In the winters, she worked in a grocery store, a variety store, and as a soda jerk. In the summers, she worked in a factory, a tobacco firm, and as a waitress. Seeing what the work did to women convinced Eloise that she did not want that kind of lifestyle:

> "If you worked in a factory, it was very hard, dirty work. The women had a very narrow vision of the world. They were also very tough—they had to be—but I didn't want to have that toughness or roughness for myself. They worked very hard for very little money. I didn't want a life like that."

With her brightness, motivation, and capacity for hard work, Eloise became a nurse. She then went on to the university, where she later became a professor of nursing.

Maturing Experiences

Maturing experiences are those that cause the person to take on responsibilities at an unusually early age, with the young person developing a competence that most peers do not yet have. These responsibilities could be given as a privilege, thrust on the young person unexpectedly, forced as a requirement, or assumed as a necessity. Early family responsibilities, early leadership roles, early independence, or early work experience can all be maturing experiences.

Regardless of the reason, such young people start building years of experience that put them ahead of their peers and often lead to additional positions of responsibility because of their maturity, reliability, and dependability. People mature because of responsibility. Then, because they appear mature, they are given more responsibility. It's a circular process, and not surprising when you stop to think about it.

- Both of Ann's parents worked at jobs and also managed the family farm. As the oldest in the family, Ann and her twin were given responsibility for helping on the farm all during their growing-up years. If they failed to carry their part of the load on the farm, it simply would not get done. "We had chores in the barn with dairy cows, anything to do with planting, harvesting, and driving tractor. Everyone had tasks they were responsible for completing. There was help if you needed it, but basically, it was your job, so get it done. We worked as a team. One of the things I remember in high school was the excitement of being given the responsibility for taking care of the farm when my parents finally took a weekend away. For the first time, we were going to be in charge without having a relative come and stay with us! It was a very big step for us."

- Because she was very tall, Catherine was automatically given more responsibility at school. She would take kids to the nurse's office and wash and bandage knees. When she was 12, the school bus had a flat tire, and the driver went for assistance. He turned to her and said, "You, big one, you take care of everything!" Catherine was also the peacemaker in the family. When her two brothers got into squabbles or their behavior got out of hand, she would calm the situation "so Mother wouldn't start screaming at us."

- Alice was the oldest of seven children and "the second mother" in the family. "I was always halfway in charge of the house. On different days, we were to milk the goats, wash or dry the dishes, or do certain things on my father's bakery truck. I couldn't leave to catch the school bus until we finished the chores. I've always been old beyond my years, and I've tended to move into leadership positions." From the time she was 8, Alice fixed on nursing as a career. At 15, she was accepted as a volunteer in a hospital, the only volunteer they had, based on the family physician's recommendation and the fact that she had been accepted into a nursing program. She "got to do" things that volunteers rarely were allowed to do, such as helping in the ER when burn patients came in from a severe explosion, helping nurses put on dressings and feed burn patients, and helping physicians with accident victims.

When I met her, Alice was the director of education in her hospital and was completing her doctorate in management, with a goal of moving into hospital administrative leadership. Throughout her life, mentoring experiences of responsibility and leadership have gone hand in hand.

Role Reversal: A Special Case of Maturing Experiences

A few of us found our roles as children in the family reversed. Instead of being able to lean on or depend on the adults, the young person instead is leaned on in ways that may not be age-appropriate.

Fernando was raised by two aunts from Mexico, who spoke only Spanish and were almost illiterate. He became the central figure in the family and very much their pride and joy.

> "I was more in control of the environment. Very often when you have parents or close relatives who don't know English, they come to depend on you entirely in order to function. Instead of taking, you give a lot. When I was 15 and a sophomore, I had to provide for the two of them myself."

Here are some additional examples from interviews:

- A girl is used as a counselor by her mother.
- A girl of 12 has to assume major family responsibilities because of her ailing mother and six younger siblings. By the time she is 25, she has racked up 13 years of experience in directing and being responsible for the welfare of others.

- A young man of 17 has to drop out of school in order to support the family when his father dies.
- A boy represents the family in school whenever his younger brother has problems. He is the one who finally tells his squabbling parents to separate.
- A boy with an ailing father works to support the family and tries to manage the violent behavior of an older brother who is into drugs.
- A girl serves as translator and handles items of business for her non–Spanish-speaking parents during the many years the family lived in Mexico.

When you are leaned on and relied on as much as these young people, you are unlikely to have the experience of growing up with mentors. Unless there are mentor substitutes, mentor bonding is likely to be weak. Chances are, you learn to be self-reliant and develop self-mentoring strategies.

Unexpected Opportunities

When people talked about their military service during America's major wars, I expected to hear about their negative experiences and trauma. So I was surprised at the positive impact that military service had for a number of them. They talked about the opportunities they had that would ordinarily not have been possible: the opportunity to break away from something or to move toward something.

- During World War II, Mitch had a deferment to complete his medical training before serving in the military. He later was assigned to the occupation force in China, arriving there shortly after VJ Day. Because of the shortage of doctors, Mitch was appointed chief of medicine of a 300-bed base hospital, the administrator of the entire medical section. He was just 26. This was his first taste of administration, a field he pursued later in his medical career.

- The Korean War provided Kevin and Cory with unusually challenging assignments because more-qualified people were not available. Kevin was only 27 when he was made a base commander responsible for 1,500 men. Cory, a public health graduate, was assigned to fill a slot designated for a medical doctor and ended up heading a preventive medicine program in Korea. Both men attribute their experiences in handling such unusual responsibilities as significant in their career advancement, and both moved quickly into hospital management on their return to civilian life.

Breaking Out or Away

Bruce showed me what a broadening and maturing experience naval service in World War II could be.

> At the beginning of the war, Bruce, following his father, was studying engineering. It was not satisfying, and he was perplexed as to what to do. Naval enlistment gave him "time out," a chance to break away from his provincial roots and discover what he wanted to become. While on sea duty, he started reading books about philosophy and began a career shift that ultimately led to the ministry.

The chance to break away—or out—is true for women as well as men.

> Carolyn lived in a small, tightly knit community where girls were expected to live at home until they married. Carolyn chafed at this constraint and saw enlistment in the Navy as an acceptable way to break away from her family and community pressures and become independent.

Karen waited for the time when she could break away from her family's religious orthodoxy.

> "I have always been a spiritual seeker, but I happened to land in a family where it was preordained that I would follow a prescribed religious path. I learned to keep my mouth shut. But

I started investigating other religions as soon as I left home for college. I looked for answers under every rock. It caused a big rift between my mother and grandmother and me. My family's religious practices didn't fit anymore. In the end, I managed to take from my upbringing and family tradition what is beautiful and useful, but I was able to let go of the guilt and suffering that I saw were ways of controlling people."

Lucky Breaks

Lucky breaks are those opportunities that are not probable under ordinary circumstances. Timing is a factor. The outbreak of war can bring disruptions in education and work that turn out to be positive for those in civilian life as well as for those serving in the military.

When I first met Helene, she was a woman scientist in her 80s who had grown up during World War I. Because of the war, there was a strong national push for people to train in the sciences, with special emphasis on nursing or medicine. Since most young men were going directly into military service, women students were more accepted than they had been previously. Helene loaded up on science courses; she liked the exactness of science and searching for truth. I asked if she was viewed as an oddity, being a woman in science at that time. She said no, that because of the national need at the time, many people were going into chemistry, and there were a number of women in the department.

Social change—the civil rights movement and legislation of the 1960s and the women's movement, for example—has afforded opportunities previously not available to some.

Owen's father was a tile-setter, the best a black could do growing up in Louisiana. After college, Owen entered government service. Later, he became the first African-American in the county administrator's office in a large urban area. He spent a decade of service in increasingly responsible health care posts before shifting to a hospital administrative position in the private sector.

OTHER FORMS OF MENTORING EXPERIENCES

Two other types of mentoring experiences exist. They are less frequent, but can be highly significant: pattern-shaping and turning-point experiences.

Pattern-Shaping Experiences

Pattern-shaping experiences are those familiar and repetitive events that have shaped the direction in which we live our lives and that we experience in a positive, growth-inspiring way. They are far-reaching as they leave their mark on us. This is particularly notable in patterns of adaptability and of continuity.

Adaptability

Take the instance of military families or other families where, because of the father's or mother's work, the family has frequent changes of location and culture. This mobile lifestyle can be a long-term positive experience for the young child, or a negative one. It was a mentoring experience for Catherine, who developed strategies for quickly surveying a new environment and making connections with people—an unconscious strategy she employs regularly. This situation also was true for Andrea, who saw how efficiently her mother coped with every move and made an instant home for the family. Also, Andrea fondly remembers how her father would take her to explore each new culture.

Such young people learn adaptability and effective ways to cope with change. Indeed, they enjoy novelty and welcome variation. Catherine, for instance, feels "rootless and restless" after a few years in the same location. Andrea needs to have some major shift in her life every five years. She might change her job, enter a new training program, or change her lifestyle—something to introduce significant change in her life.

243

Continuity

Although some of us moved around a lot as children, others grew up in very stable home and community environments. Ava grew up in a Finnish community in rural Canada. Her parents were active in the church, and her father was a founding member of the community store. Ava always knew what was going on in the community, and everyone there helped out. Her experience in her community was so positive that it influenced her career direction, leading her to the University of Toronto for her public health certificate and then directly into community nursing.

Turning-Point Experiences

Other experiences can cause such major upheavals in our lives that they can turn our lives upside down. Turning-point experiences are sudden and abrupt changes that disrupt our life plans.

- With her strong interest in animals, Melanie entered a college program in pre-veterinary medicine. That all changed with the assassination of John F. Kennedy. "With him gone," she said, "I was going to have to save the world. So I changed majors to international relations rather than striving to save the world from hoof-and-mouth disease."
- Al was in high school when Sputnik shook up the country and created the great push toward science. "That was all the focus, so I just stayed in the sciences in the college prep courses. The chemistry teacher, who always encouraged me, went out of his way to ask me to sign up for his class."

"Getting fired" is also a turning-point experience. It can be devastating, but it also can be a powerful learning experience to the extent one gains insight from the action. This was true for Sue, a dietitian. She said that getting fired was traumatic but also clarifying, because she hadn't understood who her boss was.

"Organizationally, it was the administrator of the hospital where I did dietetic consulting. In actuality, it was the father-in-law of the doctor who owned the hospital. He had been in the food business and had very definite ideas about what I should do. I hadn't understood that he was the person with the power."

Learning about power by getting fired or getting in trouble happens for a number of people. Lisa was forced to resign because of the jealousy of her boss. She concluded that "no job is a piece of cake until you learn how to deal with the boss."

Carl learned about power and politics the hard way. When he was serving as a physician in the Air Force, he wrote a complaint in response to what he felt was an unfair letter of reprimand. He quickly learned that "it's a serious thing if you turn in a complaint against anybody of higher rank." It took months of political maneuvering to get out of the political mess he was in.

"As I was growing up, my father always said that people are people, and it doesn't matter what color or race or station a person's in. But that's not true in organizations. I hadn't gone far enough in my career to know that. I learned a lot from the hard-knocks school about power politics and how things happen."

Carl learned quickly and well, to the point that he became the go-to guy in his medical practice group as the expert on organizational politics.

The Phoenix Factor[18]—Handling Traumatic Experiences

Experiences that are especially traumatic present us with a crisis that can lead either to disaster or to growth. Those that lead to growth remind us of the Phoenix in mythology. The Phoenix was a marvelous mythical bird that lived for a long time and died in a sudden burst of

---

[18] I am guided in this discussion by Karl Slaiken and Steve Lawhead, *The Phoenix Factor*, NY: Houghton-Mifflin, 1985.

flames. But as it burned, the Phoenix became transformed. Instead of being consumed, the Phoenix rose from the ashes and was born anew.

There is a Phoenix Factor in human life, too. Our crises are turning points. However traumatic, they can lead to rebirth and growth for those who can adapt to the changes and develop insights, coping skills, and inner confidence that last a lifetime.

Some events are universally devastating; others are more subtle and may be the last of a string of events. The crisis event can be characterized by suddenness and severity or by subtlety. The event can represent a loss, a threat, or a challenge for which we are unprepared. Whatever the source, we find that our normal methods of coping do not work. We feel vulnerable and have the sense that our lives are out of our control. "At the heart of the Phoenix Factor is the idea that the pain of crisis can be turned to your advantage. You already know that your life will never be the same." We grow through a crisis when we work through the experience and are ready again to face the future.

Raphael's mentally ill mother became progressively worse as he was growing up. She committed suicide when he was 16. Raphael said that dealing with all of those years and such a tragic event forged in him an "unbelievable strength":

> "I have never experienced anything since that was as bad. I can cope with anything. I am absolutely fearless of anything that could occur because I know that I can handle it. After my mother died, I went through a metamorphosis. It was a relief, a termination of a long, enduring problem. I started letting my personality show itself. And it dawned on me that there was a whole world out there of colors and sounds and personalities that were an inexhaustible source of almost everything one needs to fulfill oneself."

When Fernando was in his doctoral program, his wife was killed in a car accident that left one child near death.

> "Any close death tends to disorient you," he said. "It tends to have you reassess priorities about what you have to do now. I needed to take care of my three kids. You never recover, it changes you—it's the turning of the corner. My priority now is very clear: health, family, and job. The job will never be first."

Glenda was devastated when her husband left her, but her mentor helped her dig her way out of the ashes:

> "My mentor challenged me. He called when he heard about Jon's leaving. He said, 'You can be the martyred wife from now on and suffer, or you can make this the beginning of a whole new life.' Instantly, I chose the latter, even though that separation was terrible."

BONDER AND NON-BONDER DIFFERENCES

In this chapter, we have turned the spotlight on experiences that are formative and guiding in life, those that are broadening or maturing as well as those that are unexpected opportunities. We've looked briefly at cataclysmic experiences that can change our lives forever and remind us that the Phoenix does rise from the ashes. But now, briefly, let's look at the mentoring experiences of mentor bonders and non-bonders. Do they differ, and, if so, how?

Data from interviews suggest two ways in which the mentoring experiences of bonders and non-bonders differ. Although most of us have some experiences that are mentoring, non-bonders are more aware of and articulate about experiences they see as mentoring. Non-bonders give mentoring experiences high importance in their lives and are more likely to initiate—and even design—experiences that will be mentoring. Bonders can learn a great deal from non-bonders, who actively cultivate mentoring experiences. We need to keep this in mind as we construct our Mentoring Mosaic.

PLANNED MENTORING EXPERIENCES

Increasingly, as we move along in life and career, we have the need to plan mentoring experiences to meet important goals. Sometimes, we decide to test out the realistic "fit" of a career goal, we take a different fork in the career path, or we reassess and regroup after a major life trauma. Here are two examples:

Looking ahead from his senior year in college, Daniel wasn't sure what he wanted to do. He applied to medical school and talked to admissions people.

> "They said, 'Since it looks like you want to go into research, you can get a Ph.D. You don't need an M.D.' But I really wanted to do patient care. I was more interested in the mysteries of the human body than the cell, and I was convinced they were wrong.

> "So, I did a year of volunteer work—50 hours a week at the medical center and local kidney center—and just checked out what it was like to be in those environments. I would just go around and do whatever the nurses or orderlies wanted help doing. A lot of times, I would talk to patients—that was my main thing. A lot were depressed but were very talkative. Many were stuck in the hospital with no family members around, some with devastating illnesses. ... Many times, I would stay until 11 or 12 at night. By the time I finished my year, I was really convinced that I wanted to stick with medicine. It was all very motivating."

Karen was in the graduate program at a prestigious university and also taught composition and rhetoric. Toward the end of her second year, Karen's father was diagnosed with cancer.

"I had spent my whole first year figuring out if I really belonged in the school, and I was simply hanging in there the second year. I became torn and tormented over my father's illness: I should be helping him, but then I would not be doing my work. I was in constant crisis. The situation was incredibly difficult."

Karen's father died before she graduated. About the same time, her beloved grandmother, who lived near her parents, also died. By end of that school year, Karen realized that she needed time out. She took a leave of absence and spent a year alone in the northern California woods.

"I thought that when I was there in the woods, I would do a lot of writing and reading. Instead, I cried, slept, and walked a lot on the beach and in the woods. It was like a scheduled nervous breakdown, and I wanted to do it alone. I gave myself permission to fall apart up there and to investigate the question, 'Who am I when I am not playing all these roles I've played all my life? Who is left?'"

By the time Karen left the woods, she was over most of her grief and had new clarity about her career goals.

Planned mentoring experiences can be eye-opening, testing, broadening, or deepening. They imply conscious commitment, as illustrated by the previous examples.

BRIDGE

What conclusions can we draw from these reports of mentoring experiences? As we become aware of the mentoring potential of events, situations, and circumstances in our lives, we can do two things. One, we can keep alert to and actively seek out experiences that can provide mentoring opportunities for us in situations where we have choice. Or two, when we have no choice or control, we can be alert to our own perceptions of these experiences and their inner importance to us. We can look for the opportunities within the situation and not be blinded by the dangers we foresee. Now, let's turn to another significant element in our Mentoring Mosaic. In the next chapter, we look at the environments themselves that are mentoring, a place or a culture where amazing things happen.

Chapter 16

MENTORING ENVIRONMENTS

"It was the greatest cultural awakening a person could have."
"I felt like a kid in a candy store."
"To me, it was the Emerald City."
"We were almost making history while we were there."
"It was the medical equivalent of Camelot."

These phrases capture some of the flavor of what it's like to be in a mentoring environment as described by people who have been there. Sometimes, we chance to find ourselves in a place or culture that is particularly growth-inspiring and synergistic[19] — our Camelot. It is our interaction with this special environment, rather than a one-on-one relationship with a mentor, that makes that time in our lives mentoring. The emphasis is the group, the place, the setting, the climate — a culture that helps us to learn and grow, and that is interactive, cumulative, and endures over a certain period of time.

Much has been written about the importance of organizational cultures, the internal climate or characteristics that provide the day-to-day environment for the people in any system. An illuminating little book, *The Feel of the Workplace*, uses the metaphor of weather to describe what it feels like to function in a social system, that is, the "weather" in that region of social space.[20] The weather metaphor is quite apt: Whether people function well in an environment is a matter of the climate and their feelings, the fit. When we have a choice, we

---

[19] Simply stated, synergy is operating when 1+1 is greater than 2.
[20] Fritz Steele and Stephen Jenks, *The Feel of the Workplace*, Addison-Wesley, Reading, MA, 1977.

move to a climate that has the degree of stimulation that is comfortable for us.

In our growing-up experiences, we usually have little choice in our environments. Later, we make choices that work well for us, or not. Once in a long while, however, if we're lucky, we find ourselves in a setting that is unbelievably energizing. In this chapter, we want to look at environments that are particularly zestful and have been influential in our lives.

Mentoring environments are exciting and alive. They are creative, intellectually challenging, and/or supportive—in a word, yeasty. Look at what people say: "There was constant stimulation." "I thrived on it." "Intellectually, it was a whole new horizon." "There was a tremendous density of outstandingly competent people." "A lot of creative ferment was going on there." "It was a fantastic group of women who have met the challenges in life."

Such environments are usually bound by time and space: "It was a time when … " "It was a place where … " It's a special time in one's life where near-magical things happen. They endure during one's time in that environment, or during the time that certain people or groups are in that environment.

What does a mentoring environment look like? Where do people find them, and how do they experience them? Answering these questions is the focus of this chapter. We will take an extensive survey of mentoring environments, including the variety of settings where they may be operating, how they are formed, what they mean to the people involved, and how knowledge of mentoring environments can be useful to us.

WHERE DO THEY OCCUR AND HOW DO THEY HAPPEN?

Mentoring environments can develop in a variety of social systems, most prominently in educational and research settings, but also in work teams and professional groups, family systems, and informal groupings. They can develop in schools and universities, governmental and private research organizations, in the profit and not-for-profit sectors, and in ad-hoc groups. Although usually found in an institution or organizational setting, a mentoring environment can even be a different culture, such as living in a big city or in a foreign country.

Mentoring environments usually develop through consciously designed programs and institutions or through the implementation of the values of a gifted leader. Occasionally, they occur spontaneously in a setting devoted to another purpose, such as affinity groups. Such settings can even be converted to a mentoring purpose by the individual.

In Educational Settings
Many of us can cite a mentoring environment in our years of education and learning. Two types of mentoring environments are apparent: those created by conscious educational design, and those created by gifted teachers who are group mentors to the whole class.

Schools

Innovative Programs
Innovative educational programs often can become mentoring environments. Accelerated and interdisciplinary programs, open-classroom concept schools, magnet schools, and university demonstration schools are just a few. Not all programs succeed in their grand goals; however, those that do succeed provide a long-lasting enriching experience for the students. What the students experience is an unusual array of resources, outstanding teachers, and a feeling of privilege, having been carefully selected for the program.

- Ingrid's accelerated high school classes combined history and literature. They were taught by a pair of history and literature teachers who were an inspiring and dynamic "duo."
- Nicole was fortunate to attend the first open-concept school in Montréal, a big room with six different classes separated only by room dividers and with excellent teachers—all hand-picked. She was in accelerated literature and geography classes that catered to her needs. "We felt quite special, because we had all these interesting visitors from all over the world."

Demonstration School

Dave attended a demonstration school on the campus of The Ohio State University, one of 30 schools in a progressive education experiment during the 1930s and early '40s. The whole thrust of the progressive education experiment was one of giving maximum freedom to students. Looking back, Dave realizes that the faculty had unusual competence. His high school math teacher was also a full professor at Ohio State and had very innovative ideas about education. In his "nature of proof" class, they had unusual assignments. Dave sees this experience as a major factor in his development of the puzzle-solving skills that have been a hallmark of his career and his life.

> "We were to go out in the city and watch a traffic light with watch in hand and deduce the algorithm that the traffic light was following. 'Can you figure out the formula that the light is obeying?' It was an unconventional class, a puzzle-solving atmosphere. The deeper learning was connected with real applications so that you associated what you had learned with a branch of a tree of useful knowledge instead of only attaching it to a frame of theoretical knowledge."

Experimental schools on university campuses are known for their innovative applications and usually have a long-lasting impact on the young student. Dave's experience was outstanding in a positive direction. Claire's experience was more mixed.

"They were trying a lot of creative approaches to education. I think they were teaching the basic skills, but sometimes those got lost when we were doing all kinds of creative, wonderful things. I liked writing stories and enjoyed art—the creative things—more than learning the basics of study skills, time management, and other things that you use the rest of your life. Basics just were not emphasized and could be avoided. I ended up learning along with my children and then later in graduate school acquiring skills I should have learned the first time around."

Happenstance

Mentoring environments also develop through happenstance. Elise had a unique experience as a Depression baby going through school at a time when money was tight. Luckily for her, finances were such in her small public school district in the St. Louis area that the administration did not terminate teachers, but kept them on and had small classes.

"In high school, there were probably 40 kids who had college aspirations, so it was a select group. With the coming of World War II and the science era, we had a lot of science taught in very small classes. In physics and college algebra, we would go through the first book in two or three months. Then the teachers would continue to bring in additional challenging problems for us to work on. Sometimes the teachers didn't really know how to solve the problems, and we would work on them together the next day in class. They taught me that you didn't have to know everything; yet, they were skilled enough to be able to allow us the opportunity to go as far and as fast as we could. We had an excellent peer group, too; I learned as much from my classmates as I did from the teachers."

Gifted Teachers

Many of us remember fondly teachers who were mentors to the entire class, teachers who created a climate such that the whole group was turned on to learning. These teachers are "group mentors." Rather than singling out individual students, they encourage, stimulate, and influence the entire class.

- "They were mentors to the whole class, and if you chose to identify with them, it was a highly enriching experience."
- "He treated us like adults, like people who wanted to learn. It wasn't the teacher-child relationship with a 'you're going to learn this' mentality. He had something special to give, and his teaching was of a totally different quality."
- "They were gentle individuals, but fully in command of themselves and the students. They expected something from you, yet were fun to be around."
- "She gave all of us the idea that through song and music, you could express yourself. There was a time to express happiness, love, and even sadness. She gave us the idea that it really didn't matter if you didn't have a lot of talent individually; you still could get up and perform."

Since the individual teacher creates the mentoring environment, the climate does not usually carry over to the larger school environment or last beyond the tenure of the teacher.

In College
A number of colleges and universities have been consciously designed to provide an educational program expressing the various values and goals of the founding fathers and mothers. Such institutions often have a tradition that has endured through many student generations. Each may be noted for excellence in certain disciplines, for outstanding teaching, for world-class research, and/or for its deeply engrained values. Carefully recruited faculty and students, a key philosophy, and select programs provide a mentoring environment for many students.

The extent to which such an environment is mentoring depends both on the climate of the institution at that particular time and the fit with the young person. Sometimes, the reaction is mixed, as was Sally's experience at Pomona. At first, she found Pomona "very scary." So many people there had traveled and accomplished things, and she felt like a poor cousin. Sally also was very shy:

> "I was ambivalent. It was very exciting to have small classes and talk about ideas I'd never explored before. Intellectually, it was a whole new horizon and a lot of fun. But it was difficult for me socially, because I felt I never quite fit in. It was wonderful in some ways and difficult in others."

Mitch raves about his experience at the University of Chicago. He attended during the era of Robert L. Hutchins and found it to be "the greatest cultural awakening a person could have!"

> "The courses that were the most thrilling were the humanities. They just opened up everything—art, music, sculpture, religion. We studied all the trends from the dawn of civilization to modern times, so we had a full panorama of what happened at each stage. The most illustrious people in the program taught these courses. In the first year of humanities, we had a lecture on the political science of central Europe given by Edward Benes, the president of Czechoslovakia who had come from Prague as a Visiting Professor. I remember a lecture by Bertrand Russell. Arthur Compton, a Nobel Laureate, gave the course on cosmic rays. These were the kinds of experiences I had as a freshman and sophomore.

> "Learning how to use the tools of education was the greatest benefit. The University of Chicago's emphasis was not on the ability to regurgitate information we had been taught, but on being able to analyze and interpret what that learning meant and how it could be used."

At the time Liz attended Johns Hopkins School of Nursing, it was one of the foremost research centers in the world. She found it to be a tough clinical environment but exciting, because everything she saw was unusual.

> "The faculty would haul [the nursing students] all over the place. If we were studying something theoretical and a real-life example was to be found somewhere in a university-affiliated institution, we would go to see it. If a patient condition was so rare that we might never see it again in our lives, we would be dragged off to see it for some bedside teaching. I thrived on that.

> "It was the most stimulating environment I've ever been in—so unlike anything experienced by most students going through nursing school. I loved it! I refer back to some of those situations even now when something happens. We had a patient here with very unusual complications—I hadn't seen that particular symptomology since I was at Hopkins. Everyone was befuddled, but I knew—I'd seen it 20 years ago."

I was reviewing my data about mentoring environments with a friend and colleague who has been studying women in management in Japan. She shared that Tsuda College in Kodaira, Tokyo, provided a mentoring environment for young Japanese women at a time when the larger culture was indifferent to their education and development.[21] "It was the seedbed," she said, "a greenhouse for women." At important times in their histories, women's colleges and traditionally black universities in the United States also have been noted for providing mentoring environments for sub-groups once left out of mainstream education.

At the Graduate Level
At the graduate level, educational institutions emphasize both research and teaching, with classes smaller and more professionally focused. Those environments that are mentoring are intellectually

---

[21] Jean R. Renshaw: *Kimono in the Boardroom*, Oxford University Press, 1998.

challenging and creative, generating new knowledge as well as deepening theoretical insights.

For Don, the University of Washington's architecture school was mentoring both in terms of the architectural program and the student mix. The graduate group in architecture was small, and half were foreign students. It was an opportunity to interact with a very diverse group of people. The experience was formative for him.

"The school I'd come from was a Beaux Arts-oriented school, in terms of the architectural philosophy and approach to the educational process. Architectural schools had always viewed the physical environment as fixed and looked for behavioral changes in people to make things work. However, UW was getting a very strong Berkeley influence at that time, which was to look at what architecture really does.

"I worked on some programs in the child psychology division. The professor there was on the forefront of child psychology development. Her approach was different. Working with her, I began treating the physical environment as the variable, seeing how differently built environments would affect behaviors. We did some pioneering kinds of things. I became involved in ecological psychology. A lot of creative ferment was going on there, a broadening look at things. I learned and grew a lot just through those exposures, friendships, and interfaces."

Cornell University was a mentoring environment for two graduate students in the nutrition program, but at different times.

- Nell was struck with the many people there who were famous in nutrition history. "We were almost making history as we were there. We had an eclectic group of instructors: a biochemist, a physician with an interest in clinical nutrition, a food economist, and someone primarily interested in the international dimension. During the first week of orientation, all of the faculty talked to us about their backgrounds, primarily about their research interests, so we could begin to think about who we might want to work with in research. It's hard to tell you how meaningful it was and what an impression it made. I left Cornell knowing that I would always be involved in research."

- Right from the beginning, Julia noted a tremendous emphasis on research findings. "The presentation of nutrition information was always in the context of the most recent literature, which our professors would quote extensively—who was the investigator, the nature of the investigation, what the results showed."

Tim's experiences provide a study in contrasts. He found himself immersed in two distinctly different environments as an MIT undergraduate and then at Caltech for graduate work. Although he found MIT to be a very stimulating and mentoring environment, Caltech was quite the reverse. He attributes the difference to the posture of the faculty at the two schools at the time:

"The general attitude in the electrical engineering department at MIT was one of wanting the students to learn. The professors seemed to be there for the purpose of teaching, but doing research also. It gave them pleasure when the students did well. For me, Caltech was the precise opposite. The faculty members in the physics department were all approaching retirement age. They had been Bobby Milliken's bright young kids 30 years before but no longer were. Partly because of the snobbishness of Caltech, I think, they had fallen into the mode of getting their ego satisfaction by making life difficult for obviously capable students.

"It was really at MIT where my competence, particularly in logic, mathematics, and scientific things, was a total asset. At MIT, everyone was delighted if we learned. In the physics department of Caltech, at least at that time, the attitude was, 'We'll begrudgingly give you a degree if you can get it over our dead bodies.' The atmosphere was like a fraternity initiation. I came away from Caltech with exactly what I went there for—but with far greater emotional pain than I had any right to be subjected to. I developed competence in math and physics—the information, the tools, and the techniques. But there's no reason why it couldn't have been more."

In Research Settings

Here, we are looking at institutions consciously designed to promote, foster, and generate new knowledge, primarily university, corporate, and government research laboratories and "think tanks." Whether leader-initiated or emerging from the dynamics of the group itself, research teams at their best develop a synergy that generates a mentoring environment.

Two research teams at the National Institutes of Health had that group synergy for people I talked to.

- Brian's research team had the practice of a daily informal gathering for coffee and discussion. "The leader of the group might throw out the question, 'Well, have we discovered a cure for cancer today?' A very creative discussion would follow. Our mandate was not cancer cures, but this was illustrative of the open-ended agenda of the group, designed to foster the novel, original idea, neither restrained nor constricted by bureaucratic practice."

- Cal had a similar experience when he worked at the NIH during the late 1960s. He was animated and enthusiastic in talking about his team. "There was ferment and excitement as ideas were thrown out, explored, challenged, and developed. Out of this, new directions emerged. At the NIH, I was truly among peers, and everyone was really bright. No longer the 'overachiever,' I actually belonged there and could make things happen. I didn't have to compromise my own standards of excellence; I had the opportunity to be everything I wanted to be. It was one of those chemical reactions with the leader—his abilities and talents meshed with my abilities and talents in a way that was absolutely incredible and synergistic. In one year, I wrote nine papers, and they were first class. It was the medical equivalent of Camelot. We would meet at the end of the day and talk about politics, personalities, who's doing this, the good and the bad—really getting to know how a person thinks. It was the best part of the day for the three or four of us, the half-hour before going home. When my time was up, I chose to stay an optional third year."

Phil found Hughes Aircraft in the 1950s, '60s, and '70s an extremely stimulating environment, "not represented by only one or two but by thousands of outstanding people." The electronics company that inherited the Hughes name was started by Simon Ramo and Dean Woolridge.

"Their conscious strategy was to put together an organization with more technical competence in breadth and depth than any other in the country and then to look for areas of endeavor that could be handled only by that degree of competence.

"They created a multi-thousand-man high-powered team that functioned like a research organization. It wasn't just structured like a research organization, but it had the *personality* of one. The strategy was eminently successful. For a decade and a half, they had an absolute monopoly in the area they chose to move into. The key: They assembled an organization with a tremendous density of outstandingly competent people— Ph.D.s were falling all over each other—and gave those people broad freedom to interact with each other and do their thing.

"After a while, Hughes began to find itself constrained by an overly narrow product line, so we went into several years of frantic diversification and continued to grow. The climate didn't change, though. The breadth of competence and quality of staff and the latitude for individual and small-group freedom led to an outstanding ability to respond to that particular problem. The whole gang went out trying to do things! In a grass-roots way, a broad collection of new product lines emerged. It's neat when you can make a darned good living simply having fun. There's less dog-eat-dog politics in a research-like organization than in a conventional business organization."

Jill went to the Rand Corporation right after college. An economics major, she found the economists at Rand very responsive to her eager questioning. Their response was to share liberally.

"It was not a leader-led group, but rather a bunch of independent thinkers and researchers in a 'think tank' hothouse environment. Just sitting in on staff meetings was stimulating and eye-opening."

In Work Teams
Mentoring environments in work groups are usually leader-initiated, although ad-hoc mentoring environments occasionally spring up spontaneously to meet group needs. They function for problem solving, goal-directed teamwork, and professional development.

An Audit Group
Jim was not conscious of creating a mentoring climate when he was the supervisor of an international audit group for a multi-national company. What happened developed out of group needs and the peculiarities of the job.

"We were a small group, always traveling, always together, living at the same hotel. New people were coming in, and we were getting into new areas. Because personal things would come up and get in the way of our goals and objectives, someone had to be paying attention to the group dynamics.

"'Let's talk, have a beer, or dinner'—the opportunities were always there. We used to say we were shooting at a moving target: 'Here's the objective. But by time we get to the objective in several weeks, we've probably learned so much more about it that we've moved the objective out here.'

"We were always talking to each other. One of the principal tools of the group became known as 'gyration sessions.' Basically, they were brainstorming sessions about what we found, how the business worked, and how to improve operations in this or that department."

An Interdisciplinary Clinical Team

Jillian's mentoring environment helped her to see herself as a professional for the first time. During that early phase of her career in physical therapy, she was a member of an interdisciplinary team in a rehabilitation center, located a couple of blocks from the hospital to which it was affiliated. The group was led by a rheumatologist who insisted that Jillian start making open seminar presentations to the physicians and other professionals. Jillian's background was unique; she hadn't realized that muscle physiology wasn't being taught in medical school.

"For the first time, I began interchanging at a collegial level. Rehab fostered that because of the isolation from the hospital. People spent blocks of time there, and the administrator was a great believer in the power of food for facilitating conversation—there were luncheon meetings and breakfast meetings. I felt very much a peer, very collegial; we were all on same level. It was like being in a sorority again. Our interests were mutual but at this different level—professional as well as personal. Without even knowing it, I intuitively accepted the fact that I was a professional."

Educational Administration

As an assistant principal of her high school, Lila was part of the administrative team consisting of the principal and the four assistant principals.

"We are a real team: We work together, help each other out, bounce ideas off of each other, and do a lot of sharing. We have a close and mutually supportive relationship. We sit around a table in administrative meetings, and there's a lot of give and take, exchanges of information and ideas. My principal fosters that environment."

Nursing Management

Sherry had a similar experience with a nursing management group at her hospital. The mentoring environment developed after some group work with a management consultant.

> "I feel I can go to other group members with problems, and it's reciprocal. I draw learning from their problems and even help solve them. We bring up things in the group: 'This is bothering me. What can I do about this? Does anybody … ?' And now, we share a lot of things. Another nurse manager will call me on the phone and say, 'I have one of your employees over here, and there's something that I want to check out with you.' I don't think we would have dreamed of doing that before.

> "So the group is a support for what we're doing. We're acting both as managers and as responsible people, supporting each other. It's helped me a lot with the frustrations over our jobs."

In Professional Groups

Professional groups are associations of people in one or more related disciplines that come together for information exchange, colleagueship, and professional development. Many of these groups function as an information exchange and a means of networking. Occasionally, such groups have a strong mentoring component. Here are examples from two professional fields:

Medical Administrators

Sam was elected to what he calls "the Cadillac of medical administrators," a group limited to 50 physicians in key administrative positions in medical schools, insurance companies, public health schools, and the like. They would meet every year to discuss what was happening from their perspective and to focus on a particular problem.

> "It is exciting to be around a group of people who are self-confident enough that they are not talking to try to fill their ego needs. All of us have arrived at the top of our fields and are not stepping on anybody or trying to dominate the conversation."

Ministerial Group

Lyle found that being part of the ministerial group was "a splendid mentoring experience." A retired minister from an old distinguished family in the denomination had financed the program. He put up the money to have all of the ministers in the Northwest come together once a year for a seminar that they put together themselves.

> "There were about six of us at the time. We preached to each other and did a critique of each other. We did it without any one-upmanship. I got to know ministers with a variety of skills and styles. There was a very successful minister in Portland, a humanist minister in Spokane, and a not-so-great preacher but very able personal-relations minister in Bellevue. My encounters with those ministers had a lot of meaning for me."

In Other Settings

Families

A good example of a family mentoring environment is described in Katharine Hepburn's autobiography.[22] She describes her family pattern growing up. Her father, a doctor, chose to leave his practice at 4 p.m. every day to be with and get to know his children. She conveys the sense of excitement, of thrilling everyday experiences that were life-venturing, exploring, expanding, risking, skill-developing, courage-building, and brimming with fun.

---

[22] Katharine Hepburn, *Me*, Ballantyne Books, 1991.

Trish was part of a close-knit family of eight brothers and sisters with parents who were very active in transmitting values and providing guidance, coaching, and structure. Her parents always pushed the children to try to do the best that they could and to be honest. Family ties remain very strong, and Trish has maintained close relationships with her brothers and sisters.

In some families, the mentoring environment was most notable around the dinner table. Adrienne came from a family of conversationalists.

> "It was very lively around the dinner table, as quite an assortment of people came to our house. Daddy was an inveterate reader and used to comment on what was in the newspaper over the dinner table. My close cousins were known for being able to talk an ear off a brass monkey. My cousin Charley, who was my father's age, had little formal education; yet, he was one of the best-educated men I ever knew. He had a formidable library of classics and taught himself algebra and geometry. He was an amazing individual, but how he loved to talk! I grew up in that sort of environment."

Affinity Groups

Affinity groups are groups of people who come together because of common interests or needs. Some are planned and structured to provide aid and support for people who are coping with life problems. Examples are bereavement groups, caregiver groups, and men's and women's support groups. Many of these do indeed provide a mentoring environment for members. Other affinity groups simply evolve. Members of groups formed for one purpose sometimes discover that they have other common needs and interests, and the group becomes a mentoring environment in an unplanned way.

Carla found an affinity group at the daycare center where she dropped off her children.

As she picked up her children each day, she gradually became acquainted with other single mothers who also were going back to school and tooling up to move on. They were the ones who convinced Carla that she could do it too, showed her how, and supported her in her process. "I met so many wonderful women who were in a similar boat and were so supportive of each other. That has to be one of the most positive times in my life. I really began developing myself."

Subgroups in college can provide an environment where, for the first time, the young people feel they fit in and really belong.

Natasha recalls, "For the first time, I identified myself as an artist. All these people were very rich in their ability, and they had all been misfits in school too. There was ascendancy now for all of us who, in high school, felt outside the circle. We suddenly came into our own. It was an excellent program, 18- and 19-year-olds finding themselves, deciding what we were going to be. We were all in the same place, and we all generated off each other. When I meet people now from that period, they all seem to have remained with the art or music they started out in."

Lucy felt very much alone at the denominational college she attended until she joined the staff of the college magazine. At this time in her life, she was questioning her faith and her church. The college magazine staff gave her something she had never had before: a group environment where she could fit in and flourish.

"I'd always been a loner in high school. It was my way of handling all the chaos. I was in this church group that believed one thing, but I grew up around kids who believed in something else. In college, I began to question the church and, by sophomore year, had a lot of doubts.

"When I joined the college magazine staff, I got in with a bunch of very creative people who were also very disaffected. This was a renegade group—they were doing the same questioning as I was, and they were the intellectuals of the school. Not only did I belong, but it was there that I acquired my identity as an English major and writer—what I wanted to be."

A MENTORING CULTURE

Some of us find mentoring environments that are broader than institutions, as immersion in a totally different culture turned out for Brian during his year in Israel and for Julia in Chicago.

Brian went to Israel in the 1950s, right out of high school, along with other teens from his hometown Zionist group. For him, the history, the language, and the total culture were mentoring.

"The world of my group in high school was very narrow. Those were the Eisenhower years. I felt stultified but knew there was something else out there. I'm from a Jewish family, but I didn't know what it meant to be religious. When I was 15 years old, I got involved with a Zionist group. They were the most wholesome people I'd been exposed to, so I changed focus. After high school, I left for Israel for a year. I studied for six months in Jerusalem and then three months in one kibbutz and three in another.

"It was the most wonderful thing you can imagine. Here's this kid from a town in New Jersey out in this new country that has this tremendous enthusiasm. It was all so wondrous, beautiful, very exotic—camels, Bedouins, war. I was learning another language, a whole different culture. It was incredible.

"There was constant stimulation. Seven or eight times during the year, we went on weeklong trips in open trucks just to explore the country. A couple of soldiers with rifles and maybe a guide or two came with us. These guides were university students. ... You'd look over the plain of Galilee, and they'd say, 'You see that part over there? That's where David brought his army, and that's where so-and-so had a battle.' Suddenly, history comes alive. I gained an understanding of what it is to be Jewish and what it's like to live in another culture. My social contacts changed, and my whole focus of what I wanted to do in life changed."

Julia's mentoring environment was the cosmopolitan culture of Chicago. She commuted two days a week to Rush University from her small city in Indiana for graduate work in dietetics. Her mentoring environment was broader than the university and the medical center — it was the big city of Chicago that was, for her, "the Emerald City!"

"It was the most stimulating thing in the world for me to go to this big city where so many things were available. The academic environment was tremendous. Rush was associated with a large medical center, and they had medical students, nursing students, and biochemistry students in all kinds of graduate programs. It was just this really rich environment. The people in Valparaiso would say, 'What are you doing, going off to the big bad city of Chicago? It's such an awful place to be.' But to me, it was the Emerald City. I was meeting people my own age who were single. I ended up getting a job at that same medical center."

SELF-GENERATED MENTORING ENVIRONMENTS

Two people I talked to had self-generating mentoring patterns dating from childhood. We will meet both of them in the next chapter on self-mentoring, but here, I want to cite their creativeness in developing their own mentoring environments when they were young. For Daniel, it was the woods in Michigan; for Wil, the public library.

- The Michigan woods provided a tremendous mentoring environment for Daniel. His family spent vacations there every summer. While other family members would be involved in various recreational activities, Daniel found the woods to be a vast laboratory where he could study natural processes in the wild, a place where he could record and sketch his findings. Here, he could follow his curiosity and explore the secrets of life. In the woods and by himself, Daniel created a mentoring environment particularly suited to his needs and interests.

- The public library provided a mentoring environment for Wil. He was foreign born, dressed "funny," and didn't fit in well with a lot of kids in the neighborhood. So after school, he would go to the library and stay there until dinnertime, reading everything in sight that seemed of interest. First, he started with the boys' magazines and adventure stories, "the stuff that kids read." Then, he branched out as he learned of the rich resources that libraries provide. This started a library-use pattern that has continued throughout his life. Although he did not have many friends, he found the librarians welcoming and sympathetic and the library "a pretty nice place to be."

BRIDGE

Environments are a potential mentoring source that many of us have never considered. Broadening our outlook on mentoring environments, as well as mentoring experiences, allows us to see additional sources that are potentially mentoring and can add richness and depth to our Mentoring Mosaic. Knowing about mentoring environments can help us in several ways. We can:

- review our experience, identify any mentoring environments in our lives, and consider what being in that setting has meant to us;
- make the most of a mentoring environment that we happen to be in, knowing that it is likely to be time-limited;
- identify potential mentoring environments in the future so as to fully utilize them and engage in the process they offer;

- examine what makes an environment a mentoring one, knowing that sometimes we can convert a neutral environment to one that is more mentoring; and
- understand, as a manager, the ingredients of a mentoring climate and ways it might be fostered in a work group.

You can inventory your own mentoring experiences and environments via the guiding questions in Chapter 19. In the next section, we look at self-mentoring—first at the role of mentoring play, and then at self-mentoring strategies. We start with the significance of play in our lives and how it can play such a vital part in our mentoring life.

Chapter 17

SELF-MENTORING BEGINNINGS

Mentoring play and mentoring interests are self-generated. They are discovered by the young person alone, on his or her own initiative, or stimulated by teachers, parents, and others. Whatever the source, the interest is acquired, expanded, or transformed by the person. Interests are "mentoring" when they have impact on the direction or development of the young person. They might start as time-fillers—something to do to keep from being bored. They could start as a genuine curiosity to find out more about things, people, and the world around. They can come from motivation to develop skills, to learn how to do something, or to excel in some talent. They seem to develop naturally from the child's curiosity, if that is not stymied by other factors.

In this chapter, we turn the spotlight on mentoring indicators that come from early forms of play, the activities and interests we engaged in because of the fascination and enjoyment that they gave us. In other words, we'll look at the meaning of our play and interests *then*, the insights we have about the place of play in our lives *now*, and the relevance of it all to our mentoring process.

Mentoring play and mentoring interests are intertwined. The difference between the two is subtle and not crucial. As kids, we "played" baseball, board games, house, dress up, tennis, and dolls. We "played in" the woods, the orchestra, the field, and the empty lot. We were "interested in" nature, stamps, history, reading, dancing, singing in the choir, tinkering, and building things. We "liked to" sew, construct, swim, explore nature, hike, debate, write poetry, watch TV, organize clubs, learn things, and look at the stars. Whatever language we use, the key is that the activities or interests we pursued were those that we chose.

We want to canvas our history for those play forms that developed into longer-term interests versus those that are present to some degree in one phase of life and then seem to drop away naturally. We can follow the threads: Some early interests are dropped or discarded while others are woven into more complex patterns. Short-lived play phases have no particular mentoring meaning; other play phases develop into enduring mentoring interests.

In order to take full charge of our own mentoring, we need to be aware of our internal resources and take a thoughtful inventory of our own beginnings toward self-mentoring. Because they come from deep inside ourselves, mentoring play and mentoring interests constitute the beginnings of self-mentoring. We are tapping into a wondrous creative core of ourselves, a core on which we can consciously build mentoring strategies.

But we also want to note early interests that were shelved because of external pressure or lack of support. Those interests can resurface in later life and become compelling.

Not many of us are well connected to the spontaneous natural child we were when we were little before the socialization process started shaping us toward culturally approved goals. If we wish to heed Joseph Campbell's urging to "follow your bliss," or Castaneda's call to find the path with a heart, we may be helped as we rediscover the child within.[23]

---

[23] Joseph Campbell's famous quote is from *Power of Myth*, NY: Doubleday, 1988, p.148; Carlos Castaneda's equally famous question about the "path with a heart" is from *The Teachings of Don Juan: A Yaqui Way of Knowledge*, 30th anniversary edition. Berkeley: University of California Press, 1998, p. 82; and the "child within" is from Emily Hancock's, *The Girl Within*, NY: Fawcett Columbine, 1989.

MENTORING PLAY

We look first at mentoring play—the things we do as children on our own time, in our own way, for our own reasons, just because we want to. Although some play is socially programmed, much of it is not. If we look deeply, we could make some real discoveries. Then, we will look at mentoring interests—both those others might have introduced to us and those we discovered—that we have taken on and developed to make very much our own.

Career Path Indicators in Mentoring Play
Studying Life's Mysteries

Daniel's early memories are of camping out in the woods on the lakes of northern Michigan with his family. He would spend long hours observing nature, sketching, and pursuing his interests through books. He became engrossed in life's mysteries and, in the process, developed a systematic investigative methodology. He would first observe and collect specimens and sketch the phenomena that interested him. Then, if his interest continued, he would pursue library research on the subject when he returned home. He had his own strong internal gyroscope.

> "I'd hit on the idea that I wanted to be a paleontologist, and I'd study fossils for a couple of weeks. Then, I'd turn to weather, minerals, oceanography, and the study of animals. I would pursue it for a couple of weeks, or a summer. Or I'd get interested in something else and do that for a while."

Daniel was a puzzle and frustration for teachers who wanted him to conform to the standard curriculum because he lost interest quickly. But he was a delight to the few who could sensitively listen to him, follow his lead, and provide him with resources to pursue his investigative and creative interests. Then, he would spend long creative and productive hours pursuing his quest.

When I first interviewed Daniel, he was, at 38, a successful emergency medicine physician. His decision to pursue a career in medicine was a direct outgrowth of his childhood interests in the natural world. Yet, when I talked with him a year later, he was restless and unhappy. He and his wife were living on the outskirts of a metropolitan area but were thinking seriously of moving to Idaho or some other far-away place. He was puzzled about his restless state. Here he was, a physician with a promising career—what was wrong with him? I reminded him of his mentoring history and his strong need to be closer to nature. City or even suburban living on the edge of a large metropolis probably would not be sufficient. Daniel nodded, surprised and relieved to recognize the basis for his strong yearning.

Secret Place Underneath the Porch

Diane led a Cinderella-like existence during the Depression. Financially destitute, her family was forced to split up, and the children were parceled out to distant relatives. Diane became a "poor relation" and was made to feel that way. She found a way of coping by making a refuge for herself under the porch of the family's large Victorian home. The porch surrounded the house on three sides and had about eight steps up to the house proper. Under the front porch was a lattice and planting, but around the back of one bush, Diane discovered that the lattices were broken and left just enough space so that she could squeeze underneath. This became her secret retreat and playground.

> "Nobody knew that was my place. That was a secret I kept very well. I used to play school with the little rocks and stones. I never had a doll. I wanted a doll so desperately, I used to make them by cutting them out of the old Sears Roebuck catalogue, and I would teach my paper dolls. I collected stones and set things up like a classroom. I'd have my paper dolls sitting there, and I would teach. I taught everything. In your imagination, you can be almost anything."

Diane was absolutely determined to get an education and become a teacher. She found her way out of poverty and into teaching through a nursing school that would pay for her schooling and provide the means for her to become a nurse. Then, some years later, she became a nurse educator.

My Own Little Rolling Pin

Our third illustration of mentoring play is that of Adrienne. While Daniel followed the beat of his own drummer and Diane struggled on her own, Adrienne was surrounded by adult encouragement and support.

As a little girl, Adrienne would climb up on a stool to watch her mother making bread dough. An older cousin had seen Adrienne working with small pieces of dough to make her own little biscuits. He found a piece of cedar and hand-whittled a miniature rolling pin, then a breadboard, and, finally, a biscuit cutter for her.

> "I remember making my little biscuits and little pie dough. They were probably grubby and gray by the time I got through, but Mother always baked them off for me in a special pan. Then I got to eat them as a tea party with tiny cups at about 10 o'clock every morning. To make my own little biscuits for my tea party was special. I think that sparked my interest in foods at a very early age.

> "Mother never thought it was too much trouble or that I was too awkward to be there. She was very patient with me for all kinds of things. One day, she was called to the phone. She had creamed the sugar and shortening and added the eggs for the cake she was making. I decided that it needed more beating. I beat the tar out of it, and I think it curdled. She came back—I had practically ruined her cake, and she said, 'Oh, dear, we'll have to see what we can do with this.' I made a mess of it, that's for sure."

The experiences of these three people were quite different, but they all were filled with play patterns that eventually propelled each person toward specific career interests. Their mentor-bonding patterns differed, too. Neither Diane nor Daniel developed strong mentor bonds with adults—Diane because of the absence of respect and trust in her treatment as the "poor relation," and Daniel because advice of adults was not relevant and did not mesh with his internal compass-reading. On the other hand, Adrienne had strong mentor bonds with her mother and other adults in the family and a rich pattern of mentoring play that led naturally to her career in dietetics.

<u>Other Examples</u>

As these examples show us, many of us have signals in our play that point toward future career paths. We have seen the foretelling examples of teaching paper dolls and using the little rolling pin. Here are additional examples:

- "From very early childhood, I was always fixing somebody up, somebody who was hurt. I was always wrapping up fingers; somehow I gravitated to medicine."
- "I played with the boy next door. We mostly played war, because this was during World War II. I was going to grow up to be an army nurse, and he would be an army pilot. I did grow up to be an army nurse, and he grew up to be a navy pilot. I think that play had a powerful influence on both of us."
- "When I was 5, I said, 'I want to cook, Mom.' Mom started me cooking with little Pillsbury muffin mixes. In high school, I had a catering business. I kind of fell into it when a neighbor who did entertaining asked me over to help her dish up and serve things. As I got older and more involved in home economics classes, I started to do food preparation and hors d'oeuvres preparation. So, word got around, and I would make canapés for parties and help serve. A career as a dietitian was a natural, bringing together food and nutrition."

- "As a child, I had chalk and a blackboard, and it was great fun to play school. I liked to shape, develop, and mold, and I saw teachers doing that. School and teaching have always been such an important aspect of my own growing up and my own development, and I feel I'm making a real contribution as a teacher."

All of these examples remind us that we need to respect and pay attention to the inner forces that propel each of us to find our "path with a heart." As Castaneda reminds us,

> "Does this path have a heart? If it does, the path is good; if it doesn't, it is of no use. Both paths lead nowhere; but one has a heart, the other doesn't. One makes for a joyful journey; as long as you follow it, you are one with it. The other will make you curse your life. One makes you strong; the other weakens you."[24]

Participation in work and career is rooted in the role of play in human life. The urge toward spontaneity, self-expression, and self-realization is there from the beginning. This sense of wholeness and experience of joy is sought by people in all aspects of life, including work. We are so easily socialized to what others expect of us that we can lose our center. Finding the place of play in our mentoring history can help lead us back. The process of searching for and reconnecting with those deeply engrossing interests of earlier years can guide us in following our bliss.

MENTORING INTERESTS

Mentoring play and mentoring interests are things you do with your discretionary time, because you want to—activities you engage in by choice. You could have started through lessons you were given or

---

[24] Castenada, op. cit., p. 274.

skills you were taught, even reluctantly, but you continue them because of the satisfaction they bring you. The original source could be parents, teachers, siblings, or your own inner motivation, but the key is that you continue them by choice—because they're your discovery, and they give you pleasure.

Use of discretionary time can be suggestive of the person's talents, skills, motivations, and intrinsic interests. At the same time, activities can build skills. Sifting through discretionary activities to identify those that are or have been important can point to roads taken or not taken. Skills sharpened at an early age provide a long span of skill mastery and can account for fast tracking. Latent skills, though not fully tapped, could indicate unacknowledged yearnings for fulfillment. We need to explore what has happened to our interests over time. Are they roads not taken, neglected, stifled, forgotten, or outgrown? Or are they integrated into our present lifestyle?

Mentoring Interests and Skill Development

Mentoring interests in reading, writing, performing, and organizing surface frequently. Those process skills are significant markers for many of us. Here are some examples:

Reading
Reading is an important mentoring interest that, for most of us, dates back to childhood. What we chose to read and the meaning that our reading had for us can be strong indicators of our inner self.

For some, the process of reading was an escape from a difficult family situation or an unaccepting peer group. Lyle read "passionately" from age 7 or 8 onward, stories about young men who led upright, orderly, successful lives. Reading was an escape, giving him another world to live in rather than the one he had immediately around him. Joan found a hidden value in reading. Her mother always wanted to talk to her a great deal, so "I learned how to tune people out, but politely. I was able to satisfy her needs even as I continued my reading while she talked." Still, the content of reading was important to Joan, and she read avidly. Living in a small town did not handicap her reading.

> When she was in high school, Joan said, "I would take in a list of all the books I wanted to read, and the county librarian would order them from the city library and put them on the shelf reserved for me. I was reading things very advanced at an early age, like Winston Churchill's *The Crisis and the Crossing*—very adult books. I'm sure I didn't understand all the implications, but I read them."

Although reading may be an escape *from* a situation, it also can be an escape *to* something new, an opening up of new worlds, ideas, opportunities, and aspirations. As one person put it, "Everything that you read, if you can internalize any of it, becomes an experience that you've had without having to go through it."

- Stan took to reading biographies, right down the shelf. "I've always been fascinated by people. I read all the inventors, and then political types. What was the appeal? In the case of the inventors and explorers, I suspect it was that they did something that had never been done before. For the political figures, it was their influence on large numbers of people, their ability to help improve lives."

- In elementary school, Linda recalls that she "probably read every biography that was ever written about national and international heroes and heroines. Pocahontas, Sacagawea, Lewis and Clark, and many more. People who were achievers. People who might not have known what they were going to accomplish but, because they persevered, did well. They made their mark; they were risk-takers. They didn't sit back and let the world go by."

Writing and Word Games
Writing is another common interest, a lifetime love affair with words. Bruce played word games with his buddy when they rode their bikes around their Texas town. Some days, they would converse in Shakespearean English, another time in a Charlie Chan-type language. Later in the ministry, Bruce used his skills with language in crafting his highly valued sermons.

Vicki always loved words from childhood on: words, roots of words, and even Latin. In school, she would help other people with their papers. Later on, Vicki became the editor of a professional journal.

Lyle's writing interests started in 3rd grade, when his teacher asked the students to write a poem about George Washington.

> "I worked like crazy on it, but the teacher was sure I had copied it from some place. On the one hand, I was downcast; on the other, I was delighted she thought it was a professional poem! Years later, I had three or four short stories published in the college literary journal."

Performing
Performing via dramatics, public speaking, or debating is another way for young people to develop confidence in self-expression as well as developing platform skills. Many of us remember putting on little plays for our family, but a number of us went beyond.

- When she was in grade school, Faith recalls, "The community gave me lots of applause for my performances. I think they had a lot to do with my public speaking today because they were so appreciative. I was better at it than a lot of the kids, so I got more applause." Faith went on to become an entrepreneur.
- "Being on the high school debating team was fun," Ned said. "I think that what I put together in the years of my professional

career as a professor of medicine has required writing, speaking, and performing."

Organizing

A number of interviewees reported organizing "clubs" in childhood groups or otherwise assuming leadership roles in the neighborhood. Mitch's experience was unusual in the development of his organizing and systems skills. He was selected to be the fire marshal in high school. In this role, he completely redesigned the system for evacuating the high school during a fire alarm.

> "It was a three-story, two-square-block school. From the time the signal was given until the school was evacuated, it took 120 seconds. Everybody was out clear in two minutes. When I graduated, I was awarded the medal recognizing the outstanding high school student for both civic and scholarship activities."

Later as a physician, Mitch applied his systems skills and medical knowledge to design one of the early systems for evaluating professional competency in health care under Medicare.

Researching

Claire's enjoyment of researching topics she found interesting in high school foreshadowed her subsequent research career. She became very good at using the university library and the state's history library. When she wrote a term paper on the Pullman strike, she read all the newspapers from Chicago. She found the libraries to be "a fantastic resource."

> "In social science, we had to use the newspaper or talk to people. I interviewed people on some topics. Doing research and reading for a specific purpose was a turn-on. I find it fascinating to spend hours in the library, hunting down things. If somebody cites something, I like going back and looking at the original work to see whether they cited it exactly right or

didn't. I like to see how a thought process progresses through a number of different studies. My interest goes back to the 10th grade. I remember spending time at the State Historical Library. I was studying a number of buildings in Iowa City, where they came from and who built them. I researched the reasons for what happened and why in that library."

Incorporating Interests into Livelihood

Many of us encounter a dilemma when we ponder how to encompass our diverse interests in our livelihood. How can we avoid shutting down some aspects of our self while concentrating on others? Sometimes we shift gears, pursuing one interest into livelihood and then changing downstream, particularly in mid-life. Some of us have followed income-sustaining but unfulfilling career paths. When I talked to Wes, I sensed that he derived little satisfaction from his role as the hospital's chief radiologist. His voice was flat and his responses routine, but his eyes sparkled when he talked about his choral music. "I just love to sing," he said, and he was just waiting until retirement years to devote himself full-time to music.

The need for options, choice, and diversity is a concern of many of us and influences our decision-making and the further development of our interests. Stan chose genetics as his medical specialty, because he said it would allow him to be "a renaissance man." Ben chose emergency medicine for similar reasons. Ray has a combination role as a practicing internist and director of medical education at a community hospital. He loves the intellectual challenge of his specialty, handling complex diagnostic or therapeutic puzzles. I asked him what drew him into medical education: He said he wanted to improve the educational aspects of academic medicine and added, "There's something about me that wants to keep a foot on both sides of the aisle. I'm more comfortable being a generalist, because I'm interested in a lot of things."

Kay feels strongly about incorporating her interests in her work. She refuses to settle for a narrow career path and positions herself to keep options open. Over the years, she has had a number of roles integrating her policy knowledge, analytical skills, and ability to build coalitions. One early role as aide to a U.S. senator combined all three interests and remains one of her favorite work experiences.

Don considers himself fortunate in finding a career path in architecture that combines his many interests.

> "I was always in the process of creating things, building things, inventing things. I always had projects going. I built one of the first go-carts, just assembled from a bunch of magazine descriptions. I put engines together or built stagecoaches for my sister. Our school was very small—only 13 in my graduating class—so I took a lot of correspondence courses in languages and art from the University of North Dakota. I was interested in those subjects, but they weren't available in the school system locally.

> "One of the first things I wanted to be was a carpenter or artist, and an architect is a kind of combination. Architecture was totally devouring, allowing me to do the kinds of things I like to do, like designing and art, creating things. I enjoy conceptualizing and taking a holistic view of a project. I get great satisfaction from coming up with concepts and ideas and then putting them on paper in unique ways."

Finding Your Interests

Don searched for a profession that would allow him to reach out into many different fields. He, too, is hooked on learning and doesn't want to be limited. He finds that his many interests can be encompassed in his chosen career of architecture. But what if you don't know what your interests are? This can happen. We are so affected by social conditioning that we might not be in touch with our inner self.[25]

Russ stumbled onto a strategy that helped him. By the age of 26, he was highly successful making money in the record industry, but he also was dissatisfied. What he was doing wasn't fulfilling. He realized that to have a satisfying life, he had to discover what he liked to do. So he decided to keep track of when he started to get bored and what he moved on to next. What he liked most, he discovered, was reading and writing, so he taught himself to write. He pursued chains of reading: He read a history of World War II, which, in turn, interested him in World War I, which, in turn, interested him in the Franco-Prussian War, which, in turn, interested him in Bismarck. In time, this led him to negotiate an unconventional graduate program of his design with Harvard and move into a more personally rewarding career as an organizational consultant.

Weaving together mentoring interests can be a long, involved, and circuitous process, as Gloria discovered. By the time I met Gloria, she had incorporated several mentoring interests into a satisfying career, with management training playing an important part. She speaks of an early interest in teaching and dance:

> "I've wanted to be a teacher for as long as I can remember. I used to set up all my dolls and teddy bears, and I was the teacher. I went through the whole routine. I had a natural flair for it."

Another early interest was ballet, and she loved both performing and teaching. Clearly she had organizing ability, because from age 14 to 17, she ran her own ballet studio. "I

---

[25] Emily Hancock's book, *The Girl Within,* provides some helpful advice to women, especially on countering limiting cultural conditioning. See Hancock, op. cit., p. 274.

had recitals, rented a hall, and had the kids' mothers make costumes—the whole thing," she recalls. "It never occurred to me that I couldn't do it; I was extremely successful." That lasted until she married at age 17.

At this point, Gloria's path has taken many turns, including children, secretarial work, and, ultimately, divorce. With education a high priority, she pursued studies when she could, some years later receiving her doctoral degree. She also advanced in her work in a health maintenance organization from secretarial to analytical work, and then to an administrative post. On the strength of her presentation on how to write a job description, she was asked if she would like to become a training analyst. Her convoluted path came back to her "heart." As she has moved up further in management, teaching and speaking have continued to be hallmarks of her career.

Discovering Your Own Mentoring Interest Pattern

For some of us, our interests are clear and continue from childhood on. In the previous examples, we noted several patterns. Daniel's mentoring play in the Michigan woods continued naturally in a more complex progression. Although his particular focus of study shifted over time, his process was enduring. In contrast, Diane's teaching interest, starting with paper dolls, persisted and became more sophisticated over time. The teaching mode was always there. Don's pattern of creating and constructing diverse forms became well-expressed in his architectural career.

But for many of us, the picture is not so clear. Exploring one's mentoring history is a bubbling-up process, with new discoveries surfacing when you least expect them. That happened when I was talking with Donna about her childhood play.

Around 5th grade, she recalls, "I would have friends over, and the kids would say, 'I wish we had something or other to play with.' I'd say, 'I'll make something. You go off and play.' Using

Erector sets and the little red blocks of American bricks, I built things for others to use in our play process later. I built toy furniture for my tiny houses, painted them, sewed dresses for my Barbie doll, made a lot of things that the group could play with."

When I spoke to Donna, she was an organizational psychologist reexamining her life and career. She had just moved into a new home and felt herself in some sort of life-changing process. At the end of our time together, I was "reading the tea leaves" from our discussion. I told her:

"What is curious for me is the thread you have in mentoring play of making things to fit. That's something unusual for a child to do over a period of time. I would encourage you to do more thinking about those interests. Maybe some of those craft skills will weave into your life now in some way. Roads not taken at one time could be worth exploring now."

"It's curious that you say that," Donna responded, "because I've been looking at courses lately. I think I want to do something practical, take a carpentry course or stained glass—something I could do with the house since I'm into my house these days. You know, it's funny. I *do* feel I'm unfolding; I'm exploring and seeing things quite differently."

BRIDGE

There is value in exploring childhood interests and play in order to find those threads that can tell us more about our own "path with a heart." These explorations can help us understand our roads taken and not taken, and can help us follow our bliss. In the next chapter, we will explore self-mentoring strategies, those methods and devices we have developed on our own to help us learn, grow, accomplish, and develop. By inventorying and cataloguing these strategies, some of which we are only dimly aware, we lift them up for more conscious and systematic use in managing our own mentoring.

Chapter 18

SELF-MENTORING STRATEGIES

When you want to learn something, find something out, or make a difficult choice, how do you go about it? Do you talk to people, take a class, go to the library, read a book, check the Internet, or figure it out yourself? All of these are self-mentoring strategies, because they actively involve you in providing your own guidance and direction. You can greatly increase your effectiveness if you augment those natural approaches through conscious action. The spate of literature about finding a mentor ignores the need that all of us have for self-mentoring. Even in the best of worlds, a mentor is there only part of the time. The only one you can count on continuously is yourself.

In this chapter, we focus on self-mentoring strategies that you initiate and use repeatedly to learn something, explore options, develop skills, make connections, get support, identify goals, or make decisions— those self-guiding methods that you often use to find direction and solve problems. Whether you picked up the strategies from others or developed them on your own, they are now self-generating. You have the ability to use them, and you do so whenever it suits you.

Non-Bonders and Their Self-Mentoring Strategies
Although we all have built self-mentoring strategies to some degree, we can learn from people who have developed them to a high level. Many non-bonders have highly sophisticated self-mentoring strategies. They can point the way to identifying self-mentoring strategies we have or could develop.

Even the most sophisticated self-mentoring strategies are described by their users in unassuming terms. Their language is modest. In describing what they do, they will use such words as "I figured it out," "I tinkered," and "I taught myself." Only when you listen more deeply do you see the package of skills involved. Here are two illustrative examples of how individuals identified their needs and developed strategies to reach their objectives.

Wil's pattern was to zero in on a field of interest; read extensively in technical journals, books, and government reports; identify the key players and then strategize how to meet them to obtain information; and analyze and integrate all the data. Here is how he went about it when he wanted to build a television station.

"I got to the point where I prepared an application to build a television station in another state. Typically, this was done through attorneys and engineers. Well, I didn't have any money for attorneys and engineers, so I had to rely on myself. This process dragged out over a period of years, and, ultimately, it became apparent that competition was an issue and there would be hearings. So, I thought, 'Hell, if there are going to be hearings held, that means that I'm going to have to prepare myself and learn what hearings are all about.'

"So I started tailing the Federal Communications Commission regional examiner, who subsequently became a friend of mine. When he'd go to places like San Francisco, Portland, and Seattle for hearings on competitive issues, he'd look around, and there I would be, sitting in the hearing room. He probably wondered, *Who is this kid who is following me around the country?*. I just taught myself what the process was, and, instead of spending tens of thousands of dollars hiring attorneys and engineers, I did it myself. I already had the engineering background, but I improved on that as well in order to get myself ready. On the legal issues, I got all the books I could on the subject, all of the reports, and all of the orders of the FCC. I became a kind of curbstone attorney on communications law and was rather knowledgeable in that field.

"Years later, I found myself representing my own interests in a hearing involving outfits like Paramount, 20th Century Fox, CBS—all of whom brought in big-shot attorneys, engineers, and other highly paid professionals. And there I was, working with and against them on the basis of my scant knowledge of the subject based on gleanings."

Anna is an independent healthcare entrepreneur. She is newer in her career than Wil is in his, but she is clearly on a self-mentoring track. It is not surprising to hear her say that most of her education in college was self-learning.

"I went out and arranged a lot of my own experiences. I went to the medical school, found out about the nutrition classes, and took those. Then, I found out about a psychiatrist who was doing research, went out to his hospital to meet him, and figured out something I could work with him on and get credit for. All of this was done on my own. No one ever said, 'Here are these opportunities. Maybe you want to take advantage of them.'"

Differences in the Self-Mentoring Approaches of Bonders and Non-Bonders

Mentor bonders and non-bonders have differences in the nature and process of self-mentoring. Bonders are more likely to start out with people connections because they are comfortable in relating to them. Later in the process, they make the bridge to non-people resources. Shelley said, "I try to think who would be the best person to help me." She trusts and values people and has found them to be helpful and resourceful in any project she has undertaken. Shelley does not lean on or abuse this connection with people; she honors and respects and is given respect in turn.

Non-bonders, like Wil, are more likely to do the reverse since it does not occur to them to reach out to people as sources of help. They tend to use people in a limited way as sources of information in order to avoid raising issues of trust and control. Then, there are many in the middle, who like doing things on their own but can also connect easily to mentors and are able to go either way, depending on their needs and the resources available.

A COLLECTION OF SELF-MENTORING STRATEGIES

Self-mentoring strategies generally fall into the major mentor action categories of teacher, counselor, and guide. However, it is rather the *process* of how we make choices, teach ourselves, make connections with others, and guide ourselves that is unique. The focus here is on what we choose to combine together in our methodology, and how simple or sophisticated the process is.

Networking

We start with networking, a self-initiated strategy that is used for multiple purposes: to learn, to gain access to information and resources, to make connections, and to build relationships. Although networking as a strategy is used heavily in the professional, business, and career arenas, it can be equally important in building social networks and support systems.

Some of us are great networkers; others scarcely at all. How we develop and use our networking systems varies from intuitive beginnings to purposeful strategies and everything in between. Your networking practice can be as informal as asking yourself, "Who do I know who could help me with this?" and mentally sifting through your network database. Or, it can be a systematic process followed throughout your career and your life. In view of the rapid changes in our world, networking as a mentoring strategy is coming into its own. We need to know current networking uses and practices in order to make this a more conscious mentoring strategy. For details and examples, see

Chapters 24 and 25. Meanwhile, here is one example of networking as a planned strategy to learn, make connections, and seek advice.

> Evie was the nursing in-service director when she was asked to take on the additional responsibility of management development for her hospital. In this new role, she would have a reporting relationship to the hospital administrator. Evie felt inadequate for this new assignment and sought every means possible to learn. That was the motivation behind the networking system she developed in national and international training associations, a system that she maintained for 20 years.

> "I pushed myself. I made sure I signed up for early bird registration in order to get advance information on speakers and exhibitors. I would pore over the materials and ask myself, What do I need this year?, so that I could justify to the hospital administrator the use of my time in relation to hospital goals. By the time I got to a conference, I had a roadmap."

> At each conference, Evie made a point of meeting and talking to speakers. She also collected an assortment of conference materials for her own learning and to share with her staff and colleagues. She kept track of her networking contacts through business cards organized by category of interest or specialty and became known for her knowledge of and access to training resources and leaders in the field.

Self-Tutoring

"I figured things out … " is a self-learning approach used by many non-bonders, but it certainly is not exclusive to them. You'll hear the phrase repeated over and over, "I taught myself." All of us have some skills in self-learning. I cannot imagine anyone really using a computer who hasn't had to do a lot of self-learning with the help of instruction manuals and experimenting. Children automatically experiment. My grandson Michael uses a lot of intuitive strategies to figure out how computer games work. In fact, when he was about 10 years old, he was one of a group of children from his school chosen by a production company to test a new computer game.

Non-bonders are particularly good at figuring things out on their own from reading or by experimentation. This was Lewis' lifelong practice, including learning to ride a motorcycle when he was in his middle years. Not influenced by others, self-mentors can see things in a new light. Lewis, for instance, was one of the first psychotherapists to link existential philosophy and psychology, a truly creative breakthrough in the field. I am impressed with the use of this strategy by people who break new ground, whether as pioneers, theorists, innovators, entrepreneurs—or early leaders of our country. Benjamin Franklin, whose pioneering breakthroughs are history, consciously developed self-mentoring strategies early in life through his "Path of Self-Improvement."[26] George Washington "mulled over" his experiences in the French and Indian War:

> "As his character and his world view expanded, more meanings became clear to him. He accurately defined his failures and worked out the reasons why he had failed. This protracted self-education was to provide the greatest importance to the creation of the United States."[27]

Observing

"I watched how they did things ... " Learning by observing others can be very helpful in developing our own skills and style.

- Elise found observing helpful in understanding the details of a job. The summer after freshman year, she wanted to get a summer job waitressing at Lake Tahoe, but had never been a waitress in her life. She sat down in a restaurant and watched

---

[26] Walter Isaackson, *Benjamin Franklin*, Simon & Shuster, 2003, p. 47–51.

[27] James Thomas Flexner: *Washington: The Indispensable Man*, Boston: Little, Brown & Co., 1969, p. 38.

everything for a couple of hours and went back the next day to apply. "They asked, 'Have you had experience?' And I said, 'Oh, sure!' Just having kept my eyes open and then asking a lot of questions."

- Fernando consciously observed teachers to see which teaching styles he liked and would be right for him.
- Watching how people handled or failed to handle administrative and interpersonal matters influenced Paul's leadership style.

Observing also can be useful in learning about power and other more covert aspects of organizational life.

- Molly found it useful to observe behavior "in the room at the top, where power was, and how it was used."
- Liz needed to pick up administrative knowledge fast when she received a major promotion. She especially sought to understand the power behavior in her organization by observing others in meetings. "But you can't let some people know you're observing them because things are so sensitive."

Listening

Related to observing is listening. Early in life, Paul learned from his mother the importance of social approval. This led Paul into a life pattern of listening to people "to figure out where they were coming from and engaging them"—in college, in his psychiatric practice, and later in leadership roles in the mental health field.

Interviewing

Elise was able to put to good use the interviewing skills she developed on a high school research project years later when she was applying to medical school. Here is how she prepared:

"The year before I applied to medical school, I knew I would be asked all kinds of questions, like 'What are you going to do if your kid gets sick, lady?' and 'How are you going to put your life together?' —at the time, those kinds of questions were still legal. Well, I spent six months before my interviews talking to every woman doctor I could get my hands on: How do you do it? How do you have a family? Who cooks? I asked about what to think about things, how I should act on an interview, what I should wear, should I wear nail polish— very specific questions. From a composite of women, I put together what I felt worked for me, how I could talk about medicine and me. And frankly, I have lived out that story.

"I said I wanted to go through medical school single, that I would get married sometime, hopefully, after that, and that when I had small children, I would stay at home or work part-time. When they went to school, I'd go back to work full-time. Plus I wanted to go into academic medicine. And those are exactly the things I've done."

Researching

We can research in many ways. Non-bonders, in particular, have developed a unique process that works for them. Starting as a child, Daniel systematically observed and collected specimens, sketched the phenomena that interested him, and pursued library research on those subjects. We learned about Wil's approach earlier in this chapter.

A great many of us, bonders as well as non-bonders, use the resources of the Internet as our own reference library, experimenting with search engines and Web sites to find the access method of choice. Jill found most of the demographic and economic data she needed for her research on the Web. Jim uses it regularly to keep up with trends in the financial planning field.

Scanning

"Scan, soak, and sift" is Julia's more elaborated way of describing scanning as a strategy. Her advice to a young person entering into a professional field is "to have your eyes and ears open and soak up as much as you possibly can of everything. Even though you might not think at the time that this particular area is interesting, it adds to your life and work experiences. Later, you can sift through that stuff and either discard it or use it."

Catching Up

Sometimes, we learn useful strategies by circumstance. For Carl, that was true about "catching up." Carl's work on his family's cotton farm always meant that he started school several weeks behind the rest of the kids. In time, he learned how he could catch up within a few weeks, and this became his pattern. The confidence and skill he developed in "catching up" sustained him in college:

> "It had been a while since I'd taken trig, and when I hit physics, I didn't know what I was doing. I waded through six weeks, working very hard, spending some time with the teacher. I was persistent enough in laying the groundwork that, suddenly, everything came together. It became easy from then on. With very difficult things, I try to weave together the pieces. In time, I know it's going to click, and everything is going to be all right."

Paul had a similar experience when he was late joining his medical school class at Yale.

> "I learned the technique of skimming textbooks and got so I could summarize the content in outline form. Then, I would review notes and distill them so there was one key word that would stimulate my mind about the content and lead to a whole expansion of a given topic area."

Benchmarking

Another self-mentoring strategy involves social comparison: "If he can do it, so can I!" Benchmarking is the comparison and challenge you feel when you see a colleague reaching for a goal, and you know that if you apply yourself, you can be there, too. The person is close enough to you in competency and experience that the goal is attainable for you.

Benchmarking was a motivating force for Lil. She remembers a 3rd grade friend who did well on the spelling tests, while she did not. She was surprised to learn that if she spent a little time, she could do the same thing. Something similar happened in college. Lil had a mindset that she couldn't do well in math. Her college roommate served both as inspiration and competition: When they signed up for the same math course, Lil took up the challenge and found that she, too, could be successful.

A word of caution, of course: To be a positive strategy, benchmarking must balance inspiration and competition. Competition by itself can become destructive. In Lil's case, the competitive urge is positive and well-managed, and it drives her. She referred to another person she had met only once as "a kind of mentor" for her. Although Lil has had no on-going personal contact, she said, "I feel so competitive with this woman, it drives me crazy!" The other woman lives at the other end of the country, specializes in sports nutrition, and is frequently published in the literature. "Every time I see a new publication of hers or see her name somewhere, it just gives me a little kick in the behind and tells me to get moving."

Analytical Problem-Solving
A number of us have developed high-level skills in analyzing and solving problems. Dave developed these skills in high school. He had a teacher who challenged students with research problems, requiring them to go out into the community to collect data and then figure out, for instance, how the traffic signals are programmed to work. Puzzle-solving has become a life identity for him.

"Put a puzzle in front of me, and I just love to have at it. Jigsaw, crossword, and complex puzzles. Trying to analyze the society, or a family, or the company of which I am a part. I get my kicks out of finding the order in what appears to most people as sheer chaos. I'll find the order if it's there."

Imaging and Trying Out

Two ways people have for testing their interest in a possible future are by imaging and by trying out. Imaging is mentally picturing the desired goal or outcome, to test it for fit. Trying out involves working in an environment or in a job on a trial basis to check how well it meshes with one's interests and values, or perhaps taking a class in a new field. This is particularly useful if the desired role or environment represents significant career preparation or change in lifestyle.

All is well with Sherry when she has a clear and positive picture of a goal:

> Sherry's mother always stressed that Sherry should have practical goals. Sherry developed a talent for "picturing" to guide her to such goals. When it came time for her to think of a career path, Sherry talked to her dental assistant cousin and could visualize that as a good job to have if she married and had a family. But Sherry couldn't get into the program she wanted. At a college orientation session, a friend described the things that her mother did as a dietitian. "That picture just clicked in my head," Sherry said, and she happily followed that career path.

> Several years later, her mentor urged her to take a position with the county government, because the mentor was sure that Sherry would like the teaching. At first, Sherry resisted because, she said, "I had this picture in my head of the county as a terrible place to work." With more information and discussion, she developed a more positive image and became successful as the dietetic internship director of the county hospital.

Trying things out is useful in many settings. Kay decided to audit a German course to see if she wanted to study the language seriously.

Jim applied his finance and accounting skills broadly in several organizational settings before settling into his partnership. Adrienne took a job in a hospital to see if she really liked it. Daniel took a year off to work in a hospital to test his interest in clinical medicine. John provides one more example:

> In his residency year in medicine, John found the medical school of no help in guiding him to promising jobs. The rest of his class went into academic medicine, but he knew he didn't want that. Instead, he became "the moonlighting king" during his residency year, working in other hospitals during his time off in order to see what jobs were available and how he liked the work. As a result of his experience, he decided to practice emergency medicine in a suburban community hospital.

Identifying and Meeting Expectations

Many of us make the connection as small children between what we do and what people approve of. Many of us develop a life-long pattern of meeting adult expectations. Jenna in law school and Paul in medical school used well-honed strategies to become acquainted with their professors, find out their expectations, and become more visible. Pam, a college junior, follows a similar strategy:

> "The first couple of weeks of school, I go in every week or so to talk to the professor. I ask questions, even if I'm making them up, just talking about the literature. I let him get to know me, and I get to know him. A lot of students don't know the teacher; I can't understand that. Getting to know the teacher is half the battle, and studying is just minor in comparison. Besides, most of the professors are brilliant people and have a lot to share."

As adults, we can usually choose when and how to use these skills in order to maintain a healthy balance of meeting other's expectations and managing our own lives. Occasionally, however, meeting others' expectations can be a burden:

> Early on, Fernando would hear teachers saying, "Well, he's got a spark, he's got something in him." So pretty soon, he

started meeting those expectations, even though he didn't really do things easily. "Most things came very hard," Fernando said, "but if it took 10 hours, I put in 10 hours. It was more about meeting an expectation than learning."

Recognizing Deficits and Finding Remedies

- Sometimes, we reach turning points in our life that call for changes in career or life direction. One common turning point is when we recognize the need for additional education or training—the awareness that you can't do what you want to do without further education.
- Daniel knew he had to go to college when it dawned on him that the things he wanted to pursue could not be obtained without a college education.
- Once Claire got into dietetics, she realized that, if she wanted to be on equal terms with physicians, she needed to be as strong as they were in science. So she started taking courses. She soon realized that if she worked hard at it, she could understand the subject matter and do really well.
- Eloise wanted to do research. Realizing that she didn't have the skills, she entered a doctoral program.

This strategy also can come into play when we seek to make up for deficiencies in our earlier education or life experience. For most of high school, John skipped through academics, favoring instead sports, mechanics, and karate. He had not developed the basic educational building blocks. His biology teacher convinced him that he'd been fooling around long enough and that he had to get on with it.

"I was way behind. I began studying extremely hard, 12 to 14 hours a day. I'd go in, take a test, and still get a C. It took me six months to make up the work. When I started college, I studied harder and got Bs. Then, I took three years of calculus and was the only person in the college to take the second- and third-quarter calculus in the same quarter. I got straight As. Things started to fall into place. I understood what I had to do and what kind of knowledge base I'd need to get something out of life."

Positioning

Over the years, Kay has developed an approach whereby she continues to follow her broad interests through keeping informed and engaging in relevant activities, independent of her current job. In this way, she preserves her options and positions herself for opportunities that may arise—a good reminder from a woman who has repeatedly gone into non-traditional career roles for women.

Drawing from Within

Introspection has to do with looking inward at the conscious thoughts and reflections we have about ourselves and our world, and the way we make decisions. Some of us are very in touch with our thought processes and the logical considerations that have propelled us to choose one academic program over others, one career over another, or one path over another. Others of us seem to be guided by intuitive forces within—responding to the felt sense that a decision, an action, a path is "right" for us. Without necessarily being conscious of it, we are using these intuitive processes—drawing from within—for self-mentoring.

Yvonne has been guided by an intuitive sense of what is right for her, despite contrary attitudes and opinions of family members. Early in her nurses' training, Yvonne was assigned to observe a patient recover from surgery. She stood at the patient's bed.

> "I reached over, and I took a temporal pulse and a pulse in the jaw. I could feel it, and I could count it, and I suddenly realized I was responsible for the well-being of this human being. I was instantly transformed into a nurse! I can remember it so clearly. The sun was coming through the blinds and cast a design on the pillow. It was a warm, quiet afternoon in summer, and I remember realizing this feeling of being responsible for another

person. That was it! From that point on, I was very service-oriented, a total focus from then on. I think it validated me as a human being."

Ned has found a way to dialogue with his "inner voice mentor" on issues with a heavy emotional component, whether personal or work-related.

"I trust my inner voice more. I'll tell myself, 'I don't have all the data, but I don't need it. I'm willing to take a risk and act on this.' I will admit it when a decision has a large emotional component, when the intellectual part is secondary. I previously always felt that the intellectual part should outweigh the emotional. Now, in certain cases, I'm willing to listen more to my heart than my head.

"Earlier, I would not have admitted to myself—and surely not to others—that these were emotional decisions. Somebody asked me the other day, 'Why did you decide that?' And I said, 'I wouldn't be comfortable with it emotionally the other way. I think the other way is probably cheaper, more rational, but I have to live with it.' The way I do it is to project how I'm going to feel if it's the other way. You can't tell for sure in advance how you're going to feel, but I try to put myself there.' "

Combination Strategies

Many of us use multi-stage strategies to pursue a new interest, solve a problem, or make a decision. Recall Wil, whom we met at the beginning of this chapter. When he wants to learn something new or enter a new field, he functions completely on his own. He researches the literature on a field he is interested in pursuing, analyzes the issues, identifies key players whom he observes and/or interviews, does further self-tutoring, and takes action.

In contrast, Hal, whom we will meet in Chapter 27, is equally comfortable in tapping both people and non-people sources of mentoring. He goes through a sequence of research, self-tutoring, and analyzing on his own. Then, if he's really interested, he will seek a teacher or coach to enhance his knowledge and skill development. Hal is flexible: He can relate comfortably to a mentor, and he also can learn on his own.

Although we might not have elaborate self-mentoring strategies to pursue a goal, we will usually develop a combination of skills. Our natural style could be to combine researching and interviewing, observing and imaging, scanning and trying out—and much, much more.

BRIDGE

In this chapter we have explored an array of self-mentoring strategies and hinted at the collection each of us has developed of these strategies. This point in the book also marks the end of Part I, The Mentoring Mosaic, which has encompassed all aspects of our Mentoring Mosaic—mentor bonding, mentoring messages, mentoring models, mentoring relationships, mentoring experiences and environments, and self-mentoring.

In Part II, Enhancing Your Mentoring, the focus turns to you and to the three stages in managing your mentoring—taking stock, surveying trends, and taking action. The first step is to be clear about your current mentoring pattern, and Chapter 19 provides a systematic guide for tracking your mentoring using the framework of the Mentoring Mosaic. The chapters that follow examine mentoring needs in various life stages, trends in our culture that have an impact on mentoring, and, in consequence, the action strategies available to you for managing your mentoring.

PART II
ENHANCING YOUR MENTORING

Chapter 19

IDENTIFYING YOUR MENTORING MOSAIC

Thus far, we have focused on understanding all of the elements that go into the mentoring process and how those pieces fit together, function, and change. We have viewed this as a mosaic with a design unique to each person. With all this as a backdrop, it is time now to focus on *you* and *your* Mentoring Mosaic.

Your Mentoring Mosaic is shaped by your genetic material, by societal influences, and by other external factors. It is created, both consciously and unconsciously, by you. Your one-of-a-kind creation will be dense with design in some areas and thin in others. It is constantly shifting and changing, though the underlying structure remains solid and firm. This chapter provides a systematic way for you to identify your Mentoring Mosaic so that you can tailor a mentoring program to meet your needs.

Understanding your Mentoring Mosaic in all its dimensions can point to ways for increasing the effectiveness of your mentoring. Drawing on your portfolio of mentoring resources, you can utilize the strong parts of your structure, fill out less-developed areas, or experiment with unfamiliar mentoring strategies.

Relying on one mentoring form to manage your mentoring is limiting. With knowledge of your mentoring process, you can see alternate ways to reach your goals. You can select from your cluster of mentoring messages, models, relationships, experiences, and environments, as well as the self-mentoring strategies you have acquired.

But first, you need to catalogue your resources. You can do so by systematically noting your mentoring history, following the framework of the Mentoring Mosaic. I encourage you to create a written record of your survey, making notes or writing a narrative. The guiding steps below follow this sequence:

1. Identify Your Mentor-Bonding Pattern
2. Survey Mentoring Messages
3. Survey Mentoring Models
4. Review Mentoring Relationships
5. Identify Mentoring Experiences
6. Identify Mentoring Environments
7. Tease Out Self-Mentoring Beginnings
8. Review Self-Mentoring Strategies
9. Map Your Mentoring Lifeprint
10. Following Your Path: Life Themes
11. Managing Your Mentoring

1. IDENTIFY YOUR MENTOR-BONDING PATTERN

A good place to start is to review your mentor-bonding pattern. Your pattern of mentor bonding is the definitive influence on how prominent people mentors will be in your life and what form your mentoring takes. It also is likely to influence self-mentoring strategies you develop, and it could spill over into other design elements as well.

Was yours a strong mentor-bonding pattern? Did you have relationships with adult figures that were respectful, trusting, and relevant—or was that a missing part of your early years? If you are like most of us, yours is a mentor-bonding pattern. How would you describe it? What were the characteristics and gender of your early mentors? How have those features been replicated in later mentors? Was one mentor form—traditional, step-ahead, or co-mentors—dominant? Has that changed over the years? If only one gender, or one mentor form, would you be enriched if you sought mentors outside of that range?

Or was yours a non-bonding pattern? Did you find the major adult figures in your early life not respectful or trustworthy, or their advice not relevant to your world? If so, your mentoring relationships are likely to be sparse, non-existent, or more of a step-ahead or co-mentoring kind. The bonding part of your mentoring design will be thin, but your self-mentoring portion will be rich with actualities and possibilities. You might find that other elements more than make up the difference, particularly mentoring experiences and self-mentoring strategies—those ways you have developed to learn on your own, by yourself.

Looking at your non-bonding pattern provides you with a chance to reflect. With your current wisdom and maturity, you might want to develop some mentoring relationships that could be helpful but not confining or controlling. Should you decide to do so, you will have to do it consciously, as it is not likely to come naturally. Chapters 25 and 26 have suggestions for you.

2. SURVEY MENTORING MESSAGES

Even if we try, we can scarcely avoid receiving messages about ourselves, other people, and the environment; about our competence and prospects; and about what we should be or do with our lives. Messages are a major source of our values. We need to sort through them to understand their impact on our lives, positive and negative, and test them for relevance and appropriateness today.

You might want to list important messages by sender and message, marking their importance and the degree of power they carry. Take note of the messages that sustain you, that make you feel good about yourself and your world, messages that you want to keep, that you treasure as a source of your values.

Examine the negative messages: Are they reality-based and important to attend to if you temper them? Which ones deflate you and tear you down? Which ones can you easily discard? Which have such a strong negative valence that discarding them is not all that easy?

Which messages—both positive and negative—are relevant to your world and your work today and where you hope to be tomorrow? Which can you set aside as no longer meaningful in today's world? Can you reframe some of the negatives to take out the sting? Consider how you can use the positive messages to reinforce your feelings of competence and self-worth.

Finally, what are the messages you currently receive from your circle of friends, family, acquaintances, bosses, and colleagues? Are you in an environment where negative messages pollute the environment? What can you do to deflect, dismiss, or otherwise soften toxic messages? To what extent do you set yourself up for such messages? What do you make of your overall message pattern? The following "Steps for Managing Mentoring Messages" on page 310 may be helpful to you in answering these questions.

Steps for Managing Mentoring Messages

—Evaluate message relevance
Sift through the messages to identify those that have particular power, that have either a strong positive or negative charge. Examine the nature of the message, its history, and the time and circumstances when it was received:
- How was it communicated?
- What was said/done, and what meaning did you make of it?
- To what extent has it been a positive force in your life?
- What are your feelings about the sender(s)?

—Honor the positive message and its sender
Take time to savor positive messages. Review those special messages in your life and their meaning to you both then and now.

—Discard, reframe, or defuse negative messages
Examine the history of negative messages that had a strong impact on you. Such an examination can help you decide which messages to reinterpret or modify and which to discard. Reframe messages so they square more with present-day reality and with what you want to accomplish. You can remove much of the negative sting and restate them in a way to provide needed guidance yet sustain self-worth. Some you can discard easily; others will require considerable work. A few might remain as shadow companions, but you can learn to recognize them early and defuse them with positive messages. If the message has a negative charge, determine:
- how heavy has it been and to what extent have you felt blocked or hampered by it?
- was it apt at the time; is it still?
- does it say more about the sender than it does about you?
- was it your misreading of the message or your over-elaborating on it that has created problems for you?

3. SURVEY MENTORING MODELS

Review your collection of models from early life on. What do you make of your model collection? What does your model collection say about you? In scanning your models over time, how have they changed? Which ones have remained unchanged? What does this say about your interests, values, and transitions? Examine the models that give you a positive feeling when you think of them. Is the feeling tone one of admiration, excitement, warmth, or something else? Have your models tended to be real people you know or figures from books, television, or other media? Do you have models from legends, myths, or comic books? What do you draw from them?

What is your pattern in finding models? Did they come from your family, or did you discover them yourself? As you survey your current model collection, what long-time models continue to be useful at this stage of your life? What more recent models have you added? At this point, do you need more or different models? How might you augment your model collection?

4. REVIEW MENTORING RELATIONSHIPS

List the significant mentoring relationships in your life. How would you describe them? Have they tended to follow the traditional form, or were they step-ahead or co-mentors? Or do you have some of each? Did or do you have major mentors, or a succession of minor mentors—or a combination? Have you seen a shift in your mentoring relationships over time from traditional to step-ahead and co-mentor, or is your pattern different? Did or do your mentors resemble your early mentor-bonding figures, and in what ways? How did you connect? How did you work together? For how long? Did it change over time? What did you learn or gain from the mentor? What did the mentor do for you? How did it end?

What about the time dimension? Were these enduring mentoring relationships, or short and intermittent? In your mentoring history, do you see a succession of minor mentor connections? Where do networks and networking fit into your pattern?

How do your mentoring relationships tend to start, continue, and end? What seem to be the ways you become connected with a mentor? Which ways are familiar and comfortable for you? Which are strange and not likely? What kinds of relationships would you like to develop? How might they be helpful to you?

Looking at the present and into the future, what kinds of mentoring relationships make sense for you at this stage of your life and/or career? How difficult would these be to develop? If they aren't available, what options do you have? Chapters 25 and 26 can be helpful to you in this part of your review.

Are you, or have you been, in a toxic mentoring situation? If you have in the past, what did you do? If you are now, what can you do? Here are a few suggestions:

Some Antidotes to Toxic Mentoring

—Analyze your mentoring pattern
What are the kinds of mentors you have been attracted to, and what is the nature of your relationship? What does this say about your vulnerabilities and needs? Do you see any potentially destructive patterns that you have carried over from childhood? Do you tend to re-enact your early relationship of being submissive to an autocratic father or mother? Or do you find yourself being feisty and rebellious? Are you excessively deferential to mentors who are similar to a much-admired older sibling? Be alert to your tendencies to recreate early patterns that stifle growth. Identify the kinds of behaviors and relationships that are truly healthy for you and from which you can learn and grow.

—Manage the relationship
Identify what your needs are currently. What is now becoming toxic could have been just what you needed a short time ago. If the benefits of working with this particular person outweigh the costs, consider shifting to conditional mentoring where you can continue to value what the mentor has to offer and let go of unrealistic expectations. Remember that getting out is always a possibility.

—Try to understand the needs of the other person
Is the person responding to overload? If you're chafing because the fit of the relationship is now too tight for you, does the other person know that? Would the other person be receptive? What has been your attitude? Have you come across inappropriately? Have you created some of your own problems? Can you talk about it openly? Sometimes you can shift a close relationship to a more distant but genuinely cordial relationship.

—Keep the relationship balanced
If you need to ally yourself with a potentially toxic mentor for valid reasons, build a support network of others to whom you can turn to for perspective and support. And don't forget to look to yourself for your own internal mentoring resources.

5. IDENTIFY MENTORING EXPERIENCES

Review the events, situations, and circumstances in your life that made a mark—that influenced you, changed your direction, or guided your future development in some way. Were they maturing experiences, or eye-opening and broadening, and in what ways? Did you have some unusual opportunities or lucky breaks along the way? Has the Phoenix Factor operated in your life? In other words, have you experienced a turning point that was immensely painful and difficult at the time but caused you to move in a new direction that ultimately inspired learning and growth?

Based on your review, how do you see the overall impact of mentoring experiences on your life? How would you characterize your history of experiences that were guiding and inspired growth for you? To what extent have you initiated mentoring experiences? Can you see yourself planning mentoring experiences now or in the future? What form might they take?

6. IDENTIFY MENTORING ENVIRONMENTS

Have you ever been in an environment that inspired high levels of learning and growth and that was unusually stimulating, and "yeasty"—a Camelot? Were you in a school where the teacher mentored the whole class, made everything exciting? Have you been in a work group or a research lab or a similar place where people were creative, energized? Or, have you been in a group that was deeply sharing and caring, where you could safely talk about things that really mattered—not just one or two people but the whole group?

Review the settings you've been in to see if any of them had that effect on you, whether in school, college, community, home, work, and/or retreat. If so, describe the environment: what and where it was, how long it lasted, and what seemed to happen there. What was the impact on you? Can you spot any possible future environment that might have this mentoring effect for you?

7. TEASE OUT SELF-MENTORING BEGINNINGS

Recall your play activities as a child. Which activities have continued to interest you over time? Is there a connection to later activities and interests? What interests seemed to originate with you, and which ones were stimulated by exposure of some sort? What did they lead to immediately and later? What patterns do you see?

Were there some interests you developed but later put aside? How does that feel? Was it a natural progression, or were your interests unduly dampened? Could some of these interests still be important to you in your life?

Reviewing mentoring play and mentoring interests can provide clues, even keys, to discovering facets of yourself long hidden from view. This is the time to reexamine those dusty corners of memory for traces of mentoring play and mentoring interests, and then test their meaning for you in your current life and times.

8. REVIEW SELF-MENTORING STRATEGIES

We all have self-mentoring strategies, such as researching, interviewing, and observing, though some of us have developed them further and used them more extensively than others. Some self-mentoring strategies are quite elaborate, and others are practical ways of coping.

What can you discern about your self-mentoring strategies? You have accumulated many strategies along the way. List the important ones. What are they, and how did you come upon them? Which self-mentoring strategies are particularly well developed? What additional self-mentoring methods would you like to develop? What are you particularly good at? What strategies do you use to teach, counsel, or guide yourself? How important is this for you now? Does this tie in with the need to manage your own mentoring, or is there some other purpose?

9. MAP YOUR MENTORING LIFEPRINT

Although we have been looking at your mentoring pattern holistically—as a mosaic, a tapestry, or some other art form—you also can view it in a linear fashion, by mapping your mentoring lifeprint over time. Looking at mentoring patterns in different ways can provide new perspectives.

A mentoring lifeprint is a timeline, organized by decades, on which you can make notes about major and minor mentors, mentoring play, mentoring experiences, and the other features of your Mentoring Mosaic that you have identified. This is a way to gain further insights into your mentoring pattern. It is a variation on lifelines that commonly have been used in personal growth seminars. I find a two-stage lifeprint very useful. Use a large sheet of paper to give yourself plenty of room.

First, mark on the timeline your expected life expectancy, from birth to estimated year of death. The demographic trends in Chapter 23 provide some useful guides. Chart the ups and downs of your life according to the decades, both in your personal life and in your professional life, both your peak moments and your down times. Then, fill in your mentoring lifeprint using this guide:

Mapping Your Mentoring Lifeprint

<——>

Birth   **Time in Years**   **Death**

For each time period, include significant:
- mentoring messages;
- mentoring models;
- mentoring relationships (major and minor mentors);
- mentoring experiences;
- mentoring environments;
- mentoring interests; and
- self-mentoring beginnings.

Fill out your lifeprint and let it sit for a while to see what else occurs to you. What else needs to be added, what connections do you see, what story does it tell, how does it speak to you? Play with it. You can use squiggly lines of different colors to highlight aspects or connections in your life that seem important or surprising. Let it sit for a while, then play with it again when the mood strikes you. Since it is a mentoring lifeprint, it is continually evolving. Have fun with it. Don't despair on the down sweeps—sometimes they can be tough, but what did you learn from them? The Phoenix *does* rise from the ashes.

What does your lifeprint tell you about where you are now and where you want to be in the future?

10. FOLLOWING YOUR PATH: LIFE THEMES

Some of us have an overarching life theme that is guiding in our lives. It is a central driving force, and all self-mentoring strategies flow from this vision, image, or goal. A few of us may be aware of it early on. Others of us discover it only as we review the mosaic of our life and discover our unique mentoring pattern. Perhaps you've already identified your life theme. If not, the following examples may give you a clue.

- For Daniel, it was to study life's mysteries.
- For Eloise, it was just to see what the world was like.
- For Fernando, it was the need to gain knowledge.
- For Evie, it was a great yearning to grow.
- For Cal, it was the quest for social justice.
- For Stan, it was to develop new knowledge about important problems.
- For Tess, it was the idea that if she risked nothing, she gained nothing.

11. MANAGING YOUR MENTORING

You will find additional guides for managing your mentoring at the end of Chapter 21, "Taking Stock in Later Life," and in Chapter 26, "Managing Your Own Mentoring: Assessment Sheet."

BRIDGE

This chapter has provided a guide for reviewing your mentoring history—for looking at your mentoring world's past, present, and future. In the next chapter, we will see why this broad perspective is important as we examine mentoring needs that surface in different life stages.

Chapter 20

MENTORING NEEDS AND LIFE STAGES

Historically, mentoring has been viewed as a process that guides a young person through youth and early adulthood. That is not surprising, since life spans rarely reached beyond the middle years. The demographic picture in *our* world is far different. A child born in the United States in 1900 could expect to live to age 47 or thereabouts. Now, we expect to live and remain active well into our 70s and 80s, and a surprising number into our 90s.[28] What does mentoring look like in these middle and later years? What are our needs for mentoring, and how are they met? The answers to these questions provide the focus of the next two chapters.

Mentoring needs and practices do not disappear in the later decades of life, although they do look different. Mentoring as a process continues, but it is subtler. In the face of changes in our life pattern, we draw from our array of well-used mentoring strategies to learn what we need to learn, to cope with new problems that arise, and to make the necessary shifts from one life stage to another.

To understand the process of life-long mentoring more fully, I conducted a longitudinal study of early informants 20 years later. I re-interviewed 40 people now in their 50s to their 80s. Most cluster in the Boomer years and the few years preceding, people now in their mid-50s to early 60s. Some are retired, some are continuing in their careers. Some of those who are retired are continuing their life's work in a different context, and still others have been reenergized through

---

[28] For an extensive discussion of demographic and other trends affecting mentoring, see Chapters 22 and 23.

developing new or latent interests. From this study, these observations about life-long mentoring emerge:

- Mentoring continues in later life, although mentoring forms can differ.
- Mentoring needs shift with the stages of life.
- Mentoring patterns endure: Mentor bonders will continue to seek people mentors; non-bonders will continue to turn to other sources.
- We continue to look for mentoring models. Although some are long-lasting, others change according to our needs, and many fade away.
- Enduring models are those that exemplify values important to us.
- In periods of life review, mentoring messages are often revisited. Early messages can be valued in new ways or discarded completely.
- Traditional mentors are rarely present, except as we mentor others.
- Our people mentors are more likely to be step-ahead or co-mentors.
- Non-traditional forms of people mentoring, such as mentoring networks, become more common.
- Many of us initiate mentoring experiences for our learning and growth.
- Many activities in later life reflect important values and interests that stem from mentoring messages and mentoring interests.
- Mentoring experiences in later life include both life-changing events that happen to us and learning or enriching experiences that we plan.
- We draw heavily on self-mentoring strategies that have been useful in the past and develop new strategies to meet new needs.
- Those of us who have experienced rich mentor relationships are likely to mentor others.

SOURCES OF LATER-LIFE MENTORING NEEDS

The challenges, opportunities, and concerns that face us in later life are the result of change—changes in external situations, in our physical well-being, or in our way of looking at the world or ourselves. In these altered circumstances, we have mentoring needs that were not present before. We must learn new technologies, develop knowledge and skills previously not needed, and/or adapt in other ways. Here are illustrative examples, all drawn from interviews.

Career Crest with New Challenges

At this point in life, you could be enjoying a career crest—your career is satisfying, the rewards are good, and you can enjoy the fruits of your labor. You know that retirement is somewhere on the horizon; but right now, you are facing new challenges and opportunities.

- You accept the promotion to CEO of a complex business and need to learn quickly how to deal with administrative and political issues at the top of the organization.
- You are a medical executive in a large health plan with the challenge of setting up a wellness program for employees of a prestigious hotel chain, something that's never been done before.
- You have shifted into a burgeoning new research field and realize you must do a quick immersion in the new field in order to function effectively.

Second Career

Although you have been successful in your career, you realize that now is the time to shift gears and move to a second career.

- You decide to retire from organizational hassles and open your own business, something you've long planned for.
- You take early retirement from your role as a medical clinician to redirect your time and energies toward your life-long interest in the performing arts.

Holding Pattern

In late career, you see minimal changes ahead in your work life; your career is currently in a holding pattern.

- You are confident that you can manage your job on semi-automatic pilot and now plan to devote more time and effort to the community and professional organizations you're already associated with but never seem to have room for in your schedule.
- You now want to concentrate on developing your talents, interests, or hobbies in fields distant from your work life.
- You need to figure out ways to make work fun and exciting in the remaining years until you retire, a challenge brought about by changing conditions in your field or in your personal financial situation.
- You have just a few years before you can retire. You're hoping to hang on, but industry changes make you anxious about the future.

Retirement

You have retired from paid employment and suddenly have an excess of unstructured time.

- You are enjoying your freedom and your choice of activities, whether you use your skills in new contexts, engage in more travel, or pursue neglected interests.
- You seek opportunities to engage in activities that mesh with your value system.
- You are now taking a longer view, aiming to keep your skills current so that you can continue to engage in your profession on a part-time basis or in a volunteer capacity, should you choose.
- You wonder where and how you can maintain a sense of accomplishment and/or fulfillment.
- You are restless. You don't yet have ways to stay connected that are satisfying to you.

Health Issues

You encounter health problems that cause you pause and disruption, problems that you were earlier able to shrug off or adjust to quickly.

- You suffer a profound hand injury that prevents you from meeting your high-pressure consulting schedule and causes you to shift to research and writing in your field.
- You are beginning to experience chronic health problems that increasingly require more attention and life adjustment.

CAREER AND LIFE MOTIVATIONS

Not surprisingly, mentoring needs are closely related to a person's life stage and motivations. We can gain perspective on the mentoring needs of later life by examining our career and life motivations. A well-known model developed by Brooklyn Derr[29] in his work on career motivation offers some useful categories for analysis. I have broadened his model beyond career in order to focus on our motivations in life as well.

"Life," like "career," is more than a job, an experience, or a sequence of jobs and experiences. It has a sense of direction that comes from our desire to live out the values we believe in and find our place in the world. Derr identifies five career options that motivate people:

- getting ahead;
- getting high;
- getting free;
- getting balanced; and
- getting secure.

---

[29] C. Brooklyn Deer, *Managing the New Careerists*, San Francisco: Addison-Wesley, 1986. Abraham Maslow's *Hierarchy of Needs* is another very useful model; it appears in his *Motivation and Personality*, 3rd edition, HarperCollins, 1987.

For those in later life, I would add two additional life options:
- getting deeper (or, perhaps even better is "going deeper"); and
- getting refocused (or perhaps "refocusing").

Rarely do these options remain static. Nor are they necessarily mutually exclusive. Our motivations change over time, depending on personal circumstances and interests. One will be dominant for a while, then another. This is particularly so in later life. Determining factors include economic security, health and energy level, strength of other interests, outlets and opportunities, personal philosophy, and values.

Getting Ahead

For people in their 50s and 60s, getting ahead has a finite number on it. For some, it involves the last major career choice before retirement, or at least before retiring from a first or even second career. For most of us, getting ahead is no longer the push it was earlier. Either career goals have been achieved or have changed. Or, it has become clear that some now appear beyond reach.

Getting High

For people still in career, the motivation can be getting high through new challenges and opportunities, enjoying using one's competences to the fullest. Life continues to be exciting, challenging, and fun as you ride the crest. Or, in the years preceding retirement, motivation is strong to find ways to sustain interest so life continues to be meaningful and energizing during the remaining time.

Getting Free

Conversely, in a world with a limiting work environment and/or career future, motivation may be directed more toward getting free. Energy is spent on reducing constraints or responsibilities, planning for a career shift, or marking time until retirement. Often, the effort shifts toward getting balanced.

Getting Balanced

Getting balanced surfaces when one looks at the disproportionate time and energy spent on career. The switch occurs with a shift in awareness and desire to spend more time on personal interests and/or family life. It also surfaces upon retirement: how to engage in activities that sustain you and also maintain a satisfying social network.

Getting Deeper (or Going Deeper)

Going deeper is an additional motivation that assumes greater importance in later years—that of acting on values, exploring undeveloped or underdeveloped parts of self, and delving deeper into spiritual realms. Values take on a deeper meaning, as do finding connections and acting on them. Often, life review is done at this time.

Getting Refocused (or Refocusing)

A related motivation is refocusing, withdrawing energy from the old career and investing in a new one. For some of us, this is a clear-cut decision: You are ready to turn out the lights and close the door on what was once the center of your work life and focus instead on a new endeavor that excites you. For others, the shift is more an evolving process.

Getting Secure

The two wild cards in this are health and economics. For those of us who have faced or are facing such issues, typical motivation patterns can be turned on their heads, and getting secure vis-à-vis health and/or finances looms as the top motivation. Like it or not, we must adjust to the realities of later life, rather than what we expected them to be.

TRANSITIONING TO "RETIREMENT"

Traditionally, retirement has meant withdrawal from one's position or occupation, the end stage of a working life. In some cultures, it has signaled movement from an active life to one of contemplation and reflection. In our world, retirement has been linked for more than a half-century to reaching age 65.

Now that linkage is changing, and we do not yet have common language to talk about it. Experts talk about "the new meaning of retirement" and envision the 21st Century ushering in an era of lifelong working and learning. Given longer life spans, many of us will have multiple careers.

Whatever the time frame, life stages and needs directly influence our mentoring processes. We face specific tasks or problems as we approach the traditional retirement years.

Preparing for Retirement

Planning and preparing for retirement are tasks faced by most people at some point in their lives. Getting secure is a principal motivating factor in planning how to make the shift from active career to retirement and live on what could well be reduced income and/or reduced health care benefits. Exactly when retirement will be economically feasible and the amount of income you can realistically anticipate—these can be thorny issues.

Assuming the financial base is covered, the predominant question is how to ensure a meaningful life after career. Again, examples are from interviews.

Some of us might have a strong desire to retire:
- "I want to get out of the rat race."
- "I don't want to deal with bureaucracy anymore."
- "I've put in my time, and I'm tired of punching the clock."
- "Working in health care is not satisfying any more. It's becoming a commodity instead of a service."
- "What I have to do in my job often runs counter to my values."

Some face expectations that they *should* leave:
- "I have groomed my replacement as expected in my organization, and it's time."
- "My husband has retired and is waiting for me so we can do things together."
- "My organization does not look kindly on older employees."

Still, we all have questions and reservations:
- "How can I continue to feel worthwhile? I don't want to feel obsolete."
- "Have I made a sufficient contribution to society that I can retire without feeling guilty?"
- "Would travel and pursuing my other interests be satisfying?"
- "I'm willing to do about anything if I feel I can make a contribution."
- "What can I do that uses my skills? What else would I have to learn?"

Retirement planning is a subject that comes up in a physician group I have been meeting with periodically for 30 years. Most members of the group are in their early 60s. They find sharing their retirement questions, concerns, and strategies of great help as they move into the uncertain future.

Traumatic Career Endings

Many organizations and professional groups anticipate this major life decision by providing pre-retirement counseling. This is fine if you have the opportunity to participate in a systematically paced shift to retirement. But, if your job is unexpectedly eliminated, or if you find your financial nest egg has significantly shrunk with the vagaries of the financial markets, or if you suddenly encounter a major health problem that prevents you from working out your planned schedule, then you are forced to react, not act. Such was the case for both Elise and Ruth.

In our earlier interview, Elise described several well-honed self-mentoring strategies that she had used throughout her life to prepare for new directions—one example was her preparation for a medical school interview by seeking advice and guidance from a number of women physicians about how to present herself and handle difficult questions. I asked Elise if she had used that strategy to move herself forward in more recent occasions.

> "I was starting to do that with retirement, and then I got lurched into it," she said. She found her new chief of service very difficult to work with. Over time, the conflict affected her health. Elise had accepted her position with the provision that it be part-time, given the long commute, but the chief later demanded she work full-time and would not yield. There was a clash between the two and, given her health problems, Elise left precipitously. "Retirement was a long adjustment period for me, even in small things. All of a sudden, I didn't automatically drive to the county hospital as I'd done for years. Obviously, I didn't get to complete the planned retirement strategy I had started."

Few of the people I interviewed were faced with job loss and sudden insecurity in late career. Ruth's experience was different.

> Due to a financial crisis and massive shake-up in the hospital where she worked, Ruth's job was eliminated. At age 59, with

no retirement income on the horizon and with an ailing husband at home, she was thrust back into the labor market, her morale devastated. With the guidance and counsel of consultant friends, Ruth decided to try free-lance consulting. Moving in this direction required a major reorientation to learn about marketing and other requirements of a successful consulting practice. After several tough years, her practice began to grow, and she continued working successfully until age 73, when she made the decision to retire. The mentoring guidance and support of colleagues and friends proved invaluable during this difficult period. Reflecting back, Ruth realizes that the job loss pushed her into a new career and a new life. Although traumatic at the time, it forced her to learn and grow and to become even more effective in her work—the Phoenix Factor at work.

The Move to Retirement: Certainties and Uncertainties

For those who have been in the workforce for many years, the move to retirement can be exhilarating, frightening, or something in between. Our expectations haven't yet caught up with the demographics that point to increasing longevity, good health, and the likelihood of multiple careers over a lifetime.

Assuming economic security and good health, the question becomes one of finding a productive and satisfying use of time. For many of us, the pent-up desire for a career switch, for greater involvement in the community, or for free time to travel and pursue interests or hobbies occupies a major part of early retirement. Not being bound by time and/or organizational constraints can be freeing and exhilarating, particularly if we have planned to retire early. Consider:

- Al, who opened his own clinical services business;
- Craig, who launched a new career in the performing arts;
- Paul, who consults in his same line of work in the mental health field; and

- Dave, who volunteers his financial management skills at his church.

A significant number of us are passionate about doing work that meshes with our values.

- Fired by his passion for social justice, Cal retired early from a successful career in academic medicine in order to develop a program at his church that would make social justice and community service an integral part of congregational life.
- Values of education, community service, and helping her fellow man mean so much to Val that she reduced her consulting practice so she could be more active in the community. As an Air Force veteran with a nursing background, Val serves on the board of directors of her city's Vietnam veterans' organization, where she finds practical use for her skills in organization and management, problem-solving, and staff coaching. When she chooses full retirement, she plans to become even more active in the community.
- Kay uses her organizational and political skills in activities that mesh with her values. She does consulting for research institutions focused on reforming math and science education, serves in a leadership role for a county-wide early childhood initiative, and serves on several non-profit boards.
- Teaching is the dream of some people looking toward retirement. Vicki and Linda both want to find ways to improve the education of nurses. Jim has long wanted to teach accounting and financial planning.

However, many often face a sense of loss when leaving a job and the network of people in the organization. We can have wonderings and fears about maintaining an identity without a long-held career label. The identity question is an important concern of people who join "renewment groups."[30] Or, we feel bereft of the friendships that were organization-based, few of which carry over to our new life. Reluctantly, we realize that we have to build a new network of social and professional relationships.

Late Retirement Years

At some point in later years, our activities in the outer world decline in concert with our health and energy, and we turn inward. The nature of our work and daily activities, our health, mobility, energy level, and relationships—all of these change whether we want them to or not. We might engage in life review or contemplative practice. In the long arc of our lives, the experiences of loss, change, and inner wisdom become more frequent and more profound and require different mentoring self-management skills.

BRIDGE

Mentoring needs do continue throughout our lifespan. In later life, the elements of the Mentoring Mosaic still are present; however, they take on more significance or have different meanings. The next chapter looks more closely at the Mentoring Mosaic in later life.

---

[30] Elizabeth Pope, "Baby Boomers opt to 'renew' rather than retire," *Los Angeles Times*, August 23, 2005, Advertising Supplement, p. 1.

Chapter 21

THE MENTORING MOSAIC IN LATER LIFE

Overall, mentoring patterns have a different look in later life, that period roughly from age 50 on. Traditional mentors mostly disappear, people mentors take the form of step-ahead or co-mentors, and more reliance is placed on finding mentoring experiences from which to learn and grow. The reservoir of self-mentoring strategies and support systems we have developed through the years become more important as well. In the process of tapping our life experience and wisdom, we can find that we have a variety of mentoring strategies to help us cope and prosper during these later life stages. In this chapter, we survey the Mentoring Mosaic during this significant period.

MENTOR BONDING

Our mentor-bonding pattern is generally set early in our lives. Only with conscious effort, can it change. Examples of such pattern changes are outlined in Chapter 4 and strategies for engineering such changes are discussed in Chapter 25. Mentor bonders will naturally seek out people mentors as coaches or mentors for something they want to learn, although they also will use other self-mentoring methods. Non-bonders or limited bonders will more likely seek other modes of learning and guidance.

MENTORING MESSAGES

Many of the mentoring messages we received in our early years tend to be reinforced as we go through life. There is, however, an opportunity to reevaluate those old messages and their place and power in our lives.

Here are examples of message reappraisal in later life:

- Only in recent years has Yvonne been able to value the mentoring messages that she received from her father by his living example—messages that she ignored or discounted during her early years. Now that her ego needs are no longer dominant, she can see how much his values and the way he lived his life have influenced the development of her spiritual life.
- I commented to Val that her activities in semi-retirement seemed to be acting out her values of education, of community service, and of helping her fellow man. These were values that seemed to come directly from her parents but that she had not verbalized in the earlier interview. She agreed: "Exactly. I see that connection as a source of pride. My father and I had a rocky relationship. It's so good now to take the good things I learned from him and not focus on others—and to carry on the legacy that my parents gave me."

MENTORING MODELS

Models are generally characterized by behaviors or values that we admire and would like to emulate. Occasionally, they are models of something we wish to avoid. In later life, we tend to seek models for a specific purpose.

For New Career Situations

After the first mentoring interview, Carl found he was more attuned to "identifying people of superior quality" whom he could look to as models. From that point on, he has consciously observed people in key positions whose style he admired. This approach helped him as he prepared to become the new hospital chief of staff. He quickly listed three such models:

> "Kurt was a very gentle man, yet very strong on vision. I learned character from him. He was methodical and was able to bring people around by his systematic and reasoned argument. Mark was a good model for transforming yourself from a clinician into a manager. And I admired Chuck for his ability to understand people as well as issues."

When the board selected Linda to be CEO of her hospital, she realized she had to know more about boards and be more politically involved to be successful. The previous CEO was just such a model for her:

> "He was at ease with anyone, always just himself. With physicians, he was friendly and respectful but always firm and could say no. With staff, he was one of us. He stays in touch with all kinds of people and gathers intelligence from others constantly."

For Acting on Values

Kay looked to John Gardner as a source of inspiration, and she valued his character.

> "His character was warm and nurturing, but he also would cut to the chase. A man of principle, he drew attention to problems in the American social and political fabric and sought innovative responses. He was always involved locally in the civic culture, modeling the whole idea of citizens acting in their communities both in their professional capacities and in giving service. He was an exemplar."

For Coping with Health Problems and Aging

Louisa has amassed a number of models for dealing with health problems and the aging process.

> She admires one woman "for how she has handled numerous health problems with poise and resilience. She has not lessened her dedication to helping those in need and to social justice." She marvels at another friend "who continued to make her life rich even as she was losing her vision," and a younger male colleague who, "through grit and determination, regained greater functioning from a major stroke than medical professionals thought possible."

MENTORING RELATIONSHIPS

Mentoring relationships in middle and later years take on a different form. Scope, intensity, and duration are not as great. Because mentors serve a defined purpose, relationships are not all-encompassing. Rather, we seek a coach or a mentor to meet a current need. The search is more selective.

The approach toward the mentor search is noticeably different between mentor bonders and non-bonders. A mentor bonder's search assumes someone will be able to provide guidance. A non-bonder will tend to avoid personal entanglements and turn instead to other mentoring strategies.

Mentor forms also differ at this stage of life. The era of traditional mentors is past. Indeed, if there is traditional mentoring, we are likely to be the mentor, not the mentee. It is time, if we are ready and so disposed, for us to mentor others. But mentoring does continue; it is just the form that changes. Rather than traditional mentors, the most common forms are the step-ahead mentor—the person who is ahead of us in life and experience in an area we want or need to learn—and peers who are co-mentors.

As we move along in our careers, the technical aspects of our job have been mastered, unless there is significant change in the field of work. If we move into positions of greater responsibility or management, however, we must learn new skills, particularly in the political and managerial areas. If we move into a new career field before or after retirement, we also must learn new skills and knowledge. Although such mentoring relationships could be broad and sustained, they are more likely to be limited and of short duration.

Step-Ahead Mentor Examples

Carl turned to senior colleagues for guidance in medical management.

> "Neil showed me about transforming from clinician to dealing with management issues. I worked intensely with him. I admired Ron, another physician, for his clarity and honesty. He knew how to deal with various entities and showed me how to package issues and understand people and issues at all levels. I haven't seen anyone better, before or since."

When Linda accepted the promotion to hospital CEO, she realized that she had to quickly learn more about boards and become more politically involved.

> "I'm shy, and doing glad-handing and going out there isn't something that comes naturally. But I knew I had to do it. So, I identified people in the organization who could introduce me to the political arena and how it works. The political advocate with the health care system knew all the politicians, the issues, and the people I needed to become familiar with. I also needed to find someone who could get me up to speed about the functions and dynamics of boards and how specifically to work with our governing board. I was able to spend some time with Brad, who was a high-level executive in strategic planning at the corporate level and did lots of governing board work there."

With his decision to retire early, Craig shifted gears completely, moving from clinical pathology to the cultural arts. He knew very little about arts management, and had little conception of what the roles of "producer," "house manager," and "managing director" entailed. Several people in the arts community who had known him became step-ahead mentors. They not only urged him on but oriented him to this new world. Craig was a quick study. He could see that his interest and general knowledge in the performing arts, coupled with his well-developed organizational and analytical skills, could fill a vital community need.

> "Megan urged me to apply for membership in the Cultural Arts Commission and then mentored me in arts management and performance. She considered me as a resource in the community, seeing potential I had never considered. Jean, a retired theater professor, taught me a lot about theater production and involved me in a theater group that she'd formed. They were amazed. Here were all these right-brained people and here I was, a left-brained person. 'We think you might be managing director,' they said."

As Craig learned more about arts production, he assumed increasingly responsible leadership roles. Through his networking in the arts community, he was asked to serve as liaison between the Cultural Arts Foundation and a theater travel company. Later on, he assumed a key role in the city's New Year's Eve arts celebration.

Professional Mentors—A Form of Step-Ahead Mentors

When we reach crises or turning points in our lives, we tend to seek counseling from someone specially trained to work with people who have problems, such as a counselor, psychotherapist, minister, or life coach. Usually, the need is specific, and the time interval is relatively brief. Such professionals are credited for their great help at turning points in life.

Al and Craig are friends. Each had a mid-life crisis at about the same time. Al recommended a psychologist who had helped him when he was dealing with a divorce and a death in the family. Craig had a similar problem: an impending death in the family and then a major work crisis. Both credited the therapist with helping them deal with the life issues and career decisions.

— *Al*

> "About the time my father was dying, I went to a psychologist who taught me something deep that changed my life—a simple expression, to 'honor your pain!' We spent many hours together talking about that concept; it helped me fit everything in perspective."

— *Craig*

> "Two years before I retired, I was going through tough times mentally—all the folderol at work coming soon after Mom passed away. Al had been going to a psychologist, and he suggested I go, too. I got a lot of help in the course of working on my issues with him. My interest in the arts really came out, and I was finally willing to put the arts rather than medicine up front. He pushed me to get more involved in the arts. I was a little ashamed that I wasn't devoting 100% of my time to the practice of medicine. I don't think I'd ever articulated that before, and, of course, that's what was holding me back."

Pat found her life coach very helpful when she decided to leave a long-term relationship. The coach helped her keep moving toward the goals she set for herself. "First, she and I met and talked," Pat said. "Then, we had a weekly half-hour phone date. She prompted me to think about issues, e-mail her my questions, and then she would respond to my answers." Now that Pat is planning her retirement, she expects to call the life coach again.

Co-Mentor Examples

In later life, co-mentoring with peers becomes the dominant mentor form. In reciprocal mentoring, each person in the partnership has unique skills and competences that complement the other. Mutual mentoring describes a supportive relationship where both persons share their problems and concerns, and they draw strength, wisdom, and support from each other.

In Organizations

In three major organizational moves, as Linda has moved up the management ladder, she has found a co-mentor whose talents and skills complemented and enriched her own. It was natural when she moved into her role as hospital CEO that Linda would seek another such relationship. She found one with the chief operating officer.

> "Leslie is a planner, and I'm a visionary: I learn from her actions, and she learns from my thinking perspective. Our strengths are different. I will have the idea, and she will immediately know to how to do it. I keep her from going off too fast before everything is in place. It's a more complicated role being a CEO. So many people depend on you to do the right thing, because the margins are so thin that the smallest wrong move can tip things precipitously. Programmatic implementation with financial implications has to be thought out and planned. Still, at some time, you have to move forward. If I'm not 100% certain, my tendency is to seek more data; Leslie will recognize that it's time to pull the plug—'Let's go!' "

Co-Mentoring in Personal Life

Carl met Joel when traveling in Laos in 1974, and they have remained very good friends ever since.

> "Joel reminds me that the clock is ticking, and you only get one trip around the track. He emphasizes things like, 'Go to a hotel where you can meet Ecuadorians, not a five-star place.' He keeps me looking at things in my life that I want to do. He is a mentor for me in philosophy and in life. As to the other side of the relationship, I started him mountain climbing."

Marisa is 70, and her friend is 82. She shared a recent mutual-mentoring experience they had. By coincidence, they discovered each was coping with a major health problem: Marisa risked losing partial vision with bleeding from a retinal tear, and her friend, who already was coping with a nasty wrist fracture, now had a heart problem. They discovered each was homebound and dealing with a range of feelings and reactions to these life upsets. The telephone became their emotional lifeline. Almost daily during this difficult period, they shared their experiences, feelings, and reactions in a way that helped each woman gain perspective, patience, and a more positive outlook on the road back to health.

Spouse Co-Mentoring

Spouse mentoring is a form of co-mentoring often quite significant in later life. Linda shared about her husband, Roger:

> "Roger intellectualizes and poses questions. It drives me crazy, because he's one of those data people. My immediate reaction is often negative, but I always have to think about it. I tend to blow something off or not see all sides. He will raise a question, or 'You really should consider that.' People like Roger force me to reach beyond what I would think.

> "On the other side, when Roger was contemplating a career shift, seeking an opportunity that could work out well, I was influential in helping him sort out options. I also help him now when he gets frustrated. He's way too intuitive, intellectual, and intelligent for the people he works with. He knows what needs to be done, but he's made a pattern of telling the wrong people that."

MENTORING EXPERIENCES

Mentoring experiences are events, situations, and circumstances that are guiding and influencing. In later life, we see examples of mentoring experiences that happen to us as well as those we initiate. Happenings can be benign and happy, traumatic and life-changing, or something in between. Planned experiences that we initiate usually inspire growth or are broadening in the sense of going in new directions.

Happenings as Mentoring Experiences

Many happenings that become mentoring experiences are very positive, as we saw in Chapter 15. Sometimes they can be a surprise, something unexpected, like a wake-up call. When Carl was in his 40s, he had a herniated disc. It was a wake-up call, a motivator to go ahead and play and do things besides medicine. The result was a broadened life perspective and a widening circle of friends.

> "Starting in 1986, I shifted over to doing some personal things, rather than just medical things. Back when I was kid, it was all work and no play. I laid awake thinking about that. I've always done backpacking, so I started mountain climbing with a friend. I combined the climbing with travel: I climbed McKinley in Alaska, then the tallest mountains in South America and Russia, and, of course, in the Northwest. You meet friends and form extraordinary bonds with people all over the world. A friend in New Zealand called this week wanting me to go to Ecuador late summer or fall to do some climbing there."

Up-Ending Experiences

Most mentoring experiences are expanding or enriching, moving us to new places that inspire learning and growth. But life also throws us curves that force us to make a shift in goal focus and direction; they represent losses that can be quite traumatic. Such experiences become more frequent and more serious in later life. Losses can be in the areas of health, job, family, finances, or some combination of these: diminished capacity in health, stalemated job, family broken by death or divorce, and/or significant financial shrinkage.

Up-ending experiences make us face loss. They require resilience and flexibility in order to shift gears and move in new directions. Can we deal with the loss and gradually find growth and satisfaction in a new direction? Can the Phoenix rise from the ashes? These are difficult questions matching difficult situations. This was certainly true for Mel, who had a major stroke when he was in his late 50s. Nothing in his lifestyle could have predicted such a blow to his health. It has taken a major effort in physical therapy plus his determination to regain functioning. Seven years later, he talks philosophically about how this experience has altered his life. Now he finds himself much more selective, choosing to spend time with people where the interchange is rewarding for him and for the other person. He also is doing far deeper reading—books requiring more reflection, books that draw on his own wisdom.

> "The experience has opened a space inside me, and I'm using it in my conscious life. What's exhilarating is being in touch with and tapping those inner wisdom sources. The stroke has forced me to slow down and be more self-reflective, although the purely contemplative life is too passive for me. I do more active searching and integrating. I'm interested in integrating in order to fix the world.

> "The stroke also has required me to be much more deliberate in all the things I do. It created a mental discipline of paying attention to be sure that, when I walk or sit down to eat at the table, I'm aware of what I need to do. Everyday events now require thought; before, they required just an intuitive or habituated response. Now I am more able to think before I act. I like that."

Planned Mentoring Experiences

Planned mentoring experiences represent a meshing of self-mentoring strategies and mentoring experiences. You take the initiative to create an experience from which you can learn, grow, or find guidance.

Al's Path to Entrepreneurship

Early in his career, Al's boss encouraged him to think about becoming an entrepreneur and having his own business some day. These messages seeped into his head, and Al quietly prepared for the time when he could leave his secure position in hospital medical technology and open his own business. Over the years, his hospital role expanded far beyond medical technology to include management responsibility for a cluster of clinical departments.

Encouraged in his hospital role to become more involved in the community, Al became an officer in the credit union and also "went through the chairs" in the local Kiwanis Club. He credits his accumulated experiences—of being a staff person, a manager, earning a master's degree, and knowing people in the community—for preparing him for this major role shift. By the time he approached the bank for a line of credit, he was well known in the community. The bank officials, after checking him out, gave him the full amount requested.

His original partner was in the staffing business, so he learned the ropes of that business as well. When his partner wanted to move on to something else, Al bought him out and set up a registry business for recruiting professionals for health care settings. He now has a registry of respiratory therapists, home care aides, and medical billers. Over the years, Al's carefully planned mentoring experiences prepared him for this major occupational shift after early retirement when he was 53.

Pat's Path of Personal Growth and Spiritual Development

Approaching the half-century stage was a mentoring experience for Pat. While continuing her successful career, she resolved at that time to devote more attention to her inner growth as a person. She made a point of attending programs, conferences, and retreats focusing on personal growth and spiritual development. She practiced meditation and followed other routines to connect mind and body. Along the way, she has been able to connect with new mentors.

A decade later, Pat carefully planned her transition to retirement. Soon after all the farewells, she loaded her car with belongings, camping gear, a list of three questions she wanted to answer for herself, and took off for a five-month solo trek around the United States and Europe.

MENTORING ENVIRONMENTS

In later life, mentoring environments usually take the form of support groups. Groups can form for one purpose but, over time, develop as a mentoring environment for members, a place where they can exchange information, share feelings, and be supported when difficulties arise. Such groups play an invaluable role in later life as individual support systems dwindle with illness, distance, and death.

For Bruce, a Wednesday lunch group of eight retired men has become a mentoring environment for him.

> "It has become a men's support group. We talk about our prostates, our cholesterol levels, our impending strokes, and all those things. We share in one another's aches and pains, and we play tennis together. It's more meaningful than any group I've ever belonged to—meaningful in that we're all in the same season of life, and we share concerns with the stock market, health, family, and grandchildren."

Daniel's family provides another mentoring environment.

> "My wife and kids are very supportive and understanding of what I'm doing. They are a barometer for me. I was thinking about making a job switch for a long time, but I couldn't make a decision. When I asked them, they unanimously told me to leave and why. I knew their reasons were correct, but it was

different coming from them, especially my wife. They refocus and redirect me. They reel me back in. It's like a family council."

SELF-MENTORING

By the time we reach our 50s and beyond, we have had many years to develop and sharpen our self-mentoring skills. In these later years, we have many opportunities to use them as we move in new directions and cope with new challenges. Often, those tried-and-true strategies are called upon when we need to provide ourselves with new challenges, retool for new career and/or life directions, develop new skills, or apply existing skills in new ways—or otherwise manage our lives.

Stretching

Vicki is editor of a professional journal, a role she has held for 20 years. She has to keep up with the market.

> "You can't put out a good journal if you don't have up-to-date material. So I still put myself out there, just to get the stimulation. I'll agree to do a speech on a topic I don't really know well, which forces me to do some research. Constant change keeps me on my toes and adds variety. It's my way to give myself a little jolt of adrenaline—doing something I normally wouldn't do or haven't done. I do a lot of that."

Retooling

During the years that Carl was medical director of his practice group, he completed a master's in health care management. When he became president–elect of the medical staff, he signed on for more specific medical staff training, including a seminar on the medical executive committee and how to run it. He also attended Harvard Business School's weeklong course on leadership, one of the best seminars he has attended.

Refocusing

Eduardo's natural gifts are in the arts, from drawing and sketching to acting and creative food preparation. But he carried strong messages from his father that he had to be able to make a living and not be a starving artist. So as a young adult, he worked full-time in the insurance business.

On the side, Eduardo did some acting in TV commercials. With his bilingual skills, he had an increasing volume of requests to do commercials for the Spanish-language market. Often, the script he was given showed little appreciation for the language. Eduardo was able to convince the producers of the need for change and provided a translation more suited to the specific market at which the commercial was aimed. "There's a lot of art in that, so I became interested in journalism and writing. It was a shift from on-camera work to behind-the-camera directing and producing," he said.

Eduardo continued these parallel tracks working in each field separately until he was financially grounded. At that point, he took the leap, left the insurance industry, and opened his own translation business. Ten years later, his translation group has contracts in all of the major U.S. markets and a number of overseas markets as well. Now age 50, Eduardo has managed to marry the artistic world with the business world and plans to do more in the artistic realm in the future.

MENTORING OTHERS

Later life is the period when we are most likely to mentor others. We have experience and skills to share, and if we have been the recipients of good mentoring in the past, we are usually motivated to do so. This was a conscious strategy for Carl.

"When I was president–elect of the medical executive committee, I tried to let committee members know what I was doing. We had monthly core meetings and talked about issues. I brought on Dr. Vandenberg to be secretary-treasurer of the committee—I needed him there as an exceptionally fine clinician. I also sent information and ideas his way and encouraged him to go to courses. I started him on a project for the critical care unit. He took it and ran with it, and the team won a quality award for it."

Al, too, has been busy mentoring others from the time he started his second career in business.

"I have six full-time young people as employees, all of whom I have trained. My oldest son is director of operations. Now he's very active in the community and emulating me in a sense. Adam's learning the staffing business. Ginny handles customer relations as the receptionist and manages some specialized staffing. Sanjay, my business manager, does all of the billing. Then there's Jeremy, who does my collections. Minnie works graveyard and is there to handle requests for emergency staffing in the middle of the night. She manages the roster of people on that shift and does all the scheduling. They all have primary roles, but I have cross-trained them in other areas."

TAKING STOCK IN LATER LIFE

In Chapter 19, you had the opportunity to survey your Mentoring Mosaic and to establish a mentoring baseline. Here are additional action steps you can take to factor later-life needs and experiences into your mentoring practice.

- If you haven't already, establish a mentoring baseline using the guidelines in Chapter 19 in order to get a clear picture of your Mentoring Mosaic.

- Examine the elements of your Mentoring Mosaic to assess the changes you are facing now or are likely to face in later life. For example, you might want to review your mentoring messages to see what values were conveyed to you and how important those messages are to you now.
- Examine the trends described in Chapters 23 and 26 to identify those trends most pertinent to your situation.
- With these strands in mind, turn to Chapters 25 and 26 to consider what strategies you might use to manage your mentoring now and in the future.

BRIDGE

Chapters 20 and 21 examined the Mentoring Mosaic through the lens of time and how experiences at various life stages shape our mentoring needs and practice. In the next chapter, we focus on five individual lives to illustrate both the continuity of the mentoring process through a person's life and the diversity of mentoring patterns among people.

Chapter 22

LIFE-LONG MENTORING VIGNETTES

The continuity of the mentoring process over a lifetime is one of the strong findings from my research. Although changes do occur in our life patterns, the overall picture is one of consistency and continuity.

Throughout this book, we have focused on design elements in the Mentoring Mosaic and also on change and continuity in mentoring throughout our lives. We have taken apart the whole to examine the pieces that make up mentoring. However, we know that within any individual, these elements combine to make a whole that is far greater than the sum of its parts.

To illustrate the pattern consistency within one person's life and the pattern variability from one person to another, we look at five mentoring lives. From the 40 people for whom I have longitudinal data, I've chosen the mentoring stories of five people. They come from different backgrounds, professions, genders, and decades. Through their stories, we can trace mentoring patterns over time. When first interviewed, they were in their 20s to 60s; at the time of the follow-up interviews, they were in their 40s to 80s. These five lives illustrate the diversity and uniqueness in our patterns of mentoring through the life span.

- **Eduardo, 47:** When I first interviewed Eduardo, he was 28, working full-time in the insurance business, acting part-time in TV commercials, and pursuing other creative interests. Now 47, he has left insurance. With his Hispanic background and advertising experience, he has created a Spanish translation business serving a variety of media markets, thereby marrying his business skills with his creative talents.

- **Daniel, 51:** I first met Daniel when he was 34 and an emergency medicine physician in a metropolitan hospital. Now he is 51, living in the rural Northwest, continuing his work in emergency medicine, and combining this with his long-standing interest in art.
- **Bell, 67:** At the time of the initial interview, Bell was 47 and assistant director of nursing in an investor-owned hospital. She is now a top executive in a multi-state insurance health plan and is approaching retirement.
- **Bruce, 77:** A parish minister, Bruce was 56 when I first talked to him. He is now 77, retired, and has moved beyond his intellectual, philosophical world into the rich world of relationships.
- **Clarisse, 89:** Clarisse was 68 and a practicing Jungian analyst when I first interviewed her. She is now 89 and continuing her own inner journey during her retirement years even as she faces diminished health and energy.

Through these lives, we can glimpse the richness, continuity, and change in mentoring within individual life spans as well as variations in mentoring patterns among people. Their mentoring stories follow.

THE STORY OF EDUARDO

Eduardo at Age 28

When I first interviewed Eduardo, I wondered about his strong commitment to business and his equally strong creative pull toward the arts. What were the mentoring sources pushing the development of both business and creative interests? I asked him what came to his mind in thinking about mentors and mentoring.

"I guess the first person who came to my mind was my mother, as someone I saw as a guide or as an image of something I wanted to follow. I found what she had to say valid and trusted what she said. My father was there, but his points of view were known through Mom's filters."

—Mentor Bonding

What kinds of messages about you did you receive from your parents?
From Mom, that I was very delicate and needed protection, that I was very creative and different from everyone else. Just take it easy and know that I will always be here to protect you. Dad also protected me, but there wasn't a lot of emotional connection. He was the first one to stand up and say what he thought was right. He provided. As far as the dream he had for me, I was confused. The conflicting messages I received led me to feel he had no dream. He wanted me to be self-sufficient, healthy, happy. I was so afraid of him disliking or disapproving of me, yet he was never a violent person."

—Mentoring Messages

"In school, the mentors were the people who saw the artistic side of me. My 1st grade teacher was a nun. It was the first time I allowed the opinion of someone other than my mother to come into my life. She started to develop my drawing and painting. When she saw my work, she shifted assignments around toward what I was doing. We began sketching objects, not just filling in the coloring books we had."

—Mentor Bonding

Eduardo asked if the influence of the person had to be of a positive nature. I responded: No, I have a category that I call Toxic Mentors.
"Then my 2nd grade teacher was a toxic mentor. She was a very hardened, bitter individual. It was horrible. I got a clear sense that I was not okay. I would go to school in the morning sick to my stomach, not keeping anything down because of the fear. Then I had a lay teacher who had a troubled marriage, and her bitterness came across

to us. Evidence again that school was not a happy place. My 1st grade experience was a fluke as far as I was concerned."

— Toxic Mentors

"I didn't get joy in learning until 4th grade, when I had a teacher who appreciated me. She acknowledged me, went out of her way to be supportive, and promoted what I did and did well. Tremendous bonding occurred. I started to feel very strong and very happy. Learning became a treat.

"The next person was my voice teacher in high school. She started to develop my singing. She heard a timbre in my voice that she thought was clear. I also adapted easily and quickly to the science of reading notes, memorizing the sounds in my head. She suggested that I take on some theater arts, so the later part of freshman year, I was doing plays and stuff with the big kids. That gave me a sense of accomplishment and belonging. She continued through college as my professional voice coach. We still speak to each other, and she suggests certain things about voice, and we talk about my recordings.

"Also in high school, Ernesto, a friend of my father whom I'd known since 1st grade, became a big brother or father figure for me. I'd never had the connection with my dad of going out and doing sports. I had a problem with the smog, so I didn't enjoy playing outside. Ernesto used to ice skate and snow ski, so I started playing ice hockey and became a hockey buff. He was my coach and my friend. He would drive me to events. We had a wonderful time all through high school. Then, in skiing, I started competing when I was 17 and won some gold medals in Utah when I was 18 or 19. Skiing became my absolute joy. Then, I started coaching hockey and teaching small children how to snow ski up in Yosemite."

— Mentors

We talked about Eduardo's creative process.
"From the 4th through 8th grades, there was more drawing and painting, entries into contests, prizes won that made me realize it wasn't a freakish thing to do. High school was an artistic time period. I became the Thespian president for three years, was always in the plays, putting together props, doing backdrops, painting scenery, acting. It was a Renaissance time. I didn't get into dramatics until college. My voice teacher's boyfriend was a writer of music and published commercial jingles. He would have me do the demonstration tapes for him."

—Mentoring Interests

Then why, I asked, did you close those down when going to college?
"College represented a time of work. I had a belief that said you work hard and that's all you get to do. Dad wanted me very much to go into the business field. He wondered when I was going to finally come to my senses and realize that money was the hardcore reality of life—not the existential things. He never turned against me, but the lack of support in the artistic things I was doing was clear. So I worked part-time in insurance but allowed myself the luxury of studying something existential and cerebral like teaching and psychology. I felt like Walter Mitty,[31] living in both worlds. The arts were put aside. It was never horrible. I simply like taking the easy way out of everything, so that's what I did in my college years."

—Mentoring Messages/Values

---

[31] Walter Mitty is a fictional character in James Thurber's short story *The Secret Life of Walter Mitty*, published in 1941. Mitty is a meek, mild man with a vivid fantasy life: In a few dozen paragraphs, he imagines himself a wartime pilot, an emergency-room surgeon, and a devil-may-care killer. (Source: Wikipedia. Available at: http://en.wikipedia.org/wiki/Walter_Mitty. Accessed September 23, 2006.)

"During college, my sister came into play. We had not been close; there was too much rivalry. Later, we saw the value in each other. We established a bond that was just amazing—the understanding she has for my emotion-packed life and my career aspirations. I felt a tremendous need to be there for her and make things right. She's been one of my most major influences. I can talk very openly with her about what is going on for me—the upsets, the joys, the frustrations that come with the entertainment business and media. I also can pick her mind about the insurance-related jobs I've taken to supplement my income. She won't let me sell out on my dream."

—Co-mentor

"In my last year in college, I was heavy into my psych major. Humanistic psychology was big at the time, and I found a program called Lifespring to be both very experiential and very nurturing. There, I met Sherm, an artist, musician, and vocalist. He was very a supportive person, like a brother, and we became roommates. He represented for me friendship and freedom. This was my first experience of living away from home."

—Mentoring Experiences, Co-mentor

I knew that Eduardo had done some catering, stemming from his interest in foods picked up from his mother, and that he enjoyed the creative preparation and presentation of food. Here he mentions another mentor, Gerry, who was still important at the time of the second interview.

"Gerry was absolutely a mentor. She brought out the reality that cooking and doing all this creative stuff I've done with food can bring in money. Suddenly, I saw that people would pay for what I love to do. I said I might as well do it for money, so I started to create food, getting verbally and financially rewarded for it. I thought it bizarre—people are paying me for it. There's high drama in gourmet cooking. It's very flamboyant, very artistic."

—Mentor

But catering wasn't enough to provide the income Eduardo needed. He tried moving to another city, continuing in insurance. He soon found himself again in a rut and returned to Southern California. Then things began to change.

"Soon I was out on interviews, and I landed a commercial. Things just completely flip-flopped. I had this drive to maintain the exhilarating feeling of being acknowledged by an industry that's very tight and limiting and frightening. I did more commercials. I met many other people who were instrumental in guiding me, but they aren't people I count on or place deep trust in. They are my agents and producers. They didn't have the impact I had felt from major mentors in my past."

—Minor Mentors

Eduardo at Age 47

Through the intervening years since the first interview, Eduardo continued in insurance—and also did catering and made commercials. Three years after our initial interview, Eduardo moved to the Pacific Northwest to an executive position in an insurance company, bought land, and built a house. Two years later, he took the plunge, leaving financial services completely. He started his own business in Spanish language media advertising, a spin-off from his work doing TV commercials that married his creative talents and business skills.

"I knew there was a market. I didn't know how to get in, so I just jumped in. My timing was lucky. In 1990, the Goodwill Games were staged for the first time, and the organizers brought me in as a Spanish-speaking nations' advisor and emissary. I also knocked on doors of local ad agencies. With two accounts and the Goodwill Games, I ran with it, built the company, and here we are 15 years later. We now land 80% of local market business and do some global business as well."

—Self-Mentoring Strategies/Networking

"Earlier, when I did commercials, I would complain to the director of advertising that the copy for commercials was mediocre. He would say, 'Go ahead and change it.' If there are any cultural concerns in language that might be badly received, the script must be adapted. So I became more of a creative writer, shifting from camera to media. I focus on different styles and cultural elements of the Hispanic media. East Coast Puerto Ricans and Cubans have different accents and tag words. The southwest is more Spanglish. The Midwest is a conglomeration, a good deal of Basque plus migrant workers with border Spanish. You have to understand the publication for which the ad is intended to know what education level people have, and the range and level of Spanish. There's a lot of art in that. I became interested in journalism and writing. It was a shift from on-camera to behind-the-camera directing and producing."

—Mentoring Interests

This experience has led Eduardo to develop his writing skills. He now covers the social scene, writing a monthly column in a city-focused magazine on local trends, politics, theater, arts—both in English and Spanish. He sees himself doing more journalism in the future. But that's not all of the melding of creative and business interests. He also works with Gerry, his long-standing foods mentor, occasionally taking on catering jobs and coordinating large scale parties in the Pacific Northwest and Canada. He also does some food-related international travel.

"I'm so grateful to Renee, the editor of the city magazine. She gave me an opening, because I was not a professional writer on that level. She has groomed me and edits my work, now less and less every year.

"Gerry evolved into a 'growing old with me' mentor. She's the longest mentor to me in the foods field, and she continues to update me on trends in southern California. We're on the phone constantly. She comes up here to do jobs that are clearly at the masters level of catering knowledge, and she sends me to the people she knows are of equal caliber. Occasionally, I teach in cooking schools in the northwest, California, Spain, and Paris, with an emphasis on the cuisine of southern Mexico and Spain."

—Step-Ahead Mentors, Mentoring Interests

I asked Eduardo about a possible mentoring relationship with his partner Jay, since Jay, too, is in the arts.

"The attraction came with his being an artist; the repulsion came with, 'My God, he's an artist!' What I learned from him is that he is both talented in the arts but also a good business person. He knows the ins and outs of the production side, the elements of musical direction. On the flip side, he writes plays and composes music and lyrics. He knows what it takes to make something work, and he knows how to sell it."

—*Co-mentoring*

Eduardo's relationship with his parents has shifted over the years. He has integrated the values of his father with the support from his mother. His father, now in retirement, is consulting with Eduardo's translation business.

"Dad and I have switched roles in the translation business. We complement each other. He brings an experienced but different point of view on how to say something in a very short period of time—a 30 second radio spot. But I'm dealing with newer concepts of speech and media than what he knew from being in business long ago. He sobers me up: here's the standard; we need to be consistent."

—*Co-mentor*

When he looks ahead, Eduardo has a full agenda.

"I'd love to be able to consider retirement in my early 50s, but I love what I'm doing. I just hope my partner and I are together the rest of this time. I also hope that I can do something for the world community through the medium of writing. I want to write about things that are colorful, meaningful—not just light stuff."

Comments on Eduardo's Mentoring Pattern

Central to Eduardo's remarkable mentoring pattern is his interest in the arts and the strong messages he internalized about economic security. In the second interview, we see how he has managed to meld the two into a full-time business. Not content with a single outlet for his talents, he also continues to devote additional time to his wide-ranging creative talents. He has reappraised the mentoring messages from long ago and has established a meaningful relationship with both parents, exemplified most clearly in the co-mentoring with his father concerning Spanish language translation. In addition, he has a number of step-ahead and co-mentoring relationships with both men and women.

THE STORY OF DANIEL

Daniel at Age 34

I first met Daniel when he was a new physician partner in a hospital emergency medicine practice. He and his wife had purchased a two-acre home in a semi-rural suburb where they could have horses. Daniel commuted some distance to the hospital where he worked. He was willing to do this as a trade-off for the rural life. When I asked him what came to his mind as to mentors he may have had or mentoring influences, he responded immediately.

"They've been people I've never met. Most were people I read about and had ideas about in my mind. When I was a kid, I didn't study much; I'd do things that I wanted to do. I did a lot of art, worked on a science fair project by myself, things like that. One summer vacation, I started reading a book on Marie Curie, her life story. I was really motivated by her life story, her study techniques, the way she worked. I was also impressed and motivated by the creativity of Leonardo da Vinci, Isaac Newton, Jacob Bronowski. Those would be my main mentors."

—Mentoring Models

"Then, there were college professors who were reinforcing for me, very energetic people. When I read a book, I would think about how it pertained to me or to some problem I was having. I would do the same with some of my college professors. I would see the way they interacted with others, the way they valued what they were doing, and I would try different things that they suggested."

— *Self-Mentoring Strategy/Mentoring Models*

I asked Daniel how early that pattern had started. He guessed that it was with his father during vacations in northern Michigan.

"It's very quiet up there, and I had a lot of time to think, to observe and appreciate the natural world. The skies were so clear that I could see a lot of stars—and the lake. I would spend the day in the woods or down on the beach. I was usually the only person there. I became interested in astronomy, mineralogy, weather. I was amazed by everything around me. That led me to getting books so I could understand more. My reading both encouraged and reinforced my interest in life processes and the mysteries of life—and from there into science."

— *Mentoring Play/Mentoring Interests*

I asked Daniel about his relationship with his father.

"He was very supportive, but he was a very basic guy. He works hard and does lots in the out-of-doors. His work ethic is very important to him. Even though there wasn't an educational emphasis in our family, it was clear that whatever you do, you should try to do very well and be really thorough. Do it well enough that you're proud of what you've done, no matter what it is. Don't give up; see it through—don't let whatever it is defeat you. My father also does a lot of hunting and fishing, but he has this great respect for nature. He's probably one of the best salmon fishers in Michigan, but he'll keep only one fish; he'll turn the rest loose. There are a lot of subtle things I picked up from him."

— *Mentoring Messages/Values*

"My relationship with my father fell apart when I decided to go to college. He never understood why I needed to study. Mother was more encouraging and supportive. She would work to get things I needed—books or paper, paints. She thought it was important for us to be able to pursue what we wanted. Sometimes, she would be a mediator. My mother liked to see me read and would encourage me to go to the library and pick up a book along the lines I was interested in."

—*Mentor Support and Encouragement*

Daniel mentioned his interest in art. When did that develop?
"All along. I never really formally pursued it. I thought of going into art as late as high school. It was similar to science in a way— something you can do by yourself that doesn't cost a lot. During summers, I would always take art materials and do drawings of lakes or trees or people. I did it alone—that is something I liked. I think I was very shy, and I spent a lot of time by myself.

"I didn't start studying seriously probably until college. I just pursued what interested me. Summer vacations were the best time of the year. I'd hit on the idea that I wanted to be a paleontologist, and I'd study fossils for a couple of weeks. Then, I'd turn to weather, minerals, oceanography, the study of animals. I'd pursue each interest for a couple of weeks, or a summer. Or, I'd get interested in something else and do that for a while."

—*Mentoring Play/Mentoring Interests*

"There were always teachers who felt I could do better academically. It wasn't that I couldn't do it. Most just didn't understand that I wasn't really interested. They were supportive and encouraging, but studying didn't seem relevant at the time. Some of my science teachers and art teachers would let me come in after class and use the equipment. They didn't have preconceived notions that I had to earn an A in their class. They just cared that I was interested in doing other projects and that I seemed enthusiastic about it. If I wanted to come in after class, that was fine."

—*Mentors*

I asked for examples ...
... in art:
"I was impressed that I could make things out of clay. When the art teacher had projects the whole class would do, I'd be really enthusiastic and do a good job. She'd say to me, 'Even though we're going on to do water-coloring for six weeks, you can stay after class if you like and work with some clay and use the kiln.' I'd think up something to do, and she'd give me suggestions on the best way to do it."

... in science:
"We'd all do a routine science project, like dissect a frog. A couple of the science teachers would have other specimens, and they would ask if I'd be interested in dissecting them. I would just stick around for hours and do it. I'm more interested in the mysteries of life than I am in any formal study of something. Still, I knew I was going to college, because I realized that the things I wanted to pursue couldn't be done without it. Once that dawned on me, I put up with the requirements. I picked up on the idea that to get from A to C you had to go through B. That's why the book on Marie Curie was important. It made me realize that I was doing poorly because I hadn't been studying, as opposed to not being able to do it."
— Self-Mentoring

"In college, a professor of immunology and physiology let me use her laboratory to do what I wanted, with the condition that I always had to do well in my studies. We became good friends. I would do what interested me in the lab, and I knew she would keep me in line. She knew the other professors there, and she would check to see how I was doing in courses and give me reading materials. She was a definite mentor my first two years. After she left, I continued on with a physiology professor she introduced me to. He did animal research and had a big clinic. He was very supportive, and we carried on the same way. I was interested in their personalities and their enthusiasm."
— Mentors

Somewhere along the way, you decided you wanted to go to medical school; how did that come about?

"That was a continuation of my philosophy—the human body was more mysterious than anything else. I started doing a lot of volunteer work between my senior year in college and the following year. I wasn't sure exactly what I wanted to do. I talked to medical school admissions people. They said, 'Since it looks like you want to go into research, you can get a Ph.D. You don't need an M.D.' But I really wanted to do patient care. I was more interested in the mysteries of the human body than the cell. I was convinced they were wrong.

"So, I did a year of volunteer work—50 hours a week at the medical center and local kidney center—and just checked out what it was like to be in those environments. I would do whatever the nurses or orderlies wanted help doing. A lot of times, I would talk to patients—that was my main thing. A lot were depressed but were very talkative. Many didn't have family members around, some with devastating illnesses. I talked to a number of patients who were dying; it was strange and had a profound effect on me. Many times, I would stay until 11 or 12 at night. By the time I finished my year, I was really convinced I wanted to stick with medicine. It was all very motivating. I finally got an interview and was accepted."

—*Planned Mentoring Experience*

What was medical school like for you?

"It was four of the best years of my life; I loved it. The medical school was on a pass/fail basis, which was ideal for me. The emphasis was meeting a certain level, and then you could do what you wanted. I didn't have to worry about competing with others to get to the top. I spent time with friends in languages, music, and art, and I started incorporating those interests into my life."

—*Mentoring Experiences/Broadening*

"I became interested in pediatrics—the nicest people I met were pediatricians. There were a lot of sick kids—I was drawn to their problems. I liked surgery more, but I couldn't stand the surgeons, largely because of their personalities. I did four years of a pediatrics internship and found it rewarding—mysteries, sick kids, very hard work. It was very depressing at times, because these were kids who had something terrible going wrong and were referred to the university medical center. There was such a dichotomy: When we went out into the pediatricians' offices, we would rarely see a sick kid. In a sense, you're going 200 miles an hour in a sports car, and then you're walking backward. I'm getting all this training to help sick people, but there are not that many sick people in a pediatric practice.

"So instead of going into practice, I stayed on for a 4th year. It gave me a year to think about ways I could use my medical training to help really sick patients without being totally devastating. I ended up in emergency medicine. It dawned on me that the ER was the place you saw sick patients. You could do a bit of surgery and orthopedics. Anatomy was very important. But diagnosis was the main thing. You had to find out what was wrong. That mission filled a need I had. I also liked the idea that I could work hard for 12 to 14 hours and then leave, that it wasn't a continuing process. I was able to go home and read about what I was interested in or what I had seen that day that I hadn't known anything about. Emergency medicine gave me a sense of freedom, almost like the pass/fail system in medical school. I could do things other than just spending my whole day doing surgery or pediatrics."

—Self-Mentoring

I remarked that Daniel seemed to have a pattern—that in two critical periods of his life, he took a year out to check his interests and then made a sharp turn. He agreed.

"I head in a direction. But rather than totally committing to that direction at the outset, I head in that direction and see how things go."

—Planned Mentoring Experience

Daniel at Age 51

When I tracked down Daniel, I wasn't at all surprised to learn that he had moved. He is now living in the Pacific Northwest, 40 miles from a large city, but within commuting distance of the suburb where his hospital emergency medicine partnership is based. He and his family live on 20 acres of land where they (particularly his wife and daughter) raise and board horses. Daniel had just completed cutting a big circle through their woods for a horse trail. Their three children range from teens to a 5-year- old. Since Daniel started raising a family later in his life, he has no plans for early retirement as some of his partners have done.

That's not a problem, though. Daniel is happy in what he is doing and in the lifestyle he and his family have, living in a more rural community and enjoying camping trips into the mountains and streams of the Northwest. Nature remains central in his life. His work, although he carefully manages it so that it doesn't strip him of his energy, continues to fascinate him. His choice of emergency medicine has worked for him, because it provides the daily opportunity to be engrossed in life's mysteries. Here is how he puts it:

"Even though I find it stressful sometimes, I'm doing largely what I want to do and have always wanted to do. Other ER physicians like it, but they don't *love* it. I enjoy the hunt, trying to figure out what the person has. One day, a partner I was working with had a kid who was being sent to the trauma center in the city. The child had had a seizure. We did a spinal tap and concluded it might be meningitis. After the child left, the nurse said that when the kid came in with a seizure, she also was making weird motions with her mouth and tongue. The nurse had never seen anything like that. The CAT scan was normal, but lab work was just a little abnormal. So I found the original ER doc and said, 'Did you consider that the kid might have herpes? That could affect the temporal lobe. If you didn't start medication, the kid could have a bad outcome.' So he called the trauma hospital and then called me at home. It turned out the kid *did* have herpes. He said, 'You saved that kid's life—and mine, too.' I took more satisfaction from what transpired than anything the whole day. That's the kind of thing I live for."

— *Co-Mentoring*

In earlier years, when Daniel was trying to sort out what he wanted to do, one draw was medicine; the other was art. Medicine won out. In recent years, he has found himself drawing and painting again when he has free time.

"The art has an interesting effect on me. I just started doing a few drawings of my daughters, some watercolors, and studying oil painting again. I hadn't done anything like that for a long time. Now when I get ideas about things I'd like to explore in paint or some strong image hits me while I'm in the ER or outdoors, I make a note and put them in folders."

— *Mentoring Interests*

"Working in the ER, you see things that are an amazing part of life. Sometimes, they can be very happy and sometimes very sad. Some doctors write about their experiences in medicine. I have the idea in the back of my mind that in five or 10 years, I might draw or paint some of the things going on in the ER. Paintings can tell a story. That's how art fits in for me. Right now, I'm spending more time on the techniques, approaching the task seriously. I've studied more art than medicine in past two years. I'll go to a medical conference if there's also something going on in an art museum nearby. Recently, I attended an advanced ER course in a city where the local museum was featuring a great art exhibit on drawing people. I spent about four or five hours at the museum. I was much more drained there, looking, making notes. It was more exhausting than the exam of the advanced course, but I was also having fun."

— *Planned Mentoring Experience*

Daniel's wife and children are very understanding of what he's doing.
"They are a barometer for me. I was thinking of a job switch for a long time, but I couldn't make the decision. When I asked them, they unanimously told me to leave and why. I knew their reasons were correct, but it was different coming from them, especially my wife. They refocus and redirect me. They reel me back in. They also tell me when I need to take time off. They'll say, 'You're doing it again—look at the schedule.' They rebalance things out for me. I run things by them. We all sit around, particularly when we're having dinner, and talk. It's like a family council."

—Co-Mentoring/Mentoring Environment

Comments on Daniel's Mentoring Pattern

Daniel's mentor bonding with his father was limited, because his father could not understand Daniel's interest in learning and in probing life's mysteries. Trust and respect were present in their relationship, but not relevance. Later, when Daniel found adult figures who understood his motivation, mentoring relationships developed easily. His mentor bonding with his mother helped pave the way for this process. She understood his interest in education and was supportive and encouraging. She would mediate with his father and provide materials for Daniel's art.

Daniel stands out among the people I interviewed in terms of his strong inner gyroscope. It is not surprising that he has found his own sources and resources of mentoring—in books, nature, and research. Early in his life, Daniel developed self-mentoring strategies that have served him well through the years. Particularly of note is his ability to structure mentoring experiences for himself. His year of volunteer work to test his interest in becoming a clinician rather than a researcher is one example. His self-study in art is another.

In later life, spouse mentoring becomes important. Daniel values his family council, a type of mentoring environment that helps him maintain balance in his life.

THE STORY OF BELL

Bell at Age 47

I have known Bell for many years. At the time of our first interview, she had moved from clinical nursing into nursing management at an investor-owned hospital. Bell grew up in an extended African-American family in a Louisiana town homesteaded by her great-grandfather after the Civil War. Her grandfather believed in teachers, so Dell grew up with many teachers in her family. I asked Bell what came to her mind about mentors and the mentoring process in her life. She listed a cavalcade of people throughout her life who have influenced her, including a number from her extended family—a panoply of rich mentoring relationships.

"When I think about people who made a big impact on my life, people who have influenced the things I've done, the first person who comes to mind is my cousin by marriage who taught 5th grade. She played the piano at church and taught us piano. I have some tears in my eyes when I think the amount of energy and time she put into giving us cultural experiences that otherwise we never would have had. After all, we were a black family in this very small community in the South. Schools were segregated, and there wasn't anything else to influence us. She gave me a lot: enrichment, setting my values, wanting me to do more than just have a baby. It was done out of love.

"My cousin Edward, 15 years older, was a bright young man, a science teacher. He didn't want us to be 'common women,' so he took it on himself to teach my sister and me some 'class.' He would spend Saturday nights with us, improving our vocabulary, listening to classical music, and playing bridge. He eventually went back and got his master's and Ph.D. and is now an assistant dean at a northern university.

"I guess the most important person in my life is my mother—I could not even talk about the person I am without talking about her. She was a lady with a 6th grade education, but a Ph.D. in life. She was 32 when my father was killed in a hunting accident, leaving her with eight children. She chose not to remarry; instead, she went to work to provide us with all the necessities and extra things growing children needed. She taught us some very specific things: 'You remain a lady under all circumstances, no curlers, don't go out without stockings,' 'I don't want you to do what I'm doing [scrubbing floors and cleaning houses], but I don't want you to be ashamed. If you have to, you can do it.' There was continuous reinforcement for my sister and me—how important it was to be self-supporting and independent. At the same time, she never negated marriage. 'I want you to get married,' she said, 'but there are other things you need to achieve before you do that.' She always believed in working for yourself and not taking a handout. She would work all day, come home, cook, and still have time to see that we finished our homework and talk to us about what went on that day. I never went a day without having a hot breakfast before going off to school. She would make sure we were dressed properly, and then get herself off to work. I couldn't ask for a better mother in preparing me for where I am. As I've gotten older, I realize I mirror her a lot—my drive, my ambition, my ability to work and not mind working.

"Two others were important after we moved to California. My Uncle Ivy was in business, and I went to work for him summers and Saturdays. He was an entrepreneur, truly a sales person. He was always giving me little hints about how to be effective in selling. I never saw it as a career, but now that I opened my own business, I can see myself picking up on many of the little hints he taught me. I also realize that I'm naturally a salesperson, and I'm beginning to appreciate this ability. Also important was a history teacher, Mr. Holcomb, who always encouraged girls to participate in debates and be a part of the team. In those days in high school, you signed up for college prep or the commercial track. The lady looked at me and said, 'Are you sure you want to do college prep? Are you sure you don't want to be a secretary?' I said, 'No, I intend to be a nurse,' and I related that to Mr. Holcomb. He continually encouraged me to follow my interests and not be discouraged, because there were people who would discourage me, being black and female. The racism was subtle in 1950."

—*Mentors*

Later, Bell mentions the physician researcher who headed a project where she was a research nurse.

"Allan made a tremendous impact on my intellectual growth and on my life. He taught me to be creative, that you didn't need a Ph.D. to be creative or make important contributions. His style of brainstorming was to sit me down and ask my opinion. He gave me instant trust. He'd say, 'Here's the program, and here's my idea of what I want to accomplish. I want to do outreach around such and such problems in the city.' He didn't know how we were going to do it. That was the challenge to the team. I loved it. I could zero in on his central approach and ideas and start being creative about how we could get there."

—*Mentor*

Bell also mentions her relationship with the current director of nursing.

"Celia and I have a shared value system of nursing. I tease her: We're two southern women [one white, one black] whose basic values are the same and who are both very strong about being female. She knew far more than I did, and I wanted to learn certain aspects of management from her: her leadership style, her ability to get a point across, and her ability to write. On the other hand, I'm more politically astute, aware, calmer, and more analytical in a managerial or political situation."

—*Co-Mentor/Reciprocal*

How did you develop your astuteness?

"To tell the truth, I don't know. I've never been a militant female or a militant black. I grew up liking who I was, being sensitive at times to the fact that I was black. I have an ability to look at a situation and understand—maybe it's the listening, hearing more than one message. I am a kind of peacemaker, an intervener. Even when I was a child, my mother always reached out to me when there were conflicts or she needed an ear. I was always there—I don't know why. I can always remember listening to my mother getting up, and I could tell the mood she was in. I would be aware if she was sad or upset. Or, when she was standing at the stove thinking, I could tell if she was sad, or worried about money and how she was going to make ends meet. I'd go to her, and we'd have our little conferences where I'd sit and listen to her. She was always comfortable sharing with me. Now that I look back, that's probably where it started."

—Mentoring Experience

Not very many people who are your age could claim 40 years of experience in being sensitive to nuances, to see where people are coming from under all kinds of situations and stresses.
"I realize that I was a comfort to my mother, a human being who was there for her to talk to. Oh, and she's unbelievably fair. No matter what, she always tried to be fair to us all—never making us feel all lumped in."

—Mentoring Messages: Values

"Another key person is my second husband, who turned out to be my friend, first and foremost, and an important mentor in my life. He's an accountant. What I most value is that he respects me for my ability and knowledge. When I give my opinion, he listens; he needs and values my input as much as I need and value his. I'm comfortable saying, 'Here's a situation; let's talk about it'—whether it's personal or outside of our lives. He's the first man in my life with whom I can be open and honest and not feel that I should be something else."

—Spouse Mentoring

Why did you choose nursing?
"I was programmed most of my life. My mother used to call me Miss Helen, after the public health nurse. So in my head, nursing always

was there. My first dream was to be a lawyer. As time moved on, I became more realistic. My mother could not pay for me to go to the university. Yet, the lesson I had in my head was that I must be self-supporting, I must take care of myself. Since I didn't want to be a teacher, the easiest thing was to go to nursing school."

—*Mentoring Messages*

"After the research project with Allan, I knew I could not go back into regular nursing and find the same environment that he allowed. I was realistic. I went to work on my master's in health administration, but a confrontation with one of the instructors who was teaching hospital administration put the brakes on. Someone asked him how he hired directors of nurses, and he said it was when he found someone who was 'hot to trot.' Worse, he was also my counselor! I picked up my books, walked out of class, and never went back. I went to the dean and told him I could never sit in a class like that; I could never respect that instructor. There had been other incidents as well. So, my husband and I founded a travel business. I stepped out of nursing for two years. I found I had good selling skills and the ability to market myself and my business. But I felt I must always have that nursing skill as a backup, in case something happened. When I returned to nursing, I was hired as relief supervisor. That time was rewarding."

—*Toxic Mentor*

As I read "the tea leaves" to Bell, she reflected:
"You brought out a thought process for me. I see there can be mentoring that we are not conscious of as well as conscious mentoring. The really conscious sort probably does not occur until you are of a more mature age. For me, my current boss is my most conscious mentor. The other people—it just happened. My decision to stay on here was because I knew that I could learn from her."

Bell at Age 66

Bell has traveled a long way in her career since the time of the first interview when she was doing hospital-based nursing management. Soon after, the HMO decided to expand and open seven clinics. The person hired to oversee the expansion effort quit. Her boss and the regional health plan executive, Mike, asked Bell to take over and implement the clinic openings by the stated date. She agreed, having laid out the conditions for taking on the job. Given the time crunch, no one expected her to succeed, but she did. She hired the doctors, staffed the clinics, and opened on time. In the process, she developed the reputation: "Whenever a job has to be done, give it to Bell!"

Later, Mike moved to a national insurance company health plan and offered Bell an executive post responsible for operations. It was a career move that Bell said couldn't have been better. She learned to manage multiple systems within a large corporation and, for the past five years, has been managing a database system covering two regions, 16 markets, and close to 60,000 providers.

Bell credits Mike as an important mentor in this period of her life. Even now, if Bell needs advice, she will call Mike, even though he is no longer working for the company.

"He always made sure I had opportunities to be seen and heard. If the right job came up, I always had the chance to bid it."

—Mentor

Becoming experienced in corporate governance, systems, and technology was a big shift for Bell. In addition to mentoring from her boss, the company has a well-established development program for managers. Managers at her level are required to take courses in project management, accounting, and communication skills. When she worked in the hospital world, management was not in an economic position to assist staff other than on-the-job training.

Information technology is an area where Bell coaches her managers, especially three new managers she plans to bring up to speed before she retires. The challenge is how to use information technology to meet the needs of providers, to anticipate and fix problems that may arise, and to stay in compliance with the law.

"In the systems world, there are two arenas of politics you have to learn about—one related to the technology and the other to the business. There often are problems around development, delivery, and implementation of systems. It's tricky. When I'm doing a cost-benefits justification, there's always a question about what perspective to take and where to place the emphasis. Those can be career-breaking decisions if you aren't careful. Less experienced managers have a lot to learn here."

—Mentoring

What are your plans after retirement?
"Several of us want to provide supplementary services to seniors on Medicaid. On the basis of an earlier corporate job starting up and rolling out Medicare products, I think there's a real need for services. I don't know how serious the company is, but they tell me they're looking for an administrator for an initiative in this area. I'll probably volunteer my services to get it started."

Looking back over her career, Bell provided this summary of the people mentors who have helped her throughout her career:
"Allan [the pediatrician researcher] was my first career developer. He put the bug in my ear: You can do other things than nursing. I was validated, I had options. I could stay in the clinical field without having to provide bedside nursing. He said, 'Use your brain for other things.' Along came Celia [director of nursing], who was not only a friend and mentor but absolutely a developer. Certain things I learned from her I still use: my management style, how I document my communication to my managers, how I create an agenda. I learned the skills of management from her. From Ted [the regional health care executive], I learned the politics of management. He used to tell me, 'Listen, listen, listen—and then speak. You want to know what other folks are thinking and feeling before you express your opinion.' My husband is my

stabilizer, listener, and confidant. We dream together, we scheme together, and we enjoy our family together."

—Mentors

Comments on Bell's Mentoring Pattern

In contrast to Daniel, we see in Bell's pattern strong mentor bonding early in her life and the panoply of people mentors who followed. It is natural for Bell to reach out and learn from people. It is also a natural corollary for her to mentor others. The value systems (mentoring messages) in her extended family were consistent and strong. Mentor bonding took place with both men and women, making it natural for her to seek help from all people who fit her interests and value system. It's important to note the variety of mentoring relationships in Bell's life: traditional (Allan), step-ahead (Mike, Uncle Ivy, and her cousins), co-mentoring (Celia), and spouse mentoring.

THE STORY OF BRUCE

Bruce at Age 56

When I first interviewed Bruce, he was 56 and a long-time parish minister at his church. He listed a cadre of ministers, professors, and writers who provided intellectual stimulation and were powerful mentoring models for him in the worlds of the intellect and of religion.

"I had never imagined that a clergy person would be a mentor to me, but Bill was so intellectually stimulating in his sermons and seminars. I was a young man in college, fascinated by ideas; Bill was surely in his early 50s. My mind was reaching out hungrily for fresh ways of understanding the world, and he just happened to fill all those needs. He was a student of ideas, and he gave me a picture of what a rich, broad intellectual life could be. He encouraged me, without saying it in so many words, to begin a lifetime of reading and study, a path I subsequently followed. I sat at his feet, figuratively speaking, listening to him, admiring him. He became the most conspicuous mentor in my life up to that point. It was Bill who influenced me to go into the ministry later on—I didn't realize it at the time."

—Mentor

"Another mentor was a philosophy teacher at my university. This was after the war [World War II]. I came out of the Navy so hungry to study and to learn that my mind and spirit were like a sponge. Professor Fallon opened me to the world of philosophy that I had known before only by having read one or two books. All these figures in philosophy greatly stimulated me, gave me models of a way of life, an intellectual life. These people modeled values, ideas, and concepts. I brought my own judgments and biases to it, but they showed me what life could be about."

—Mentoring Models

"I went to Cambridge in the fall of 1949 to start graduate work at Harvard. I would visit ministers of my denomination in the Boston area. One modeled for me what being a minister could be like. I don't think I ever had a mentor in terms of a close, personal relationship. But both he and Bill invaded my unconscious to the point where it slowly became apparent to me that I wanted to be a minister. Consciously, I had planned to seek a university post as a philosophy professor, but I came to a kind of crisis—was teaching philosophy really what I wanted? I became aware of flaws and concluded that an academic career would be too narrow and sterile. Besides, I was interested in religion as much as philosophy.

"Other mentors that I had in this period were figures I met through the pages of books. Albert Camus is the outstanding one, and I became entranced with existentialist philosophy. Camus was more a humanistic existentialist, not quite so pessimistic and dark as Sartre. The other figure that greatly influenced me in those years was Eric Fromm, the psychoanalyst."

—Mentoring Models

"When I became a minister in my first job in Albany, there was a senior minister in a nearby city who became my mentor, but in a different sense. Doug was not an intellectual model, but he was an experienced person who could teach me the ropes of parish ministry. I was terribly green. When we would go off to various ministers' meetings together, he would advise me on the practicalities of everyday professional life. He was a wise, senior counselor who took me under his wing."

— Traditional Mentor

"In more recent years, my mentor was the director of religious education at the church. She has particular skills in group leadership and group dynamics. She is able to listen carefully and to discern what is going on in a group situation, in board meetings, in committee meetings. Her sensitivities were far beyond my own perceptions. I could teach her in the world of concepts, books, and ideas—that has always been my forte. She had skills in other areas that I have needed and depended upon. So we traded off our different strong points and made a good team."

— Co-Mentor/Reciprocal

We turned then to his family background.
"My mother was the dominant figure in terms of force of personality and exercise of power. She was the one to be feared and the one whose tongue-lashing or viewpoints were likely to be decisive. My father was an absentee figure, a traveling salesman away much of the time. Even when he was at home, he did not relate warmly. But I was greatly attached to him and sought his approval. He was a gentle, non-violent man, rather quiet and genteel. I thought his way of being in the world was much more desirable and worthy of emulation than my mother's. My mother was very critical of my father. It was not a happy marriage. I loved my father and wanted to behave like him, yet I feared being like him. I was torn."

— Mentor-Bonding Deficits

"My father influenced me to go to a technical institute for chemical engineering. He didn't know who I was, and I didn't know who I was, and being a chemical engineer was far away from my interests and temperament. It was not right for me, but I was influenced by his nonverbal messages. I had learned to read him, all the cues. On the positive side, he was a very great influence in shaping my values and my personality."

—Mentoring Messages/Values

"My mother and I had a combative relationship. I was rebellious. She was frustrated in her own personal ambitions and poured them into her sons. She pushed my brother and me to achieve in every respect. If we failed to meet her expectations, she made us feel very guilty, as if we were 'shiftless, unambitious, ne'er-do-wells.' It was the standard guilt-inducing, high-achievement push."

—Mentoring Messages/Toxic

"A few teachers stand out. One conveyed to me the beauty and possibilities of the English language. I was fascinated with her class, the way she presented the material, and I was sorry when the bell rang at the end of the class. Reading and study were honored in my home; books and learning were honored. My interest in reading and writing just seems to always have been part of my world."

—Mentoring Messages/Values

"There was a friend of mine, Robert, through junior and senior high school. We were inseparable buddies. We played word games when we rode our bikes. Some days, we would converse in Shakespearean English, another time in a Charlie Chan-type language. He was a mentor in the sense of a peer whose interests and talents meshed with my own. Ours was very creative play, and it gave me a deeper love of and appreciation for language in its many forms."

—Mentoring Play

"I spent summers with my aunt and uncle. One summer, I went to a Methodist camp, an experience that had a mentoring effect on me. It was the people. I wasn't into theology and didn't care. But the people seemed to be loving, warm, accepting, non-judgmental, non-critical— just the opposite of my mother. It was okay to be myself."

—Mentoring Experience/Eye-Opening

"After high school, I started at a technical institute. Very quickly, I realized it was not my world. I tried to fit in, but it all seemed alien to me. Then the war intervened, and I joined the Navy when I was 18. I would probably never have taken the initiative to leave home without that. The Navy was a searching time for me—who am I and what do I want to become—a transitional period accompanied by great confusion and a feeling of being lost. The turning point in the Navy came in China, the day I was ashore, lonely, wandering around. In a bookstore there, by some mystery, I pulled off the shelf Will Durant's Story of Philosophy and another book. Together, they changed my life. It was like flipping a light switch, and I knew what I wanted: I wanted to be a philosopher. It was a magnificent religious experience. It showed me who I was. Those two books set the direction for my life for all the years subsequent. They gave me a sense of possibility. When I came out of the Navy, I went to the university."

—Mentoring Experiences/Time Out/Eye-Opening, Self-Mentoring

"The Navy experience allowed me to break away from my provincial roots. I had never really traveled, hadn't been much out of Texas. Overnight, the Navy brought me to San Diego, housed me in huge barracks of men from all over, taught me the discipline of the armed services. It was instant transition into a new world, and it was good."

—Mentoring Experience/Broadening

"The one mentor who hasn't been mentioned is the girl who had the grace to want me as her husband. She took the initiative. You see, in my world, women took the initiative—that was the world of women I knew. She opened for me the world of relationships. She taught me more than any mentor ever has about the deep emotional dimensions of life. She did for affect what the books did for intellect. She also opened up the world of travel, theater, art, and music. She expanded my world over a thousand-fold across the years. I did not know the skills of relating emotionally, did not have the courage. She was the one who made the demands for me to grow in directions I found threatening and fearful. She gave me no choice."

—Spouse Mentoring/Broadening Experience

Bruce at Age 77

By the time of the second interview, Bruce had been retired for 10 years. I asked him what happened in the years before retirement and in his move into this new life.

"I had a long interval focusing on career. Unfortunately, my career too often predominated over family. That was a syndrome of working men at that time—focus on career and on earning money. So, retirement marked a huge transition in my life. By definition, I was no longer career-oriented. I had no office to go to. I had to remake my life completely, whereas before, I had been totally absorbed in the church. Essentially, what I've been doing has been remaking, reshaping, reorienting my values, my commitments, my interests."

—Self-Mentoring

How have you gone about that?
"Interestingly, that happened in a way I could not foresee. My planning went into setting up an office in my home, to have a place to function. I thought I would devote myself to reading, writing, and the ways I'd always developed intellectually. Then things began to intervene. I agreed to join the board of the church-sponsored retirement home, becoming immersed in trying to save that institution and in issues of

assisted-living and health care. Then, I was called on to fill the needed role of bioethicist at the regional Veteran's Administration facility, on the institutional review board. These two positions opened a whole new world to me. Before, I had foreseen retirement as sitting in my chair and absorbing the wisdom of the ages!"

—Mentoring Experiences/Broadening

"But more important than these experiences has been a Wednesday lunch group of eight of us retired men, all of whom come out of the church and know each other. It has become a men's support group. We talk about our prostates, our cholesterol levels, our impending strokes, and all those things. We share in one another's aches and pains, and we play tennis together. It's more meaningful than any group I've belonged to—meaningful in that we're all in the same season of life and share concerns like the stock market, health, family, and grandchildren.

"The unique thing is that these men are minimally defensive in protecting their own egos. We share ideas, largely politics, but we talk about our feelings about growing older, our sense of loss when someone dies. We share intimately the last season of life—retirement and aging. That has proved to be more meaningful and important to me than almost anything else. Again, it's totally unplanned. It is a group in which I can express myself."

—Mentoring Environment

"For decades, I used the pulpit for the measured sharing of ideas, thoughts, and concerns. In contrast, I find myself in the lunch group speaking up, uninhibited, because of the level of trust. There is nothing I cannot share with this group of men, and that's rare. Interestingly, and totally unexpected, that experience of sharing and opening myself has permitted me to open up with my wife in a way I've never done before. I carry our lunch conversation home and find myself talking to my wife about what we shared. I'm more inclined to open myself to her than I have ever been. I had been armored in the classic sense.

"She, in turn, has helped me discover another whole dimension of life. I now see how narrow living only in the head can be. There's a whole world of feelings that are really more important—that's where one lives. That defines a person more than ideas. If you can open your heart in the Buddhist sense, to be in touch with your deepest feelings—that really defines who you are. Now, we take care of one another; we don't want to lose the other. When she had her surgery, I wanted to be with her. I didn't feel obliged. You protect your foremost essence."

—Spouse Mentoring/Self-Mentoring

"The Wednesday lunch group opened a portion of me that I had locked out for fear of being rejected, being seen as foolish—all kinds of fears. The older you are, there's less to lose. You don't worry about status. I can risk more, because there's less that I need to conceal, less that I'm afraid of showing. It's been freeing. After 77 years, I've continued to grow, to open myself up, and let who I am be expressed emotionally and verbally. Somewhere in my mind, I knew I needed to do this, but I didn't quite know how. I certainly didn't have the courage until I found myself in circumstances—the lunch group—where it just happened.

"Those of my age are going through a great deal of life review. As I've gotten to know myself a lot better, I've had a chance to be reconciled to what I've done and have been in my life—my parenting, my marriage, my career. I'm so vividly aware of my shortcomings. I've gone through the remorse, contrition, agonies, and regrets about so many things. The loss of the closeness of my children, how much more my marriage could have been. Even my career would have been different were I to go into it again."

—Self-Mentoring

Comments on Bruce's Mentoring Pattern

Early mentor bonding was weak in Bruce's life. He rejected his mother and her values but admired his father's personal style and values. Initially, he followed his father's suggestion regarding career only to conclude the field was not right for him--that his advice was not relevant.

Bruce's service in World War II allowed him to break away from familial expectations and enlarged his vistas (time-out and broadening experiences). Much self-mentoring followed in the direction of his reading. Mentoring models helped him shape his career path, and mentoring relationships helped him learn the ropes of parish ministry. Overall, the depth of his reading and the models he sought to follow heavily guided his intellectual development.

That was the nature of his mentoring in the intellectual and career arenas. In his emotional development, the nudging of his wife and the mentoring environment of the men's support group opened him to the importance of the emotional/affective world and his need to develop those long-dormant parts of himself. His determination to find a way to discover these parts of himself (self-mentoring) has been the dramatic record of his post-retirement life.

THE STORY OF CLARISSE

Clarisse at Age 68

When I first interviewed Clarisse, she was a practicing Jungian analyst in a large Canadian city. She has lived much of her life there, with long time spans also in the United States. I first met her when she was attending graduate school in California. Knowing something of her background, I was eager to interview her.

What comes to your mind when you think of mentors and mentoring influences?
"A sense of richness, of the number of people who have been there for me at different times with affection and confidence in me, who somehow helped me on my way and spurred me on."

Who are some of the people who flash through your mind?
"Two teachers at the private high school I went to. Janine taught English and French; she was tall and pretty and took a real interest in

me. Marie was a little more distant until later. Once, when my parents went for a brief holiday, Janine came and stayed at the house with me. When I went to the university, I had regular visits with them. When I was a senior in college and was reading a lot of philosophy, they were the ones I could talk to about ideas. Both were important to me because I was a terribly lonely kid, really alienated from my mother and unable to express affection to anybody."

—Mentors/Mentor-bonding Deficit

You mentioned you had minimal contact with your mother and that you couldn't do things quite up to snuff for your father. Did you have any other family members?

"My mother's cousin and her husband lived in Ontario. They were warm, affectionate, and loved me very much—that was very important. They were parent surrogates. I had them when I was 12 and 13, and then Marie and Janine were reinforcing."

—Mentor Bonding/Surrogates

"Marianne, the dean of women at the university, became a spiritual mother to me. When I arrived at the university from my private high school, I was not yet 16, really too young socially and emotionally. By December, I was in a state of nerves. I went to talk to her about taking a temporary leave. She was very understanding. The leave was arranged, and the university agreed to hold a scholarship for me until I came back.

"Hugs were always important to me, because I never got any at home. When I said goodbye to Marianne at Christmastime, she offered me a hug. From then on, I kept in touch with her when I came home at holidays. I was very close to Marianne and that's how I decided to train to become a dean of women. She not only supported me in that career choice, she groomed me to be her successor. So I went on and did my master's at Teachers' College, Columbia University, in student personnel administration, and then I did a professional internship without salary with her. The president of the university concurred in all this but wanted me to get experience on another campus first. So I was offered a job at the University of Toronto that I accepted. Then, during summer school, I met the man who soon became my husband. During that era, the fact that I was married made me 'unsuitable' for the position, and the university would not consider hiring me.

"Marianne was so important to me. I was devastated when she died of a heart attack. More than a mother figure, in a real sense, Marianne was my mother—we were like soul mates or kindred spirits. I meant so much to her, too. I was like the daughter that she never had. I felt totally accepted just as I was. She took me into her heart, and I was always fine in her eyes. Nobody took her place."

—Mentor Bonding/Mentor

"Later, I became principal of the private school where Janine and Marie were on the faculty. I had long been unhappy in my marriage and wanted out, but I waited until my boys were 13 and 15 to divorce. Marie was a very sensitive and wise woman in the interior, symbolic sense. She noticed the changes in me, watched my own inner development, continued to rejoice in my progress, and affirmed who I was. That relationship transformed into a deep friendship. Marie is a role model of wisdom, maturity, and breadth of vision."

—Mentoring Model/Mentoring Relationship

"Virginia Satir was another important influence. In reading her books about the pain that can exist within families, I began to see the systems model and how I could have been more helpful to parents, teachers, and girls at my school. The school was a living laboratory about families and family pain. That's what led me to want to study families—plus my own family. I wanted to apply those techniques to parents and family education, so I went to UCLA to the behavioral science graduate program. There, I was challenged on every level; I had never before learned to be assertive. I got in touch with my intellectual capacity and felt affirmed as a competent person by one professor who relied on me to do creative things in his summer program. I was doing honors work on my exams even after being out of school so long. I was then in my mid-50s. My faculty advisor believed in me, gave me a free hand to do whatever I wanted, and was extraordinarily supportive about my thesis."

—Planned Mentoring Experience/Mentoring Relationships

"Off and on through the years, I read a lot of Jungian books, including several by women who did their richest writing in their 80s. They became role models for me in terms of women who continue to be productive, valued, and growing on into their later life. That was probably my first sense that life goes on increasing in depth and complexity as you get older."

—Mentoring Models

"I was already doing educational counseling in private practice. The Jungian decision was a result of one client who had some remarkable dreams he'd never had before. It was then that I started reading more Jungian books, including June Singer's Boundaries of the Soul,[32] a detailed description of how an analyst works. I was very excited—that's the way I wanted to work. I was already 64, so I let the idea sit for a while. In the fall, I got the courage to phone Mark, a Jungian analyst. He had known me from Family Place, where we both did work—he just handed me the brochure for training! An important aspect of my decision was that age, wisdom, and maturing experience all are valued by the people who follow the Jungian approach, in that philosophy. So, as I approached the age of 65, when the rest of the world is retiring, I was admitted to the training program. Having doors open to people at 65 to begin a new kind of training—and having the money to do it—is a luxury."

—Self-Mentoring/Planned Mentoring Experience

---

[32] June Singer, *Boundaries of the Soul,* Anchor Books, 1973.

Clarisse cites several Jungian therapists who have been mentors to her in this latest life transition. Among them are Marian and Andrew.

"Marian has been the most beautiful example of a woman doing her work in her own way. She had this marvelous combination of femininity, clear thinking, humor, and depth—and a spiritual dimension, too. I was privileged to be able to go to Toronto and work with her once every month. She helped me work on my feminine side and also on the part of me connected at an unconscious level to my father that limited me because of always having to please him.

"I felt validated by Andrew. He asked if I would co-lead seminars with him. I've listened to him when he's been in emotional pain. So there's been a lot of important sharing. I've never had a relationship with a man before where there's a lot of love but no sexual involvement. He was so affirming of me as the wise woman. He gave me a vote of confidence for entering the training program and helped me prepare for it."

—*Mentoring Relationships*

Clarisse also learns from younger women and, in turn, mentors and provides a model for them.

"I'm amazed at the number of rich, affirming contacts I've had from people senior to me and also younger. Mostly, they're younger, from their 60s down to their 40s, but I don't feel the age difference. Younger women see me as the grand old woman. They say, 'I wish my mother would be like you.' Early on, I accepted that it's important to be that kind of a model, to accept the fact that I am. People seem astonished that I'm still studying and attending workshops. In workshops, I always share the things that are hard for me, the vulnerable side. Sharing is very revealing."

—*Mentoring Models*

What is the satisfaction you get from mentoring other people?

"One part of me is an educator. Plus, elders have some responsibility to pass on what they've learned or be supportive in the way others have been supportive of us. It feels good to be able to give in that way, to be useful."

What influences the kind of person you are likely to mentor?
"People who want to grow, who are dissatisfied with their lives in a constructive way."

What would cause you to terminate a relationship?
"Usually, it shifts into friendship."

—Mentoring

What about the future?
"One thing I have to watch is that my old achievement motivation doesn't drive me to spend more energy than I should. I need to accept that my energy flags badly. I have to make sure that what I do is enhancing my total person and not just a job or project separate from me as a person."

Clarisse at Age 89

Clarisse is the oldest person I interviewed. When we first talked of her mentoring at age 68, she had embarked on yet another career—that of a Jungian psychotherapist, a role she continued actively until her 80th year, retiring completely at age 82. I was immensely interested in those years as well as the years of her final retirement and retreat to a more private, contemplative life. I knew that her physical health had caused a significant decline in her options. When it became clear that she was gradually losing her vision, she closed her practice, sold her car and condo, and moved to a retirement home. Since then, she has completely lost her sight and has moved to an assisted-living facility. In this late stage of Clarisse's life, we see an extensive pattern of self-mentoring and co-mentoring through books-on-tape and discussions with friends. Clarisse is very clear about the nature of her mentoring process. I had noted that, at change points in her life, she always turned to reading.

"My reading shifted every time I changed professions. When I became the principal of the private school, I knew very little of the field of education. So I read extensively. When I went to UCLA, I shifted my reading to family education topics. Then, when I did programs with and for women at the women's resources center, I read all sorts of the things on group work and communication."

—Self-Mentoring

So your reading has followed your changes in career rather than preceded them?
"I would undertake jobs that felt challenging and rewarding even though I didn't know much about the field. I would immerse myself in reading while I was learning on the job. That's what I've always done."

—Self-Mentoring

In retirement, through talking books and articles, Clarisse "reads" widely in the literature of human potential and spiritual development. I asked whether she has found enough people who share her interests to have a forum in which to discuss.
"There are very few people I can talk to about these ideas. The couple that reads books on tape for me does understand. Also, one of my visitors is very knowledgeable in both philosophy and quantum physics and is writing a book in this field—we have the deepest conversations. Another friend is a highly trained counselor and teacher who looks at counseling as a spiritual profession. When we share what's going on in our lives, we have a wonderfully deep sense of connection. But he's not interested in the scientific aspects. Another friend I met at church loves Deepak Chopra. So we share and enjoy tapes of his, although she is not into reading in the field of scientific exploration."

—Co-Mentoring

Later, Clarisse told me she was surprised at the number of men friends she has in her later life and the richness this brings to her. During her growing-up years, she had frequent arguments with her father and there was no display of affection toward her from either parent. Reflecting back, she realizes she had no real friendships with men until after she experienced love and affection from her second husband.

—Co-Mentoring

Six years ago, Clarisse published her autobiography, which had a surprise follow-on.

"A friend and I had been working on the idea of conscious living and conscious dying, and I was reading about death, consciousness, and spirituality. I sensed somehow that when I finished the autobiography, I was going to die soon, that I had finished what I was on the earth to do. And then I didn't die. There was a painful period of rethinking where I was, realizing I had a lot more work to do before my soul would let me die, that the choice wasn't mine. It meant I had more to learn. Several months passed before I really developed a sense of renewed excitement about learning more of what the spiritual life is all about.

—Mentoring Experience/Eye-Opening

"At this point, I went into semi-retreat for three years, because I was really trying to probe the whole field of spirituality. I was very mystified by the idea of enlightenment—it was totally new to me. That was a turning point in my life, along with the transition into blindness and further limitations. I didn't have any guidance on what to read. I just read—especially women writers who had achieved some breakthrough. I had no knowledge of Eastern religion at all, so I began reading in that area.

"After three years, I felt I had been in retreat long enough. I was on a plateau, and I was ready to see people again. The usefulness of the retreat period had ended, and it was time to move on. I still had energy and didn't need to be so introverted."

—Planned Mentoring Experience/Self-Mentoring

Again, in the pattern of your life—when you're in a new place, a new stage of life—you've turned to reading to develop the skills or the understanding for the path you're following.

"Right. In the past seven years, I've been devoted to exploring spiritual dimensions. There's always been a dialogue between what I was reading and what I was thinking about or sensing. That's when science, especially quantum physics, became really important to me. The study of cosmology and the evolution of consciousness on our planet have been really exciting."

—Self-Mentoring

Clarisse has occasional "down" times. She talked about several weeks of "being becalmed; kind of stuck and lethargic."

"When we get stuck with feelings of loss and limitations, it separates us from our creative center. One of the things I've learned is that I must not focus on physical limitations. If I do, I can get depressed easily. I need to dwell on what is still so very rich in my life. I'm really lucky to have my mental faculties, for which I'm eternally grateful.

"A line from poet Joseph Campbell is deeply important to me: 'It is the gift of a lifetime to be who you are.' I feel that in addition to being a gift, it's a task. In this advanced old age, it's important to *be* rather than to *do* because you're limited; you can't *do* anymore. Being more than your body is the essence of it."

—Self-Mentoring

Comments on Clarisse's Mentoring Pattern

Clarisse's two parallel threads are apparent throughout her life—her learning and connections to people, and her self-generated studies through reading and discussion. We note in Clarisse a pattern of going ever deeper on her spiritual path. In late-life stages, connections with people shrink, and many of us, like Clarisse, are forced to rely more on ourselves and on self-generated mentoring behaviors.

BRIDGE

Through these five lives, we can see more vividly two overall characteristics of mentoring: continuity throughout an individual life span and mentoring diversity among people. We also see that each of the five has a combination of mentoring strategies that can be drawn on at will, tapping both people and non-people sources but in quite different ways. As life moves on, each will face additional challenges that they are likely to handle according to their lifelong mentoring strategies. In the next two chapters, we step back to gain a broader view, to understand important societal trends that affect mentoring needs and influence mentoring practice.

Chapter 23

TRENDS INFLUENCING MENTORING

"Mentors" and "mentoring" are now part of the vocabulary in a way that was missing 20 years ago. Just entering a "mentors or mentoring" search on Amazon.com brought up 397 book titles![33] This growth of interest is coupled with a number of social and economic changes that affect mentoring. The two most significant trends have to do with demographics—the age and composition of the population—and the structure of work organizations. Changes in both realms have important implications for mentoring as we chart our mentoring life journey. Additional trends of significance to mentoring include changes in Internet technology, programs of professional associations and educational institutions, and the growth of networking.

DEMOGRAPHIC TRENDS

- People are living longer and healthier lives than ever before.
- Living into the 80s and 90s is increasingly common.
- The huge crop of Baby Boomers is beginning to reach the traditional retirement years with far greater health, energy, and longevity than previous generations experienced.
- Traditional "retirement" is expected to give way to multiple careers reaching into later life.
- Later careers will provide the opportunity for many to activate values and pursue interests.

---

[33] Searched http://www.amazon.com/ on July 11, 2005.

The bulk of people approaching retirement age are Baby Boomers, the group that has marked our culture in every decade. Boomers, the generational cohort group born between 1946 and 1964,[34] defined the youth culture in the 1960s and '70s; the dual-income household in the 1980s and '90s; and now, Boomers are likely to redefine retirement itself.

In 2006, we are seeing the first wave of Boomers reach retirement age—and this is only the beginning. According to a recent Conference Board study, 64 million Boomers, over 40% of the U.S. labor force, are poised to retire in large numbers by the end of this decade.[35]

The impact of the Boomer group already is visible in health clubs and retirement communities. In a recent five-year period (1997–2002), the number of people aged 55 and older joining health clubs jumped 350%, prompting an estimated one third of all U.S. clubs to revamp their facilities, equipment, and exercise programs for an older clientele.[36] "Leisure World" retirement communities plan to drop the word "Leisure" because it sounds too sedentary for a generation more active than ever. Only 2% of this group thinks "senior citizen" is an appropriate term to describe them.[37] The literature abounds with phrases like "60 is

---

[34] Boomers born 1946–1954 are considered "leading-edge" Boomers; the 1955–1964 group is considered the "trailing" Boomers.

[35] The Conference Board, "Managing the Mature Workforce," Report #1369. September 19, 2005. Available at: http://www.conference-board.org/publications/describe.cfm?id=1007. Accessed September 23, 2006. The Conference Board, "America's Aging Workforce Posing New Opportunities and Challenges for Companies," September 19, 2005. Available at: http://www.conference-board.org/UTILITIES/pressDetail.cfm?press_ID=2709. Accessed September 23, 2006. Note: The Conference Board is known for the quality of its economic research and the preeminence of its membership.

[36] "Flex Appeal," *AARP Magazine*, March/April 2005, p. 15.

[37] Kimi Yoshimo, "Leisure World May Retire Its Name, Image," *Los Angeles Times*, March 13, 2005, p. B1 and B8.

the new 40." Such phrases are gaining currency in ordinary conversation. Indeed, some Boomers resist the term "retiring" and talk instead about "refiring," and a recent popular book on the subject is entitled *Don't Retire, REWIRE!*[38]

Most people who are 65 today can reasonably expect to live another two decades.[39] Cultural observers follow these trends closely.[40] What are some of the implications of such an increase in life expectancy? Marc Freedman, an adviser on aging to government, corporations, and foundations, believes this new kind of aging has the potential to harness Baby Boomers' energy to benefit society.[41] Retirement expert Helen Dennis refers to this phenomenon as a "retirement revolution," and she explains, "Thirty years ago, retirees may have been looking for more of a rest. Today's group is saying, 'Give me a little rest, but then I'm ready for the next challenge.'"[42] Psychologist and aging expert Ken Dychtwald goes even further: "In the years ahead, you'll enjoy boundless ability to customize your mix of work and play and gather

---

[38] Jeri Sedlar and Rick Miners, *Don't Retire, REWIRE!* Alpha Books, Indianapolis, 2003.

[39] Walt Duka, "Will Your Ship Come In?" *AARP Bulletin*, March 2004, p. 24.

[40] Gail Sheehy, *New Passages*, Ballantine Books 1999, p 139. Sheehy has altered her view of life stages and now sees the years 45–85+ as the "Second Adulthood" — the middle years between 45 and 65 constituting the "Age of Mastery," and the years from 65 to 85 or beyond as the "Age of Integrity." For earlier work on life stages, see also Daniel J. Levinson, *The Seasons of a Man's Life*, Knopf, NY, 1985.

[41] Marc Freedman, *Prime Time: How Baby Boomers Will Revolutionize Retirement and Transform America*, Public Affairs, 2002.

[42] Quoted in Walt Duka and Trish Nicholson, "Retirees Rocking Old Roles," *AARP Bulletin*, December 2002. Available at: http://www.aarp.org/bulletin/yourlife/Articles/a2003-06-26-retireesrocking.html. Accessed September 23, 2006.

the resources you'll need to fund the power-years lifestyle of your dreams."[43]

Age and Employment

More and more older workers want to remain in their jobs for both personal fulfillment and financial reasons. According to The Conference Board report,[44] 55% of older employees surveyed said they were not planning to retire because they found their jobs interesting. A significant 74% also said that they were continuing to work because they did not have enough financial resources, and 60% needed to retain medical benefits. The historical linear life plan is becoming obsolete. Boomers want to work on terms more customized to their needs. They want to "ratchet back" and give up responsibility, yet stay involved and active.

The need for economic security and health-care coverage is clearly a driver for many who are worried about possible changes in Social Security, reductions in pensions, and/or decreased health-care coverage. Others want to engage in work they feel passionate about. When William Safire said farewell to readers of the Op-Ed pages of the *New York Times* recently at age 75, it was not to retire, he said, but to change careers in order "to keep [those] synapses snapping."[45]

How our institutions will respond to this shift in the meaning of work and retirement is not yet clear. Organizations in the United States have not had the flexible work patterns of some other countries that allow a phasing-out of careers. Most companies still want only full-time employees. As a result, retirees have had to turn to "bridging jobs"

---

[43] Ken Dychtwald and Daniel J. Kadlec, *The Power Years: A User's Guide to the Rest of Your Life,* John Wiley & Sons Inc. 2005, cited in *Time,* Inside Business, November 2005, p. A32.

[44] The Conference Board, op. cit., p. 393.

[45] William Safire, "Never Retire," *New York Times,* January 24, 2005, p. A17.

elsewhere in order to work part-time until they choose full-time retirement. In the future, we are likely to see a shift. Companies will have to broaden their policies to include alternative forms of employment. Not to do so threatens organizations with the loss of too many experienced workers from the Boomer group. A recent *Harvard Business Review* article, "It's Time to Retire Retirement," makes this abundantly clear,[46] as does the recent Bureau of Labor Statistics finding that more than half of the workers in the United States are age 40 or older.[47]

Characteristics of Boomers suggest a fruitful role for them past the traditional retirement age. The trait most attributed to Boomers is their willingness to give maximum effort. They also are rated as highly results-driven, very likely to retain what they learn, and low on their need for supervision. This suggests that Baby Boomers are eager workers who are well suited to be brought back as consultants and mentors after their retirement.[48]

There is a caution, however. The percentage of men drawing Social Security retirement benefits at age 62 increased from 17% in 1965 to 54% in 2001.[49] Most working people do not look forward to working forever,

---

[46] Ken Dychtwald, Tamara Erickson, Bob Morison, "It's Time to Retire Retirement," *Harvard Business Review*, March 2004. Available at: http://harvardbusinessonline.hbsp.harvard.edu/b01/en/common/item_detail.j html?id=R0403C. Accessed September 23, 2006.

[47] Bureau of Labor Statistics cited in the *Los Angeles Times*, March 31, 2005, p. A23.

[48] Judith Lindenberger, MBA, and Marian Stoltz-Loike, Ph.D., cited in "Why Mentor? Mentoring is a Strategic Business Imperative." Available at: http://humanresources.about.com/od/coachingmentoring/a/mentoring_boom. htm. Accessed September 23, 2006.

[49] Robin Toner and David E. Rosenbaum, "In Overhaul of Social Security, Age Is the Elephant in the Room," *New York Times*, June 12, 2005. Available at: http://www.nytimes.com/2005/06/12/politics/12age.html?th=&emc=th&pagew anted=print. Accessed September 23, 2006.

especially people who have jobs that are uninteresting, stressful, or physically demanding. Fewer than 10% of people 65 to 75 are in poor health, but many prefer not working.[50] They are eager to retire and question their employment prospects in their middle to late 60s.

As we can see, attitudes about retirement vary greatly depending on family responsibilities, pension projections, health-care coverage, spouse retirement timing — and the amount of "fun" people are having in their current work. All of these changes in demographics and in attitudes about retirement reinforce the need for self-managed mentoring. In this vast sea of change, there are no well-established routes to the future. We must be mentoring pioneers.

TRENDS IN ORGANIZATIONS

The other major trend that so strongly impacts mentoring is change in the world of work, encompassing both technology and the structure of organizations. The concept of career usually is associated with work in organizations. How is organizational life changing, and what are the likely effects on people who are "in career" or nearing the end of the conventional career life cycle?

- Organizations face continued pressures to flatten their structures and rely on a smaller flexible workforce.
- The focus is on training and retraining staff to keep up with change.
- New economy companies create a mixed environment for people who work in them. Though exhilarating, the 24/7 pace can be exhausting.

---

[50] John Tierney, "The Old and the Rested," *New York Times*, June 14, 2005, p. A23. Available at: http://select.nytimes.com/gst/abstract.html?res= F50B17FB345C0C778DDDAF0894DD404482. Accessed September 23, 2006.

- Many companies lack the basic infrastructure and experienced leadership to provide mentoring.
- With some major industry sectors in a state of flux, health care and automobiles prominent among them, employees face increasing pressures and uncertainty but with diminished support.

In light of these organizational conditions, it is easy to understand why mentoring is minimal or non-existent in many traditional workplaces, from manufacturing to services. In the case of many new economy firms, organizational or "facilitated" mentoring is missing as well.[51] Although the employees have an exhilarating sense of achievement and the opportunity for creative freedom, they are concerned about the stress of a 24/7 life, the constant change and uncertainty, and the difficulty of balancing work and family/personal life. They do not want to return to the bureaucracy of traditional firms; however, they *do* report missing the communication, organizational infrastructure, and experienced management that traditional firms offer. The challenge for start-up companies as they grow is to avoid recreating the unproductive aspects of hierarchy, while creating working environments that are collaborative and agile, where mentoring can happen.

Retraining staff to keep up with change is a huge challenge. The knowledge and skill requirements combine technology savvy, analytical thinking, and interpersonal skills. This combination could be a magic formula for American workers, suggests MIT management professor Thomas Kochan: Jobs that involve all three qualities are harder to duplicate with machines or with low-wage workers abroad,

---

[51] Wendy Cole, "Stay Connected." *TIME.* March 10, 2003. Available at: http://www.time.com/time/archive/preview/0,10987,1004404,00.html. Accessed September 23, 2006.

whether the jobs are in health care, education, financial services, or any other field.[52]

Yet, there is no guarantee, given the increased volatility of the job market. Career trajectories are far less predictable than they used to be, according to Yale economist Robert Schiller, and swings in income over the course of a person's working life are far greater.[53] We live in turbulent times, trying to keep afloat in a condition of "permanent white water." Where we used to be able to anticipate a calm portion of the river to catch our breath, now there is no calm around the bend.[54]

An illustrative example is the health care field, which is undergoing considerable turmoil. Health professionals report that it is increasingly difficult to build mentoring relationships within the organization. They lack the time or ability to find willing, experienced mentors, since many senior practitioner-manager positions have been eliminated. One person calls this situation a "thinning at the top." This dearth of mentors is reported in many clinical fields, ranging from occupational and physical therapy to nursing and pharmacy.[55]

There are a few hopeful signs. Half of the companies surveyed in The Conference Board study are concerned about the potential "brain drain" with so many mature workers expected to be leaving. One-third of the companies have conducted workforce planning studies,

---

[52] Thomas A. Kochan quoted in "Middle Class No More," *The Washington Post National Weekly Edition*, January 10–16, 2005, p. 20.

[53] Robert J. Shiller, "American Casino," *Atlantic Monthly*, March 2005, p. 34.

[54] Peter B. Vaill, *Learning as a Way of Being: Strategies for Survival in a World of Permanent White Water*, Jossey-Bass, 1996.

[55] Anne Federwisch, "Keys to Finding a Mentor," *Nurseweek*, November 10, 1997. Available at: http://www.nurseweek.com/features/97-11/mentor2.html. Accessed September 23, 2006.

and half have some form of mentoring program in place to share and transfer knowledge. The Conference Board has also set up a task force on "Strategic Workforce Planning" that will report its findings around the end of 2006. Its mission is far-reaching:

> "Once limited to calculating the gap between talent supply and demand, workforce planning is now a far more sophisticated process akin to risk management or supply chain management. Today, workforce planning generates multiple, data-driven forecasts based on a variety of scenarios, enabling an organization to adjust and respond quickly to immediate and future changes to its business requirements."[56]

The focus of the study is long-range and ground-breaking, and it may lead to vastly expanded mentoring programs. For the present, however, the number of organizational mentoring programs remains small.

TRENDS IN PROFESSIONAL ASSOCIATIONS

As mentoring systems in organizations diminish, professional associations have assumed greater responsibility for the guidance and assistance of their members. Three trends are notable:

1. Mentoring programs sponsored by professional associations and occupational groups are varied, widespread, and growing.
2. The Internet is widely used in the development and administration of mentoring programs.
3. Some programs, which were originally established to meet the needs of women and minorities, have broadened to serve the needs of all members.

---

[56] The Conference Board, op. cit., p. 393.

Examples

- MentorNet, the E-Mentoring Network for Diversity in Engineering and Science, was founded in 1997. By 2003, the program had more than 10,000 active members.[57]
- The Committee on the Advancement of Women Chemists (COACh), formed in 2000 to mentor tenured women chemists, sponsors professional development workshops. Some 95% of the chemists who have participated in these workshops report that they have gone on to mentor other women.[58]
- WorldWIT (Women, Insights, Technology), a global e-mail networking group with outposts all over the globe, was formed in 2000. It now has more than 4,000 members and is growing.[59]
- Nursing associations have many mentoring programs. One such group, the American Association of Nurse Anesthetists, links new members via partnerships with experienced members through a listserv.[60]

---

[57] MentorNet: The E-Mentoring Network for Diversity in Engineering and Science. Available at: http://www.mentornet.net/. Accessed March 6, 2006.

[58] Pamela S. Zurer, "Coaching Success," *Chemical & Engineering News,* February 28, 2005. Available at: http://pubs.acs.org/cen/education/83/8309coach.html. Accessed September 23, 2006.

[59] Liz Ryan, WorldWIT CEO and Founder, "Do Ask, Do Tell." Available at: http://www.worldwit.org/ColumnEntry.aspx?C=2&E=127. Accessed September 23, 2006.

[60] American Association of Nurse Anesthetists Press Release. "Group E-Mentoring in Nursing Seeks Nurse Mentors," April 13, 2005. Available at: http://www.aana.com/news.aspx?ucNavMenu_TSMenuTargetID=62&ucNavMenu_TSMenuTargetType=4&ucNavMenu_TSMenuID=6&id=850&. Accessed September 23, 2006.

TRENDS IN EDUCATIONAL INSTITUTIONS

Although colleges and universities have traditionally provided advisors for students, mentoring programs are now on the upswing, particularly at the graduate student and junior faculty levels. Trend indicators include the following:

1. Colleges and universities are strengthening mentoring programs for undergraduates, graduates, and alumni.
2. Developing and maintaining a mentoring program is included in the responsibilities of a number of key academic dean positions.
3. Mentoring roles and responsibilities are spelled out in detail for student mentees and faculty mentors.
4. Universities have established programs to mentor junior faculty toward research and tenure goals.

Examples

- The Missouri Bar connects junior bar members with experienced lawyers for a year. Pairs are matched according to interests, practice area, size of practice, special abilities, and location. An administrator monitors the program, maintains the database, assigns mentors, and collects data.[61]
- Widener University School of Law sponsors a network-mentoring program pairing alumni, practitioners, and judges with first-year law students.[62]

---

[61] The Missouri Bar Mentoring Program. Available at: http://oldsite.mobar.org/lpmonline/mentoring.htm. Accessed September 23, 2006.

[62] Widener University School of Law Mentoring Program: Mentoring Guide for Students. Available at: http://www.law.widener.edu/departments/career_development/career_management/mentoring_students.shtml. Accessed September 23, 2006.

- The University of Kansas School of Medicine offers a thorough faculty mentoring program that includes such activities as orientation, research and publication collaboration, teaching enhancement, and clinical duties.[63]
- Graduate schools in library and information studies are active sponsors of mentorship programs. The University of Southern California sponsors a library faculty mentoring program,[64] and Yale University's program supports the professional development of librarians.[65]

MENTORING TECHNOLOGY: THE ROLE OF THE INTERNET

The development of the Internet and the expansion of its use have had a profound impact on mentoring. With its global reach, the World Wide Web is a tremendous resource for many forms of mentoring, providing a rapid and efficient way to obtain information and to communicate with others.

The Internet began operations in 1969, with usage doubling year after year. By the mid-1990s, it had become "ubiquitous as the new infrastructure for learning, business, science, entertainment, and

---

[63] University of Kansas School of Medicine: About the Mentoring Program. Available at: http://www.kumc.edu/som/facdev/mentoringoverview.html. Accessed September 23, 2006.

[64] Library Faculty Mentoring Program: University of Southern California. Available at: http://www.usc.edu/isd/about/faculty/mentoringpolicy.html. Accessed September 23, 2006.

[65] SCOPA Mentoring Program for the Yale University Library. Available at: http://www.library.yale.edu/scopa/mentoring/mentoring.html. Accessed September 23, 2006.

commerce."[66] And by 2005, Google was processing 1 billion searches a day, up from 150 million just three years earlier.[67] The next generation clearly is growing up online rather than adapting to the technological possibilities in their mid-adult years. By 2003, more than 2 million children aged 6 to 17 had their own Web site, and 29% of kids in grades K-3 had their own e-mail address.[68]

One basic use of the Internet has been as a library reference desk for research and problem-solving. According to SearchEngineWatch.com, as of January 2003, there were 319 million searches per day at the major search engines, with users spending more than 90 minutes per day on searches. Those numbers are growing exponentially.[69]

Self-mentoring is enhanced by the immediate access to information provided by the Internet. All that is needed is computer access, a good search engine and search strategy, and a few keystrokes. Now, regardless of where people live, it is possible to tap into the equivalent of a great library. The caution here is that the Internet is not a library of evaluated publications selected by professionals. Its offerings range from peer-reviewed, academically solid research and established reference sources to unsubstantiated opinions and out-of-date information. It is more of a self-publishing medium, a bulletin board

---

[66] Edward Lazowska and Roy Pea, "Reasons for Optimism: Possibilities for Hardware and Software," *Planning for Two Transformations in Education and Learning Technology*, National Academies Press, Washington, D.C., 2004, p. 90–91.

[67] Thomas L. Friedman, *The World Is Flat: A Brief Introduction to the 21st Century.*, Farrar, Straus and Giroux, 2005, p. 153.

[68] December 2003 survey by Grunwald Associates, quoted in Micah L. Sifry, "The Rise of Open-Source Politics," *The Nation*, November 22, 2004, p. 20.

[69] Regents of the University of California. "Internet." October 27, 2003. Available at: http://www.sims.berkeley.edu/research/projects/how-much-info-2003/internet.htm. Accessed September 23, 2006.

containing everything. Specific sources have to be evaluated by the user. A further limitation is that access to some of the most useful sites is limited to paid subscribers, registered members, or registered students.[70]

The Internet also is widely used as a connecting and communicating resource. Many of us would be lost without our e-mail capability. Educational institutions and professional associations with far-flung constituencies learned the value of Internet communication early and pioneered forms of networking and distance learning. Electronic networking has exploded as research communities use the Internet widely to make contacts, develop relationships, and foster research.[71] Alumni associations feature practical tips on networking to maximize career futures through face-to-face contact and the Internet.[72]

A number of these same universities and associations also use the Internet to establish and maintain mentoring partnerships and to manage mentoring programs. Through e-mail, forums, and one-to-one communication, a variety of distance mentoring forms are in use. They range from short exchanges of information and problem-solving to longer and deeper relationships, depending on the amount of trust that has built over time. Web sites have even generated a new language for the nontraditional forms of mentoring enabled by the Internet: telementoring, Internet mentoring, virtual mentoring, e-mentoring, techno-mentor, cyber-mentor, and mentoring forums, to name a few.

---

[70] A hopeful trend is the Public Library of Science site, where the policy is free access to research papers that are published in full. See http://www.plos.org/ for more information.

[71] Phil E. Agre, "Networking on the Network: A Guide to Professional Skills for Ph.D. Students," version 11, June 2003. Available at: http://polaris.gseis.ucla.edu/pagre/network.html. Accessed September 23, 2006.

[72] One example is the UCLA Alumni Association's Networking Tools. See http://www.uclalumni.net/NetworkingCareers/otherresources/NetworkingTools.cf m for more information. Accessed September 23, 2006.

Certainly the Internet is a comprehensive mentoring resource for the wired generation, but what about seniors? A new study finds that the number of people ages 65 or older who use the Internet has jumped by 47% since 2000, making this the fastest-growing group to embrace the online world. Despite these increases, only 22% of Americans older than 65 go online compared with 75% of those ages 30 to 49. Once people become adept on the Internet, however, they don't give up.[73] In the decade ahead, we can expect an increasingly wired generation of retirees.

THE SELF-INITIATING ROLE OF THE MENTEE

Traditionally, junior people have been expected to await the appearance of a mentor and then be receptive and responsive to mentoring overtures. This is no longer true. Attitudes, expectations, and behaviors are changing dramatically.

Instead of following the mentor's lead, mentees are increasingly initiating mentoring partnerships. The passive, responding person in an organization, whether employee or student, is giving way to the assertive person who is looking after his or her own needs. In fact, many organizations—from businesses to graduate schools to professional associations—are urging junior people to be proactive in seeking mentoring and in managing mentoring partnerships. Self-initiated mentoring may be a particularly useful survival strategy in

---

[73] Katie Hafner, "For Some Internet Users, It's Better Late Than Never", *New York Times*, March 25, 2004. Available at: http://tech2.nytimes.com/mem/technology/techreview.html?res=9F05EEDF15 30F936A15750C0A9629C8B63. Accessed September 23, 2006.

companies where technologies can quickly become obsolete or outsourced, and the need for staying current is strong.[74]

USE OF THE MENTORING TEAM

One-size-fits-all mentoring programs do not work in today's world. More practical is to have multiple mentors, simultaneously or over a lifetime. Sometimes, mentees can participate in a mentoring circle where a mentor facilitates the learning of a group of individuals.[75] Or, you can develop your own "mentoring team," as graduate students at the University of Michigan are urged to do.[76] Students there are encouraged to:

- Search for several faculty members who " ... are knowledgeable about your work and can speak to its quality. The team can serve as your safety net in case any of the professors you work with leaves the University or if irreconcilable issues later develop."

- "Be creative ... consider your peers, more advanced graduate students, departmental staff, retired faculty, faculty from other departments, faculty from other universities, and friends from outside the academy as potential mentors. All of these people can help fulfill your needs and serve as part of your professional network."

- " ... look for a balance of both junior and senior faculty. ... Faculty members who are different from you can contribute valuable insights into you and your work."

---

[74] Gordon Shea, *Making the Most of Being Mentored*, Crisp Publications 1999, p. 10.

[75] Lois J. Zachary, *The Mentor's Guide*, Jossey Bass, 2000, p. 4.

[76] *How to Get the Mentoring You Want*, pp. 6–7. Available at: http://www.rackham.umich.edu/StudentInfo/Publications/StudentMentoring/ contents.html. Accessed September 23, 2006.

THE CHANGING SHAPE OF MENTORING RELATIONSHIPS

Concepts about mentoring are clearly changing. Today, mentoring is viewed more broadly as a journey of personal growth and development, not just for promotions. It's more about learning than power. "A successful career will no longer be about promotion; it will be about mastery."[77]

Mentoring relationships are not about who you know, but rather about who knows what you need or want to know. Cheryl Dahle, senior writer for *Fast Company*, has written an interesting article on the changing concepts of mentoring.[78] Although her focus is on ways of mentoring for women, her observations are applicable to both men and women. I have summarized her views in the "Mentoring Rules" chart on page 409.

---

[77] Michael Hammer, quoted in "Executive Coaching or Mentoring—Which Way Should You Go?", *Direct Link*, A Quarterly Publication of the Association of California Nurse Leaders, Fall 2004, p. 1

[78] Cheryl Dahle, "Women's Ways of Mentoring," September 1998. Available at: http://www.fastcompany.com/online/17/womentoring.html. Accessed September 23, 2006.

Mentoring Rules

Old Rule

"Mentors and protégés [mentees] should have a lot in common."

New Rule

"Sometimes, mismatches work best."

If you connect with someone like you, the "potential for discovery" can be low. Try pairing with someone who will challenge you. Differences can be the best part of the match.

Old Rule

"Look for your mentor higher up on the food chain."

New Rule

"A good mentor is anyone you can learn from."

The ideal mentor can be "anyone from anywhere inside or outside of the organization. Peers can serve as handy mentors when you have no obvious senior role models to look to."

Old Rule

"Mentoring is one-on-one."

New Rule

"Mentoring works best when you mix and match."

Not many people have the time to be a one-on-one mentor. "In fact, you are better off diversifying your mentor portfolio" and having a smorgasbord of mentors—some are the bread, others the beef, and still others the dessert.

Old Rule

"Mentors pick their protégés [mentees]."

New Rule

"Protégés [mentees] pick their mentors."

Don't wait for a mentor to find you. Look for mentoring on your own.

Old Rule

You're either identified as a mentor or a mentee.

New Rule

You can be both a mentor and a mentee. Everyone needs mentoring at times.

"Reverse mentoring" meets the needs of people to learn new technology, or to check assumptions about others who are younger or older, are of a different gender, are of a different cultural background, or differ in some other ways. You need a mentoring mind-set that allows you to learn from those around you, no matter who they are.

BRIDGE

In this chapter, we looked at a variety of trends that affect mentoring. One in particular needs greater attention, that of networking. We devote the next chapter to networking and mentoring and how they work together.

Chapter 24

NETWORKING AND MENTORING

Networking is burgeoning. Experts say that formal mentoring relationships in organizations cannot keep pace with the fluid environment of this new century, so we must form learning networks or clusters of professional relationships that will contribute to our individual and career development.[79] So how does networking relate to mentoring?

Mentoring and networking are two strands of human development that have operated independently until recent times. With the increasing complexity of our fast-changing world, each has branched out until they now touch. Both enrich personal learning and growth. Used together, they constitute a powerful force for managing mentoring. In this chapter, we trace developments in both fields that point to the importance and inevitability of networking as a mentoring strategy.

Traditionally, the mentor is an older, wiser, trusted counselor. The hierarchical difference between the mentor and mentee is sharp and pronounced. In the research reported in this book, however, mentoring is far broader than traditional mentor relationships. Peer mentoring and other mentoring forms must be included. Current trends reflect this

---

[79] Kathy E. Kram, *Mentoring at Work*, University Press of America, 1988, p. 148; Beverly Kaye and Devon Scheef, "Harness the Power of Mentoring, Networking to Help Your Career," from *National Business Employment Weekly*, March 2, 2005. Available at: http://www.ctrc.com/appTips/KayeMentoringNetworking.pdf. Accessed September 24, 2006.

greater leveling of power in mentor–mentee relationships, as the mentoring literature demonstrates.[80]

Networking, the other guiding strand, has its origins in the community practice of neighbors helping each other through extensive kinship and friendship networks, and also in the commercial world of buying, selling, and marketing. Increasingly, networking also is seen as a way to strengthen peer relationships, based on shared values and interests and a communication process that builds trust.

The coming together of these two strands is propelled by recent social and economic change. On the mentoring side, there is a recognition that traditional hierarchical power structures of mentoring are diminishing—that you can no longer rely on senior, older, and wiser advisors, many of whom have disappeared. At the same time, step-ahead and peer, co-mentoring relationships are on the rise. On the networking side, there is increased recognition of the importance of building relationships beyond making contact for selling and marketing—that you no longer can rely solely on selling yourself or focusing on your own needs. When you are dependent on others, you must invest in connections for the long haul, knowing that, over time, you will need each other. In this convergence of the two strands, we can see that the mentoring strand reduces the power differential between mentor and mentee while the networking strand builds relationships and two-way exchanges.

Used together, networking and the elements of the Mentoring Mosaic constitute a powerful base for managing your mentoring. Corporate

---

[80] Kram, op. cit., p. 411; see p. 139–158 in *Mentoring at Work*. See also Linda Phillips-Jones, *The New Mentors and Protégées: How to Succeed with the New Mentoring Partnerships*, Coalition of Counseling Centers, The Mentoring Group, Grass Valley, CA, 2001, p. 92–93; plus numerous Web sites on "peer mentors."

career development consultant Beverly Kaye and her associates have coined the term "mentworking" to describe this melding of mentoring and networking. Mentworking is seen as "a process of giving and receiving by participating in relationships in which everyone is a learner and a teacher. ... Each 'mentworker' receives and gives brain power to others, creating multiple short-term learning teams."[81]

With the melding of mentoring and networking as our focus, we look at networking in greater depth: what it is, why it is important now, what it looks like in different fields, and how it relates to mentoring. The two chapters that follow take a "how-to" stance, outlining ways you can develop, use, and maintain your network contacts to manage and enrich your mentoring, both as a mentor and as a mentee.

NETWORKING—WHAT IT IS

Networking is not mentoring. Rather, networking is an on-going process for developing professional and/or social relationships. To manage your mentoring effectively, you need a network of relationships: professional relationships if you are still in career; task and/or social relationships if you are shifting from career to other activities. Networking requires a mind-set that focuses on building reciprocal relationships that have the quality of both giving and receiving, teaching and learning. To sustain your network, you need a well-developed data bank in order to access information sources and make people connections.

---

[81] Kaye and Scheef, op. cit., p. 411. For more on mentworking, see Beverly Kaye's Career Systems International (CSI). Available at: http://www.careersystemsintl.com/mentwrk.htm. Accessed September 24, 2006. Also, see Jeff Westover, "Industry Sources." Available at: http://www.collegerecruiter.com/pages/articles/article167.php. Accessed September 24, 2006.

In a way, we already "do" networking when we socialize at a conference or an event, when we introduce people who should know each other because of their common interests, when we seek out the opinion of a knowledgeable person in our field, and when we help along a junior person on a new project. We seek out and are challenged by people in our field whose views are intriguing, novel, and insightful. We listen to people whose advice is reasoned, thoughtful, and well informed—as well as people who question and challenge our thinking. Responsible networking encourages us to do all of this and more, but in a systematic, coordinated, and ethical way.

NETWORKING ORIGINS AND RECENT HISTORY

Although networking has had a great deal of press since the mid-1990s, it is not new. People have formed networks from the earliest days of human history, networks of common bonds and/or shared interests.

The early ties that linked people together were ties of blood or community. Family helping family, neighbors helping neighbors—a web of reciprocal ties, obligations, and exchanges. Frontier America was known for its hospitality to travelers, quilting bees, barn-raisings, and neighborly support in time of need. People were giving without keeping score and without immediate expectation of return. Almost as ancient are trading networks that developed through shared interests and the necessities of livelihood.

Recent history is different. Community ties have weakened with our increasingly mobile society and rapid change. In modern times, there have been two divergent networking postures. On the positive side, new groups entering the workplace—particularly women and minorities—recognized the need to develop networks akin to "the old boys' club," the informal web of connections that influence career development and direction. Many innovative programs spring from this motivation.[82]

On the negative side, networking acquires an unsavory reputation when used as a sales and marketing tool to get information, impress a potential client, or make a deal. A number of interviewees reported networking experiences that were unpleasant, uncomfortable, or exploitive:

- Marisa disliked the "strutting" people were doing when networking.
- Janet avoided networking when she saw it as "pretending to be a friend." She thought it was phony.
- Diane didn't know how to start a conversation without "being pushy" and sounding artificial.
- Jim found that he had to evaluate what people were telling him to see if it made sense—or if the person afraid of his competition was trying to steer him away.

Writers on networking acknowledge this negative history. They deplore the fleeting transactions glorified in the "Cult of the Deal"[83] and the practice of "schmoozing," getting something from someone with no benefit to the other person.[84]

Also, with the advent of the Internet, it is all too easy to use technical means to find information on the 'Net and lose sight of the human connection. Professor Phil Agre of UCLA's Department of Information

---

[82] See especially Sheila Wellington and Catalyst, *Be Your Own Mentor*, Random House, 2001, Chapter 6, "Your Number One Success Strategy: Networking."

[83] Wayne E. Baker, *Networking Smart: How to Build Relationships for Personal and Organizational Success*, McGraw-Hill 1994, p. 44.

[84] Diane Darling, *The Networking Survival Guide: Get the Success You Want by Tapping into the People You Know*, McGraw-Hill 2003, p. 17.

Studies is adamant that electronic communication is wasted unless we use it to seek out, cultivate, and nurture relationships with other human beings.[85]

Responsible, Ethical Networking

Experts in the networking field urge us to build and manage networks of personal and organizational relationships in "intelligent, resourceful, and ethical ways."[86] They see networking both as a skill and an attitude: a process of gathering, collecting, and distributing information for the mutual benefit of you and the people in your network. The key phrase is "expecting nothing in return,"[87] and the emphasis is on building relationships. It is in this sense that I use the term "networking" here.

Networks refer to the horizontal connections between and among peers based on shared interests and/or values and trust. They can seem invisible because so much of the meaning is bound up in relationships—the links, connections, communications, friendships, interests, trust, and values that give the network its life. To understand the process of networking requires a shift from thinking about things to thinking about relationships.[88]

Networking and "Permanent White Water"

We turn to the question of "Why now?" As discussed earlier, today's world is increasingly mobile and complex. Exploding technologies, heightened time pressures, and incessant change in other aspects of life loosen family and community ties as well as organizational ties.

---

[85] Agre, op. cit., p. 405.

[86] Baker, op. cit., p. 415.

[87] Donna Fisher and Sandy Vilas, *Power Networking*, Mountain Harbor Publications, Austin, TX, 1991, p. 15–27.

[88] Jessica Lipnack and Jeffrey Stamps, *The Networking Book: People Connecting with People*, Rutledge & Kegan, New York and London, 1986, p. 112, 138–42.

The job market is increasingly volatile. The information revolution is constantly accelerating. One important result is that career paths are less predictable, and swings in fortune over the course of a working life are greater.[89]

Peter Vaill, a noted observer of social and economic change, likens today's tempo to a condition of "permanent white water," regularly taking us out of our comfort zone and asking things of us that we never imagined would be required. Words people use to describe the turbulence and confusion: "the blind leading the blind," "being on a roller coaster," "a see-saw" or "a merry-go-round," events "spinning out of control," and "something out of *Alice in Wonderland*."[90]

As we struggle to stay afloat in these white water conditions, we find that orderly mentoring programs have diminished. Mentoring programs do continue in corporations and businesses with a strong mentoring tradition, though in streamlined versions better adapted to conditions of rapid change.[91] Even with the desire to mentor others, few people have the time or the energy to do so. Brad's experience is illustrative.

> An executive in a large defense technology corporation, Brad is responsible for a sizable department and has 20-plus attorneys reporting to him. The fast-changing tempo of the company is so great that he frequently comes home with the desire simply to crawl into bed and pull the covers over his head. The work pace is grueling, and things are changing so fast in his industry that

---

[89] Shiller, op. cit., p. 399.

[90] Vaill, op. cit., p. 399; see p. 14–15 of *Learning as a Way of Being*.

[91] Mentoring consultants have been very inventive in developing products for this changing market. For examples, see Corporate Mentoring Solutions Inc. (available at: http://www.mentoring-solutions.com/) and Career Systems International (available at: http://www.careersystemsintl.com/solutions.htm); both accessed September 24, 2006.

Brad worries about his future. Now 50, he will not be eligible for retirement until age 55. He worries that if his job is eliminated, which easily could happen if contracts are canceled, he could be too high-priced to find another job within the company for these five crucial years. Given Brad's situation, mentoring others is simply not in his field of vision.

The impact of "white water" is not limited to business. Pat said that "white water" is hitting her state government agency hard.

"People feel overwhelmed. They feel they are drowning with all the changes happening so fast. There's a major system reorganization going on in the seven divisions that pay for mental health services. The plan is to pool funding for better coordination. That's very scary for everybody. No one knows how it will affect their job. They have to do their current job, plus participate in planning meetings to help the new entity get created."

Under these circumstances, where is the time, energy, and inclination to mentor others?

The "Strength of Weak Ties": Networking and the Mentoring Mosaic

All is not lost, however. In Chapter 13, we talked about the "strength of weak ties" and noted that having a number of weak ties can be very strengthening. There is value in cultivating minor mentoring relationships. Although minor mentors are not strong in all three factors of attraction, action, and affect, they can have significant impact on your learning, guidance, and growth—whether you are in the early stages of career or transitioning to something completely new and different.

This is where networking comes in. Networking usually begins with a sharing of information or connecting people to each other. But it also is an important way to flesh out your Mentoring Mosaic, particularly in the areas of mentoring experiences and minor mentor relationships. Since networking is built on the concept of horizontal relationships rather than the hierarchical relationships so characteristic of traditional mentors, it is a natural source for finding a peer mentor—or, in the principle of reciprocity, of being one.

HOW NETWORKING PRACTICE DEVELOPS

I have been particularly interested in how networking develops and where it is common practice. I expected to see networking prevalent in business and commercial sectors, but I was surprised to see that networking is an established tradition in other fields as well, as illustrated by the examples that follow. Particularly notable is the prevalence of networking in the fields dealing with "public" goods— such as public health, community development, and other public policy arenas.

Networking can be a deliberately acquired skill as it was for Evie (see Chapter 18), who developed her networking practice when she was charged with quickly mastering a new area of work. Or, it can have intuitive origins, like Stan's innate curiosity about people. Or, familial patterns can have a role, as they did for Jill, who saw two different patterns in her Missouri families. She gravitated toward her father's community-oriented family rather than her mother's more aloof patrician family members.

Networking in Practice

Just as networking origins are diverse, networking practice in occupational fields also is varied. Given job mobility, multiple careers, and the increasingly interdisciplinary nature of many fields, it is not surprising that networks and networking frequently cross boundaries.

Jim started his networking through organizations and associations. He credits the Financial Planners Association with helping him launch his accounting business and still maintains connections with the alumni group of the "Big 4" accounting firm where he had his professional start. A friend of his, an avid networker, has established several formal networking groups over the years. One network that limited membership to a single person from any occupational group proved to be the source of a number of Jim's clients. Aside from business, Jim likes to be connected with the larger world and finds networks focused on other common interests.

> "Members of the UCLA Bruin Professionals networking group have something in common. I run into them at games, at the university summer camp, at the touchdown club. It's a sense of community that's important to me."

Kay's networking pattern simply evolved. Looking back, Kay realized that she started developing networking skills in student government in college, in a national student association, and later through connections in graduate school.

> "The school was the magnet in the country for folks who were interested in the formulation and implementation of public policy. The common idea was service to the nation, whether from careers in government, business, the non-profit sector, or some combination. The reason that the school was so good that way was because the professors, staff, alumni, and even students knew all sorts of people—in Washington, in New York, around the globe—and got them together.

> "Given how encompassing an interest in public policy can be, you never know where people from earlier in your career are going to surface. Very few of us have pursued straight-line career paths."

Kay said her early networking was interest- and volunteerism-driven, "an opportunity to continue my political and policy involvement."

Now, Kay has a tremendous network of people in almost any area of public policy. She often has drawn support and guidance from her network as she has moved into diverse roles in government, business, education, and non-profit organizations.

Stan is the elected leader of a national scientific organization and also a major player on a current frontier of science. His networking practice stems from his lifelong curiosity about people.

> "After my junior year at college, I spent the summer at the Woods Hole Oceanographic Institute, where I stayed in the dorm with other students, mostly grad students. I went out of my way to meet people, and I kept up with them later. If I had an appointment or a dinner engagement, I would send a follow-up note, perhaps about the logical conclusion of the discussion. I would take a risk, figuring that the other person might remember me better. When I went to someone's home, I'd send a courtesy letter but also create some basis for a future contact.

> "When I go to meetings, I try to get the list of participants with contact information and then make some follow-up contact. You'd be surprised. Years later, people come to me at a conference and say, 'You wrote a note to me, and I remember that.'

> "Networking increases social contacts, which can help you find mentors in your life. When I travel, I tap into the network of people I know I'd like to see or people who can direct me to other people of like interests. It's all preparation. It's not willy-nilly."

Dee is the development director of a non-profit community center serving low-income and homeless people. I asked her how she developed her skills and her positive attitude. She credits her master's program in public health with learning the importance of networking, a function so essential to her role in a community agency.

> "I see networking as meeting people and developing relationships, externally and internally. I've always felt it was

an important skill—making contact with, communicating, and understanding people. When I moved to fund-raising, I observed others who were really good at networking, especially people in executive leadership roles. I noted the ease they have in starting a conversation, the genuineness that comes through, their articulateness, and how they give enough information to keep people engaged."

Connectors

Some networkers are especially known for their ability to bring together, physically or electronically, people who have mutual interests or concerns. These connectors can serve as models for us as we hone our networking skills:

- Stan often links people who have common interests but don't know each other. He will forward a document, an e-mail, or a note to one person about another, CC'ing a copy to the third party. Thanks to him, Jill connected with a key person in Korea, and they plan to meet on her next research trip there.
- Pat first developed networking skills in the Peace Corps when she was posted to a small village in Thailand a number of years ago. Today, as she plans conferences, Pat is always looking for ways to link together community psychiatrists who live and work in remote communities. Her successful programming efforts at a recent national conference left the group clamoring for more. At other times, Pat has been on the receiving end. A colleague in Pat's network received a listserv question from a contact in Norway asking if anyone was doing studies on the impact of computers on people with mental illness. Knowing of Pat's work in the area, the colleague forwarded the message to Pat. The exchange that followed ultimately led to an invitation for Pat to participate in a conference in Norway.

In this era of constant change, network connections are portable assets that travel with you wherever you go. Since you can no longer count on staying in an organization for a lifetime, you need to maintain a strong network system, both inside and outside the organization, in order to access mentoring resources as you move on. Combined with your other mentoring strategies, networking can constitute a powerful force for managing your mentoring.

BRIDGE

These two chapters have surveyed the trends most likely to impact mentoring. They serve as a backdrop for taking action. In Chapters 25 and 26, we focus on strategies by which you can enhance your mentoring. With knowledge of important trends and your own mentoring process, you can identify those strategies most useful for managing your mentoring as both a mentor and a mentee—now and in the future.

Chapter 25

MANAGING YOUR MENTORING—AS A MENTEE

Change is the driver of mentoring needs—change in your personal situation or life stage, but also change in the economy, in technology, in the world at large. During childhood and our post-secondary education and training years, life and occupational trajectories can seem fairly clear. In the early stages of a career, you find there are certain expected pathways for acquiring training and being noticed—unless you are in an emerging field. It is natural to listen to and accept the advice of older, wiser, and trusted counselors.

Later in life, the future can become murky as you cope with external threats and opportunities, health and family issues, and shifting internal needs and priorities. "One size fits all" might work for early career movement in a stable profession, but it frequently doesn't work later on and rarely during unstable economic conditions. Counselors are fewer, life experiences may point you in a different direction, and advice that is available may not fit with your present-day reality. Usually, this progression toward managing your own mentoring occurs naturally. You are far more ready to listen to your own inner counselor—your inner mentor—and test others' advice against your own values, experience, and perceptions. You size up the situation and ask yourself, *Would this work for me?* This is where versatility in your mentoring practice pays off.

The goal in self-managed mentoring is to become a more effective person by increasing your mentoring range—to be more comfortable and at ease in using a variety of mentoring forms and self-mentoring strategies. As you broaden your mentoring repertoire, you have more tools, skills, and strategies on which to draw. You can identify models, philosophies, and values relevant to the situation in which you find yourself. You can tap your array of self-mentoring strategies to gain information, analyze data, and seek support, as well as to network and build mentoring relationships.

HOW TO SEEK MENTORING

Broadening the goal from "finding a mentor" to "seeking mentoring" is a significant shift. It allows us to think "outside the box" and to be more open, creative, and receptive to alternative forms of mentoring. "Seeking mentoring" reminds us to tap both people and non-people sources. The more aware we can be of our present mentoring process in relation to all the possibilities, the more likely we are to enlarge our mentoring repertoire. The wider the net, the more mentoring resources we can draw in.

As mentees, we tend to use and overuse the methods most familiar and comfortable for us. Depending on our mentor-bonding pattern, we seek men or women mentors, less often both. We seek traditional, step-ahead, or co-mentors, rarely all three. Those of us who tend to seek only major mentors fail to maximize the use of minor mentors. We use a few tried-and-true self-mentoring strategies to learn new things; it does not occur to us to try others that could be equally or more useful.

By this time, you are aware of your mentoring pattern and have a grasp of your current life and career motivations, your resources, and your mentoring needs. In this chapter, we look more closely at your needs, the mentoring resources available, the extent to which they match your preferred style and/or comfort level, and the process of connecting with a mentor.

Identifying Your Mentoring Need

Usually, you want to learn something, develop specific insight and knowledge, become more proficient in a skill, make a connection, obtain guidance, or solve a problem. You are the seeker of help for yourself. Usually, you have choice. You can take a class; apply your present self-mentoring strategies or try new ones; design a mentoring experience for yourself; seek a mentor; or network to see what kind of help is out there. But first, you need to be clear about your mentoring need.

Perhaps you've tried to set up a mentor relationship with one or two people, but it hasn't clicked. Sometimes, the lack of fit with a mentor is the result of an inadequate definition of the mentoring task. Suppose you've been looking for expert advice on a project and have found no logical person to help you. The problem could be an inadequate definition of the mentoring need, as Ruth discovered.

> Ruth kept looking to others to guide her on a book project—someone to steer her through the difficult writing process. Several people she contacted sincerely tried to help her, but the direction that seemed right to them wasn't for her. "My problem was that I wasn't sufficiently clear about what I wanted for the book myself. I guess the approach I communicated was, 'Tell me what will sell, so I can turn my data around and try to make it fit.' Meanwhile, I was feeling uncomfortable. I was too dependent. I realize now that I needed someone to help me think through the process, not do the process for me."

Ruth realized she really wasn't ready for a mentor. When she finally worked out for herself what she wanted to say, she was able to move the project further along and come up with a co-mentor solution. "Looking back," she said, "I think I was avoiding taking responsibility for my own data and my own conclusions."

Ruth's experience is a reminder of one of the basic tenets of problem-solving: understanding the problem. The presenting problem often is not the real problem. With a fuller understanding of the problem—in this case, the mentoring task—a feasible solution often will emerge spontaneously.

Scanning Mentor Possibilities

Let's suppose that you are clear about what you need and your preference is to connect with a mentor who can help. How available are mentors for what you want to learn or do? What are your options? Further, suppose you have done a search and found no logical mentor, nor a way to make a connection. Mentor shortages are very real as organizational structures and roles are changing so rapidly. It is entirely possible that there is no one person who can provide the kind of mentoring you need. You've tried putting various people in the role, but somehow it hasn't worked for you. What now?

Maintaining an Effective Networking Strategy

Are you unduly limiting yourself by focusing on finding *the* right person? Could you cobble together a mentoring team of people who could help you with various aspects of your problem—people who have some skill or knowledge that could be part of the solution? They might not even have to know each other. You are the one who puts together what they have to offer to solve your mentoring problem.

Many of us have well-practiced, comfortable ways of making contact with other people, but these ways can sometimes fail us when we change direction. Does your network of contacts reflect your current interests? Perhaps you need to expand your present network, maybe even build a new one.

You need not stumble in developing your skills in this area, since numerous networking guides are available.[92] Many networking guides are business-oriented, while others have a broader focus. One excellent source directed toward academic communities but equally useful for professionals in other fields is Phil Agre's guide to "Networking the Network," available online.[93] In it, Agre outlines specific steps toward building a professional network, observing that, "If there is no community waiting for you, you will have to go out and build a community, one person at a time." He then goes on to explain how, and he augments these steps with full descriptions of the process and with many examples. In brief, see the "Building Relationships" chart on page 429.

---

[92] Among others, see Lipnack and Stamps, op. cit., p. 416; Fisher and Vilas, op. cit., p. 416; Baker, op. cit., p. 415; Darling, op. cit., p. 415.

[93] Agre, op. cit., p. 405; see p. 2–7 of "Networking on the Network."

Building Relationships

1. "Know your goals" and what you care about. "[O]nce you can explain what you care about, then you can build a community of people who also care about that."

2. "Identify some relevant people," those with whom you have some mutual interests. Look for commonalities—shared values, shared goals, and shared interests—and then find a language to talk about them. Practice explaining your area of interest in a way that puts the interests you share with the other person in the foreground and other elements in the background. Also, identify the collection of people who don't know each other but ought to. You will be providing a public service if you serve as the go-between.

3. Make contact: Write to them, talk to them at meetings, and get out there. Remember that network-building takes time and that you are making a long-term investment.

4. "Your single most important audience is actually not the power-holders of your field ... but rather the best people of your own professional cohort ... especially those who are a few years further along than you. These people share your situation and usually will be happy to talk to you."

5. Find ways to follow up: Pass things along to them, exchange drafts of what you're working on, and invent helpful things to do. Approach this activity as ordinary cooperation among equals. "Make sure you're exchanging these favors out of courtesy and respect and not as phony politicking."

If you are a networking beginner, I encourage you to follow Agre's lead. But there are many other sources, too. You can find an array of networking strategies on the Web as well in the books previously cited. Don't overlook alumni associations and professional organizations, many of which have taken up the networking torch for their members. One of these, the UCLA Alumni Association, offers workshops and sponsors a Web site with a section devoted to networking. "Networking Tools" provides a list of practical tips for building an effective network.[94] Here are a few:

- " ... Networks, like support groups, must be cultivated and created. They do not just happen."
- "Look for a connection when talking or writing to others. Find out what you have in common."
- "Practice the '2-foot rule.' Let everyone within 2 feet of you know that you're looking for a job."
- "Choose members of your network based on information, not a position."
- "Keep in touch with professors and instructors."
- "Create a system for keeping track of your network."

Lastly, consider a variety of places where you can connect with people with whom you share similar interests or values. In addition to business and professional meetings, venues for networking could include your book group, the locker room at the gym, your neighborhood association, the community world affairs forum, Internet networking sites, or a support group. Develop the habit of "trolling for mentors," as one person aptly put it.

Use a Combination of Mentoring Strategies

It helps to move beyond your usual sphere. More resources are available if you are receptive and skillful in tapping them. Is the dearth

---

[94] UCLA Alumni Association, op. cit., p. 405.

of mentors truly a function of a scarcity of desired mentor skills? Or, is your definition of a suitable mentor or mentoring experience too limited? Your options increase when you devise a combination of mentoring forms into a system that will work for you.

Self-mentoring strategies and other non-people mentor forms become more important as you move along in years. Chapter 15 provides examples of people who use mentoring experiences to expand horizons or work through dilemmas. Chapter 18 has examples of people resourceful in using self-mentoring strategies. Consider new ways to collect information, master skills, or obtain guidance. When tackling a new subject area, consult the literature before deciding additional moves. Take a class and consciously network with other class members. Spot people who could meet a piece of your mentoring need, a special niche. Make connections with people who could help you in their areas of expertise.

Assuming you have experience in your chosen field, consider peers who might help you move forward, one-on-one, in groups, or via the Internet:

- One small informal women's writing group has functioned for years. In earlier days, the women met together physically; now they use the telephone. At a regular time each week, two or more are on the phone reading aloud and critiquing each other's work. The group is characterized by mutual respect and effective counsel as they co-mentor each other. All are published writers.
- Jill plans to join the independent scholars study group in her city, a group of people with background in research but presently without a home in a university. Here, she would have the opportunity to continue her research interests in a supportive environment.
- A pediatrician with a specialty in genetics, Sally used her network of contacts across the country to gain a new perspective on difficult cases. The ability to send pictures via e-mail added to the usefulness of that method and the value of

the advice received. Over time, Sally became known as the "e-mail queen" of the cranio-facial group.

Finding the Fit in a Mentoring Relationship

If you are looking for a mentor, what kind of relationship are you seeking? What Goldilocks bed would not be too hard or too soft but "just right" for you?[95] What mentor form do you prefer: a traditional, step-ahead, or co-mentor? Could you build on the "strength of weak ties" and develop a minor mentor connection that would be helpful to you and satisfactory for the mentor?

The Life Cycle of a Mentoring Relationship

Most mentor–mentee relationships begin in a minor mentor way. You have a single, short-term need, and the mentor is able to help you. Usually, a mentoring relationship evolves according to its usefulness to the two parties. At early stages, you have invested little and are free to advance or discourage further contact. If the interaction has been satisfactory, the relationship builds to a level that feels appropriate to both people.[96]

As you increase in your mastery of the mentoring goal, you'll usually notice a gradual shift in the power relationship between you and the mentor. You are ready to assume more responsibility and need less guidance or a different kind of guidance than earlier. This can be a delicate point. How that shift is handled influences the outcome of the relationship. The natural course is for a leveling of the power difference between the two of you.[97] If that does not happen, you might have to withdraw some of your investment in the relationship

---

[95] See the "Goldilocks Theory of Mentor Matching" in Chapter 14, p. 205.

[96] Remember that in networking, reciprocity is the name of the game. If this is a peer relationship, consider what you have to give the other person in return.

[97] See "The Dynamics of Mentoring Relationships" in Chapter 14.

in order to avoid an outright rift. The important point is to appreciate and value what you have gained in the relationship, and to show that appreciation in an appropriate manner.

It never hurts to make note of what you have learned about your mentoring practice from each mentoring experience that you have.

BRIDGE

Managing your mentoring has two sides—as a mentee and as a mentor. This chapter focused on ways to manage your mentoring when you are the person who seeks mentoring—that is, the mentee. The chapter that follows looks at the flip side: managing your mentoring when you are the mentor. Looking at both sides of the mentor–mentee relationship encourages you to review the balance of your relationships. As well as receiving help, to what extent are you, or could you be, helpful to others? What resources or connections can you provide that would be viewed as useful? Consider this reciprocal aspect of networking as you review the material in Chapter 26.

Chapter 26

MANAGING YOUR MENTORING—AS A MENTOR

This chapter is addressed to those of you who want, or need, to be more effective as a mentor of others. Maybe you are a parent, teacher, coach, manager, volunteer, or simply an interested person. Somewhere or somehow, mentoring is important to you. Perhaps you have been a mentor, but your experience was not as satisfying as it could be. Or, your work requirements thrust you into a mentoring role that was uncomfortable for you. Maybe you never have been a mentor but want to be one. Or, perhaps you have felt that the demands placed on you to mentor others were excessive. So, either you have had no experience or you have sensed something was missing in your mentoring of another person. Or, perhaps you simply want to check out how you stand as a mentor.

Can a Non-Bonder Be a Mentor?

If you're a non-bonder, you might have found mentoring, or the idea of mentoring, daunting. Your early relationships with adults might not have been as positive or rewarding as you would have liked. Those close to you were not respectful or trustworthy. Either that, or their advice was not relevant. They did not have the skills, talents, or insights that would be useful in your world, so you learned to go it alone.

Not having a mentor-bonding pattern in your life does not mean that you are unable to be an effective mentor. However, it *does* mean that it's not likely to happen spontaneously. Luckily, you have had many experiences since then. Possibly, you have observed some mentor behaviors that you thought you could probably do, but you have held back, not trusting or not knowing where and how to begin.

<u>Not Trusting</u>

If the answer is not trusting, take a look at your more recent relationships. Most likely, you have had some experiences with people that were not traumatic and were even positive. Could you be locked into old untrusting patterns that do not fit with present-day reality? Reviewing the experience of late bonders described in Chapter 14—the "untils" and the "becauses"—might be helpful. Late mentoring, either as a mentor or mentee, can happen when you have new experiences that cause you to reexamine old patterns and allow yourself to be open to change.

<u>Not Knowing</u>

If the answer is not knowing where or how to begin, the following pages can help you map out a practical plan based on knowledge about yourself that is realistic and doable. The first step is to assess what you can bring to the mentoring relationship.

ASSESSING WHAT YOU HAVE TO OFFER

The first step toward becoming an effective mentor is recognizing that you're not as effective as you would like to be and that you really want to change. That motivation alone is a big step toward change. Then comes a clear and specific appraisal of your strengths and your limitations. From this self-assessment, you can build a practical action plan, tailored to your needs.

Action

What is it that you have to offer a mentee? What particular knowledge and skills do you have that you are willing to share with or teach to someone else? Are they technical skills or communication skills? Is it knowing the ropes in an organization, knowing how to cut through red tape, or other insider knowledge? Do you have good entrepreneurial skills: Have you picked up knowledge and skills to set up and run a small business, or to go out on your own on a business venture? Are you a good listener? What are you good at, and where do you excel? What do others seem to admire or value in you?

For instance, you could be particularly good at understanding different cultures, teaching yourself new technologies, setting up systems, making presentations, making complex ideas easy to understand, analyzing problems, simplifying work, finding useful sources of information, easing tension between people, or applying technical or clinical skills in your work. The list is endless.

Keep those skills in mind while you look at the kinds of mentor behaviors that mentees find helpful. The form beginning on page 437, Measuring Mentoring Potential, lists a variety of action roles that mentors take to assist mentees. These roles have stood the test of time, and they come from the experience of many mentees. You can identify your strengths and abilities on these dimensions.

Remember that even the most effective mentors do not take all of these action roles. The mentee might not need that sort of assistance, and mentors are not equally good at everything. But this will give you a starting point, a profile of the kinds of mentoring behaviors you have available and those that you might want to develop or improve. The list is illustrative, not exhaustive. New action roles continue to emerge in our changing world. In fact, you might want to add them to the list.[98]

---

[98] If so, I would be interested in hearing from you. Visit my Web site to send me your experience with mentoring action roles: www.mentoringmosaic.com.

Measuring Mentoring Potential: Action Roles

Action Roles	Low to High 1 2 3 4 5	Examples: He/She ...
Prodder		"pushed me to achieve high standards." "kept prodding me if I allowed myself to slack off." "was very clear what was wanted from me."
Teacher–Coach		"taught me how to set priorities." "taught me to develop interpersonal skills." "guided me on problems." "said 'Let's see how you could have done it better.'" "taught me to write scientifically."
Technology Guide		"taught me how to do lab research." "helped me with new computer technology."
Feedback-Giver		"gave me a lot of positive and negative feedback." "let me know if I was going off track and helped me examine the situation."

Action Roles	Low to High 1 2 3 4 5	Examples: He/She ...
Exposer/Eye-Opener		"opened my eyes, got me interested in research."
		"helped me understand the politics of the organization."
		"helped me to understand why I have to look at the total impact that something has on the place."
Door-Opener		"made training available."
		"included me in discussions."
		"said, 'I want you to represent me on this committee. Here's the information; here's our view.'"
		"would delegate to us."
Idea-Bouncer		"encouraged me to bounce ideas off of him in a way that brought things into focus."
		"eloquently spoke for professional issues."
		"would discuss issues, problems, and goals with me."

Action Roles	Low to High 1 2 3 4 5	Examples: He/She ...
Allower/Entruster		"set me loose to set up a totally new position for the clinic and make it work." "allowed me to do all the buying and close the ledger at end of month."
Challenger		"made me really look at my decisions and grow up a little bit." "challenged me, forcing me to prove my point. I found out if I believed what I recommended or not."
Culture Guide		"showed me what the world was like in terms of race relations." "showed me how to survive in that political climate."
Other Action Roles:		

Although action is the most visible part of a mentor's behavior, it does not stand alone. Remember the mentor bookends in Chapter 11. Three essential elements sustain a major mentor–mentee relationship: attraction, action, and affect. We discussed action as the role most visible and central, but, like books on a shelf, action requires support. The solid bookends of attraction and affect are required to bolster a mentor–mentee connection. So, in addition to assessing your abilities in the action roles of a mentor, you'll need to look at these essential ingredients as well.

Attraction

We know that mentees must be attracted to a mentor as an example or exemplar of something they would like to be, do, or become. What are your model strengths? What are you a good example of, or an exemplar?

What is it in your knowledge, skills, or way of being that draws people to you? Are you a good example of some skills or behaviors to which a mentee might aspire? Not that you have to be a star or celebrity, but do you have some skill, knowledge, or ability that people recognize and value? The major point here is that, as an aspiring mentor, you need something in your kit bag that appeals to and would be valued by a prospective mentee. This is an important reason for assessing what you have to offer.

Most likely, your style will not appeal to all people—but it certainly could to some. In mentor matching, the fit is the thing. Remember the Goldilocks Theory of Mentor Matching in Chapter 14: The mentee could find this mentor too hard, or that one too soft, but a third one just right! Some of us thrive with "Exacters" while others of us do better with "Evokers." The old adage that it takes different strokes for different folks holds true when it comes to mentor–mentee matching. Remember, too, that the lack of fit could have more to do with the other person's mentor-bonding pattern than with you personally.

Affect

The other bookend supporting the action roles is affect—that is, the mentor's positive regard for the mentee. Positive feelings toward the mentee might be minimal at the start, but a relationship is not likely to develop if the mentee does not feel respected or valued by the prospective mentor.

We know that mentees must feel respect from the mentor. What kinds of mentees would you want to work with? What kinds turn you off? Even if you would not feel comfortable with some mentees, you might be able to use your contacts to introduce them to a mentor who could help them. No one says you have to do it all. One of the best things you can do is know what you have to give and what your limits are. Then, you can be a referral agent to someone who can better meet the mentee's needs. (Be sure this is a genuine action on your part, not sloughing off an unpleasant task.)

Of course, non-bonders might run into problems. Some non-bonders I have talked to find themselves impatient with mentees and even with teaching their own children. If this is your tendency, you'll need to be selective about the kind of mentee with whom you connect. Either that, or you will need to work on your attitude about learners. If neither of those approaches make sense, you could be more effective as a referral mentor, providing aid by referring the mentee to others who can meet their needs better than you can.

But that's not the only possibility. You could have great aptitude for being a peer mentor.

BECOMING A PEER MENTOR

If you have a history of comfortable interactions with peers, consider the possibility of becoming a peer mentor: a colleague mentor or a co-mentor. This is the most likely mentor relationship to develop through networking. Remember that in peer relationships, there is an equalization of power. You connect with each other because of overlapping interests or goals. You have mutual or complementary strengths and skills.

Many of the action roles in "Measuring Mentoring Potential" are applicable to any of the three mentor forms: traditional mentor, step-ahead mentor, and co-mentor. Your style, your optimum way of being with mentees, will become clearer in the following discussion about connecting.

Connecting

Who do you want to mentor? Do you have someone in mind who is seeking help from you or whose performance you are responsible for? Or are you thinking of mentoring in general?

If you have no prospective mentees in mind, consider networking in groups to which you belong. Can you spot people who could use a little help and then volunteer your assistance? If you do not have the kind of help that is needed, connect the person to someone who does. When you can, follow up: Find out how that worked and how else you might help.

Most likely, this step requires you to take the initiative. How easy is it for you to reach out to people and for people to feel comfortable with you? Are you more at ease with junior people who have much less experience or skill than you, or are you more comfortable in a peer or co-mentor relationship? Can you use some of your self-mentoring strategies to help you bridge to another person?

Goals

Set small reachable goals for yourself. Consider the array of mentoring possibilities: Could you be good at short-term skill-coaching, career advising, teaching a new technology, or troubleshooting? You could start with a goal of becoming a good minor mentor. If being a mentor is new and strange for you, you might want to take it slowly. Again, effective minor mentoring may be an appropriate goal. Do what you can do, and do it well. Start in a limited way that would be acceptable to you and to the mentee.

Mentoring Models

Perhaps you have good observation skills. Chances are that you've observed others who are mentors. Is there someone whose style looks familiar and comfortable to you who you might use as a model to try as an approach, or at least build on? You probably have learned a great deal from books. Are there mentor behaviors you have read about that might be comfortable for you?

Expectations

You will find it useful to be open and explicit about the way you would like the relationship to go. It is natural to take small "testing-the-water" steps in the communication and negotiation process. The more open you can be about your strengths and limitations about being a mentor, the more the mentee will be encouraged to be equally frank. Be sure that the two of you are clear as to when and how you will communicate with each other. The more explicit you can be, the better. Most relationships that snag occur because the implicit requirements of the relationship are not stated or even known during the mentoring process. Here is a good rule of thumb: When you do become aware, when you feel a "pinch," consider how you can communicate it. A problem exists, of course, if the mentee is more aware of problems in the relationship than you are. Your ego can be on the line, and there can be a lot of hurt on both sides. Can you take feedback? How do you like it to be given? Can you communicate this to the mentee?

Continuing

Often, relationships start in a "toe-dipping," minor mentor way. This gives both you and the mentee time to test the relationship without much commitment or investment on either side. The relationship could evolve without much discussion. Should it become more formal, the two of you might want to communicate something about the purpose, frequency, and duration of your contact. Many minor mentor relationships continue very well on an unspoken, mutual basis. If and when there are problems, however, more open discussion is indicated.

How are you in sustaining relationships over time? How frequently do you want contact, or would you prefer not to be bothered except in certain situations? How do you handle feedback? What is your preferred style of giving and receiving data about yourself? What is the mentee's preference? The more that the two of you are clear and can operate on the agreed-upon level, the more likely your mentoring will have a positive outcome.

Concluding

Endings in mentor relationships happen by transformation, rift, or drift. (See "Mentor Endings: Concluding a Mentoring Relationship" in Chapter 14 for more information.) All mentoring relationships do end. What is your expectation about this one? How would you like it to end? What is your experience? Pay attention to how you handle it and how you feel about it. Periodic introspection about your mentoring experience is helpful.

Debrief yourself. Either during the process or after the relationship ends, use some method, such as journal writing, to review the recent pairing: Describe what you did, what happened, what you learned from it, what you liked about your performance as a mentor, and what you would do differently another time. Debriefing is one of the quickest ways to improve your abilities as a mentor.

PARENTS AS MENTORS

Parents have a responsibility for their children for the better part of two decades. As a parent, you will have a hand in your children's mentoring for a good portion of that time. The guides above can be useful in improving your skills to mentor your children. But you can do more to guide them into a rich mentoring life. Here are useful actions that you can take:

- Look honestly at your attitudes and behavior toward your children. To what extent do you show respect for the young person, to what extent can they trust you, and to what extent is your advice relevant? Do you need to shore up your relationships with them to provide a mentor-bonding environment?

- Acquaint your child/children with a variety of mentoring models that represent the basic values of the family.

- Look honestly at yourself to see the kind of mentoring model you present. If you don't like what you see, how might you change? If that's impossible, what could you do to offset the negatives?

- Don't expect that "one size fits all." Identify, if you can, what you have to offer your child, what the other parent offers, and what other intimate and extended family and/or close friends can offer, both as models and potential mentors.

- As disappointing as it might be, and hard on the ego, recognize that you may not be the adult to whom your child can easily bond. If that is the case, do what you can to facilitate the bonding with appropriate others. Examine, too, your mentoring style to see if a change of behavior on your part could make a difference.

- Your family could have a built-in step-ahead mentor in the form of an older sibling or relation. Do what you can to make that relationship a positive one.

445

- Try to become aware of the mentoring messages you are sending purposefully or inadvertently to your child. If some are not what you would like, look at what you might do to counteract them.
- Do what you can to shield your child from negative messages that are coming from otherwise well-meaning people.
- One basic communication skill for all parents to develop is the art of active listening, not only to the words of the child's message but to the feeling tone that accompanies it. Active listening is a skill that can be developed.
- Be aware of the kinds of mentoring experiences that are likely to be constructive in your child's life and foster those when you can.
- Encourage the development of mentoring play and mentoring interests.

As an addendum, here are two parents-as-mentor stories from interviews. Al describes his mentoring of his sons during two interviews 20 years apart. From the first interview:

> "I'm trying to teach them how to work under stress, because I think it's a stressful world. They know I love them, I give them support, I go to all of their events, but I've added something extra: dealing with stress by talking about coping strategies. Sometimes, I put stress on them; sometimes, it comes from some other source—like my son and his math. He's excellent in math but, in the 7th grade, he psyched himself out and flunked the first two math tests. So, I sat down with him. I said, 'You're dealing with a pressure situation. How are you going to handle it? Do you know the facts? Let's go over the facts.' Sometimes, he knew the facts; sometimes, he didn't. 'Okay, that's why you prepare. Try to learn everything that you're supposed to know and be prepared.' He has successfully learned how to deal with this pressure of being afraid of taking a math test. He's now getting all Bs and As."

Now, 20 years later, Al is using this same systematic mentoring process to prepare his oldest son to take over the family business.

Lacey's parenting style exemplifies respect and response to a young child's needs. This is how she describes it:

> "I think my kids have been a tremendous influence in terms of my parenting. When Michael was a very little person, he began to be verbal and ask questions. I made a very clear decision at that point that I was going to take the time to answer him and not fob him off with the usual parent responses. It was sort of an epiphany—that it was going to take a lot of time, and that I consciously wanted to take the time, rather than 'I'll tell you later; you're too young to understand.'

> "I also talked to my husband about this approach. I knew we wouldn't have opportunities for very long. I think it made me a more honest parent as a result. I knew I couldn't speed by. I needed to show up, stop, and answer all of both sons' questions regardless of how long it took, how complicated the response might have to be, or the more questions that might result from the answers. I really made a conscious decision not to brush their questions aside.

> "That's been the basis of our relationship as a family. The boys are interested in the world around them, and they know that they can ask questions and that they will have a dialogue— that what they say and want to know is important."

We conclude this chapter with a few questions to help you assess your present status in managing your mentoring, both as a mentor and a mentee.

MANAGING YOUR OWN MENTORING

Assessment Sheet

1. At this stage of my life and career, my motivation is (getting ahead, high, free, deeper, refocused, balanced, secure) because:

2. Comparing my motivation with demographic trends and career opportunities, I want to consider these goals:

3. My current mentoring needs are:

4. Reviewing my mentoring lifeprint, my mentor-bonding pattern, and my Mentoring Mosaic, I need to be aware that:

5. My self-mentoring strategies that are well developed and useful are:

6. The external trends and aspects of my mentoring process that could be obstacles to my career and life objectives are:

7. Reviewing trends, my goals, my strengths, and my limitations, my next steps in managing my mentoring are (as mentor, as mentee):

BRIDGE

These two chapters have stressed the importance of enlarging your mentoring repertoire and suggested ways to increase your skills both as a mentor and as a mentee. The final chapter illustrates enhanced mentoring.

Chapter 27

ENHANCED MENTORING

Throughout this book, we have looked at mentoring through a broad lens in order to capture both people and non-people mentoring. We noted earlier how leaning on one form of mentoring, to the exclusion of others, can create problems. "Don't put all your eggs in one basket" is the folk wisdom. A corollary, applied to mentoring, might urge us to "collect more baskets"—to expand our mentoring resources and move our mentoring skills to another level; to extend our reach, both as a seeker of mentoring and as a mentor of others. This approach, which I call "enhanced mentoring," puts us in the active role of managing our portfolio of mentoring needs, skills, and strategies.

To illustrate this broad-brush approach to enhanced mentoring, we turn to several examples. The interview data portray three people in their 60s and 70s who are still active in their careers. Although their patterns and styles are quite different, all three draw on people and non-people mentoring sources as they actively direct their own mentoring processes and as they mentor others.

THREE VIGNETTES

Hal: Music, Magic and Medicine

When I interviewed Hal, I had no idea that he would be such a good example of a rich and fully formed Mentoring Mosaic. He illustrates the happy consequences of following one's interests and being guided by curiosity.

Drawing on a capacity for self-learning as well as for learning from instruction, Hal has made managed mentoring a high art form.

Hal was the physician in charge of a hospital nuclear medicine department when I met him. He was, I learned, one of the pioneers in the hospital nuclear medicine field.

His office didn't look it, though. Instead of framed credentials, the walls displayed a jumble of marvelous photographs taken on his travels. As we talked about his non-medical interests, he told me he was a drummer and showed me the practice pad he kept in his desk along with a pair of drumsticks. A semi-professional musician, Hal has played percussion in symphony orchestras, studied Dixieland jazz, sung in barbershop quartets, and much more. At the time of our interview, he was not only into drumming, but he also was studying sophisticated magic tricks as well. He also had a print shop in his basement and gave lectures on typography.

Professionally, Hal was trained as an internist and then practiced with his orthopedic surgeon father for eight years. Wanting to specialize, he decided to take a residency at the Veteran's Administration in metabolic research. A risky venture, a big step, since he had four children and didn't want to ask his father to help. But trying new things was as natural to him as breathing.

In time, he concluded that academic medicine didn't have a strong enough pull, and he returned to a clinical setting. There, he found himself attracted to the new field of nuclear medicine. Hal's intellectual curiosity and his pattern of self-learning made him a natural for entering a pioneering field, especially one where there was little training available and most was on a self-taught basis. To pursue his nuclear medicine interests, he acquired his knowledge on the job, studying books about radiation and nuclear physics.

Hal's approach to this challenge was typical of his "wanting to learn something." He has a well-developed study strategy that made this career change highly successful as well as stimulating. He employs the same strategy whenever something new has caught his interest. First, he explores the subject thoroughly, by reading, practicing on his own, and taking classes. When he needs instruction on finer points, he searches out a teacher or coach. What Hal has developed into a high art form is the process of self-learning, of developing new bases of knowledge and skill.

<u>Comments on Hal's Mentoring Pattern</u>
How did it happen that Hal developed such broad mentoring interests? For him, it began with strong mentor bonding with both parents who were into a wide range of activities, hobbies, and interests. They served both as mentors and as models for acquiring new knowledge and skills. He credits his mother with his artistic development and his father for his interests in sports, printing, painting, and more.

Hal's Mentoring Mosaic presents a pattern of learning on his own, and only later, if needed, seeking a teacher or coach. This pattern of learning was particularly apt when he needed to gear up for the revolutionary new field of nuclear medicine. No one was available to guide him or provide instruction; he had to do it on his own. Hal's mentoring approach has served him very well as he has "craved more knowledge and learning" throughout his life.

Jill: Co-Mentoring and Global Reach
Jill is a management consultant and researcher studying organizational and societal change with a focus on how it occurs and how we live with it. She also is an expert on gender issues and changing gender roles. Cross-cultural studies are important in her work, and she has lived, worked, and done research in such different cultures as Iran, India, Japan, Korea, and Fiji.

Throughout her life, Jill has followed the beat of her own drummer. When she was little, her mother, grandmother, and aunt all tried to curb her independence in order to make her fit their very conventional ideas of appropriate behavior. Jill loved her mother dearly and could not understand why her mother, normally so loving and supportive, would go along with her grandmother instead of standing up for Jill.

All through school, Jill kept looking for strong, effective women models. When she became the first woman doctoral candidate in a graduate school of management, she was frustrated that the only woman on the faculty was taking a subservient role. It wasn't until Jill joined a support group of women doctoral students that she discovered mentoring relationships with women that were helpful and supportive.

Jill describes the mentoring relationships with men earlier in her life as ambiguous, often because of sexual overtones. One senses her hesitancy even now, as she describes her co-mentor relationships with Alex and Randy.

- "Alex [a well known author] and I spar intellectually. In the process, he makes me clarify what I'm thinking. Earlier, I felt that I had to defend myself, but I have come to realize that he values me and enjoys the interaction. Something similar has been true with Randy, a professional editor, who volunteered his editing services. He argues with me, but also keeps asking, 'When are you going to have another chapter for me to edit?'"

Jill's Mentoring Mosaic is filled with self-mentoring, mentoring experiences and environments, and mentoring relationships of the co-mentoring kind. Here are two co-mentoring examples with women:

- For a number of years, Jill shared a management consulting practice with Elaine. Over time, their co-mentor relationship has remained strong although the focus has shifted. Recently, Elaine introduced Jill to key people she needed to talk to for her research in Korea, and Jill helped Elaine sharpen the focus of the memoir she was writing. Periodically, the two go on writing retreats together.

- Jill and another friend and colleague, Chris, use the same methodology in their research. They help each other with research problems and critique each other's work. They share academic knowledge, skills in computer technology—and also personal experiences.

For self-mentoring examples, including networking, Jill talks about her use of the Internet in her work:

- "Much of the research I did 10 years ago in Japan took me months. I had to find the sources and then had to get them to trust me. The material was mostly in Japanese, and I had to arrange for translation. Now I can get a lot of material on the Internet and in English. There has been an internationalizing of data. Part of globalization is the need to access data from all over for international trade, and English is the universal language. The charts I consulted today were traditional sources from government and newspapers, all available on the Internet in English. It's really exciting doing research today."

- "Research is one way of using the Internet. The other way I use it is connecting and communication. I belong to several different support groups, some on the 'Net, some in reality. Because they all have Web sites, I can access information quickly. Then there is e-mail. The beauty of e-mail is that it's not time-dependent. In the past, I didn't want to call or send faxes at inappropriate times, so I used to get up in the middle of the night. Now, I can set up appointments by e-mail. Even with vast differences in time zones, I can do it at my, and their, convenience."

- "I have mentors, too, who help me. One man, a director of Korean studies, has been wonderful in introducing me to new people via the Internet. He lets them know that I will contact them. What a blessing! When I first started international consulting, I had to make a call and wait for callbacks. Eventually, I'll meet these people in person and interview them. A former student, an M.B.A. graduate, sends e-mail at least five times a week. He still asks me questions 20 years later. He's also a data source; He does research on the Web and sends me material that he thinks will interest me.

Jill uses the Internet not only to obtain data, make connections, and transmit information, but also to maintain and strengthen relationships. She is an avid networker in person as well as on the Web and has developed effective ways to approach people at meetings to introduce herself and discuss mutual research interests.

Comments on Jill's Mentoring Pattern

In Jill, we see how early experiences stimulated a deep and abiding interest in gender and cultural differences that have become the focus of her research. She has built a life-long pattern of inquiry, using mentoring experiences and environments, self-mentoring, networking, and co-mentoring around the globe.

Ned: A Smorgasbord of Mentees

Ned had a long career in academic medicine before becoming a key executive in a multi-state health plan. Over the years, he has enjoyed a rich assortment of traditional and step-ahead mentors. He also has mentored many junior physicians in pediatrics and medical genetics. Now in his late 60s, Ned is nearing the end of his chosen career. This seemed a useful time to explore his views on mentoring both as a mentor of others and as a person managing his own mentoring process. Here, we focus on his philosophy of mentoring, his approach, and the strategies he uses both in mentoring others and in self-mentoring. First, he paid tribute to his mentors, observing, "When they're gone, you miss them terribly." Then he turned to my questions.

As to his experiences mentoring others during the past decade, Ned said he seems to have had "a smorgasbord of mentees." Prominent among them are young people interested in medicine, ranging from a junior colleague who wants to become a medical director to two grandsons whose career interests are medicine—and auto mechanics. He also is coaching his 6-year-old surrogate granddaughter in ice skating. Recently, he planned and participated in a formalized mentoring program in medical management for a female departmental chief who was being groomed to be chief of pediatrics. He describes his general approach and how he looks for a coach when he needs to learn something.

- "It's my mission to teach. My fiber is to learn new things while I'm teaching others. If I had to teach auto mechanics, I'd break everything down to its component parts and put it together in an organized fashion. My skill is explaining things in a way you can remember. I am a coach who knows how to get things done. Mentoring also involves advocating for someone you believe in, and steering the person toward—or away from inappropriate—career choices."

- "When I need to learn something I look for a coach—someone who does what I want to do and does it successfully. If a coach is not available, I wind up getting a book and reading about the topic, though that approach is not as easy and reassuring. I need someone to guide me along, to titrate the information so I get it right. Just reading in books is not as good as having a guide. My ice-skating coach used to say, 'I want you to do the same jump, at the same height, at the same spot, to the same notes in the music, each time.'"

Ned has well-honed self-mentoring techniques.

- "When I have a problem, I try to gather information on how others have handled a similar situation. I picture myself going down each of those paths—seeing in my mind's eye the one that feels the most comfortable, considering where I am on my life line. I consider myself at the end of a career now, and that makes certain choices easier. I trust my inner voice a lot more than I did years ago."

- "My life involves research, looking things up—sometimes for me, sometimes for friends, sometimes for patient information, and sometimes to learn new things to broaden my horizons. Years ago, a great deal of time was spent going to the library. Now I hop on the 'Net, get a search engine, and go to it. The Internet constantly serves to verify and answer questions for me."

Several years ago, Ned had massive heart surgery. After recovery, he became interested in cancer genetics. Given his background in genetics, he thought, maybe he would pursue this field part time when he retired. "It was part of my attempt to re-invent myself. I decided to go to a two-week mini-fellowship at the City of Hope, but I was not going to go with little knowledge. I jumped on the 'Net, searched for articles from MEDLINE—books, organizations, information the public was getting, everything I could learn beforehand. That way, I could get closer to the cutting edge and benefit from the information and the mentoring that I would receive. It turns out that some of the best information came from the accounts and testimonials of patients when they spoke with us at the course. But having prepared myself for six weeks in advance, I was able to ask them intelligent questions."

<u>Comments on Ned's Mentoring Pattern</u>
In Ned, we see the multiplier effect in mentoring. Those of us, like Ned, who have good experiences as mentees, are more likely to reach out and mentor others. Forming mentoring relationships becomes a natural thing to do. But note that Ned taps other mentoring resources as well; he has developed self-mentoring to a high level, trusting his own inner voice and applying traditional research methods to the Internet.

Comments on the Three Vignettes

I chose these three vignettes to illustrate that different routes can lead toward enhanced mentoring. The directions taken by Hal, Jill, and Ned were in part innate, in part a reflection of the influence of mentor bonding and mentoring experiences in their early lives, and in part their own conscious decisions. Human beings have amazing adaptive capacities: When one route doesn't work, another is taken. Circumstances change. Along the way, opportunities may open up, or close, or remain unchanged. To enhance your mentoring is to maximize opportunities and adjust to losses—to live out your values and to be agile in your mentoring dance of life.

ENHANCED MENTORING IN THE FUTURE

Awareness of mentoring and its value has increased dramatically in recent years. As we have seen throughout this book, the need for mentoring extends beyond fostering development over a traditional career. Longer life spans, the prospect of multiple careers, and the desire to balance career and non-career interests will generate strong mentoring needs for continued learning and creative aging. The stories of Hal, Jill, and Ned provide useful examples of self-managed mentoring into late career. Despite the uniqueness of their patterns, all three tap an array of people and non-people mentors, and all have a variety of self-mentoring strategies that they can apply. Many of us will turn to self-managed mentoring, since we are the only ones available to manage our mentoring process throughout our lives. The more conscious we are of our Mentoring Mosaic—of our mentoring process past and present—the more effective we will be.

We live in exciting, albeit bumpy, times. As we become more aware of our mentoring assets and more skilled in applying mentoring strategies, we will enrich our mentoring. We will do more self-mentoring as we discover tools for self-learning and gain comfort in using them. The Web generation has no timidity when it comes to exploring new electronic venues for pleasure and for learning. Even those of us who pre-date the digital age will use the Internet both as a data source and as a contact base for interest groups, user groups, and other networks. Bonders and non-bonders alike will gravitate to the Web, though the bonders will be more likely to combine Web activity with personal interaction. At the same time, we will become increasingly aware of the lifelong value of active networking as a way to ensure the continued richness of human relationships as well as access to information, skills, and advice.

On a personal note, I can attest to this process. As I have lived and breathed mentoring over the years—most recently in writing this book—I have explored the nooks and crannies of my own Mentoring Mosaic and found myself trying out less familiar mentoring forms. I also have applied mentoring strategies in new ways. I have discovered that using these strategies more fully and creatively does, indeed, enhance one's mentoring. Perhaps you will, too.

INDEX OF INTERVIEWEES

GENERAL INDEX

Printed in the United States
101566LV00004B/75/A